COMPUTER LITERACY FOR IC3™

UNIT 3: LIVING ONLINE

John Preston

Sally Preston

Robert L. Ferrett

INTERNET AND COMPUTING CORE CERTIFICATION
GLOBAL STANDARD 3

Prentice Hall

Boston   Columbus   Indianapolis   New York   San Francisco   Upper Saddle River
Amsterdam   Cape Town   Dubai   London   Madrid   Milan   Munich   Paris   Montreal   Toronto
Delhi   Mexico City   Sao Paulo   Sydney   Hong Kong   Seoul   Singapore   Taipei   Tokyo

Library of Congress Cataloging-in-Publication Data

Preston, John M.
   Computer literacy for IC3 / John Preston, Robert L. Ferrett, Sally Preston.
    p. cm.
   Includes index.
   ISBN-13: 978-0-13-506499-3
   ISBN-10: 0-13-506499-6
   1. Electronic data processing personnel—Certification—Study guides. 2. Computer literacy—Examinations—Study guides.
3. Computers—Examinations—Study guides. 4. Internet—Examinations—Study guides. I. Ferrett, Robert. II. Preston, Sally.
III. Title. IV. Title: Computer literacy for IC3.
   QA76.3.P743 2009
   004—dc22

2009004932

VP/Editorial Director: Natalie E. Anderson
Editor in Chief: Michael Payne
Director, Product Development: Pamela Hersperger
Product Development Manager: Eileen Bien Calabro
Editorial Project Managers: Melissa Arlio, Virginia Guariglia
Editorial Assistant: Marilyn Matos
AVP/Director of Online Programs, Media: Richard Keaveny
AVP/Director of Product Development: Lisa Strite
Media Development Manager: Cathi Profitko
Editor, Assessment and Media: Paul Gentile
Editorial Media Project Manager: Alana Coles
Editorial Assistant, Media: Jaimie Howard
Production Media Project Manager: John Cassar
Director of Marketing: Kate Valentine
Marketing Manager: Tori Olsen Alves
Marketing Coordinator: Susan Osterlitz
Marketing Assistant: Angela Frey
Senior Managing Editor: Cynthia Zonneveld
Associate Managing Editor: Camille Trentacoste
Production Project Manager: Ruth Ferrera-Kargov

Manager of Rights & Permissions: Charles Morris
Senior Operations Specialist: Nick Sklitsis
Operations Specialist: Natacha Moore
Senior Art Director: Jonathan Boylan
Interior Design: Frubilicious Design Group
Cover Design: Frubilicious Design Group
Cover Illustration/Photo: © Steve Coleccs/iStockphoto
Illustration (Interior): Black Dot Group
Director, Image Resource Center: Melinda Patelli
Manager, Rights and Permissions: Zina Arabia
Manager, Visual Research: Beth Brenzel
Manager, Cover Visual Research & Permissions: Karen Sanatar
Image Permission Coordinator: Jan Marc Quisumbing
Photo Researchers: Sheila Norman and Kathy Ringrose
Composition: Black Dot Group
Full-Service Project Management: Black Dot Group
Printer/Binder: Webcrafters Inc.
Typeface: Adobe Garamond

Microsoft, Windows, Word, PowerPoint, Outlook, FrontPage, Visual Basic, MSN, The Microsoft Network, and/or other
Microsoft products referenced herein are either registered trademarks or registered trademarks of the Microsoft Corporation in
the U.S.A. and other countries. Screen shots and icons reprinted with permission from the Microsoft Corporation. This book is
not sponsored or endorsed by or affiliated with the Microsoft Corporation.

Pearson Education Ltd., London
Pearson Education Singapore, Pte. Ltd
Pearson Education, Canada, Inc.
Pearson Education–Japan
Pearson Education Australia PTY, Limited

Pearson Education North Asia Ltd., Hong Kong
Pearson Educación de Mexico, S.A. de C.V.
Pearson Education Malaysia, Pte. Ltd.
Pearson Education, Upper Saddle River, New Jersey

Prentice Hall
is an imprint of

10 9 8 7 6 5 4 3 2 1
ISBN-13: 978-0-13-506499-3
ISBN-10:   0-13-506499-6

INTERNET AND
COMPUTING CORE
CERTIFICATION

CERTIFICATION ROADMAP

Whether you're seeking further education, entering the job market, or advancing your skills through higher ICT certification, IC³ gives you the foundation you need to succeed.

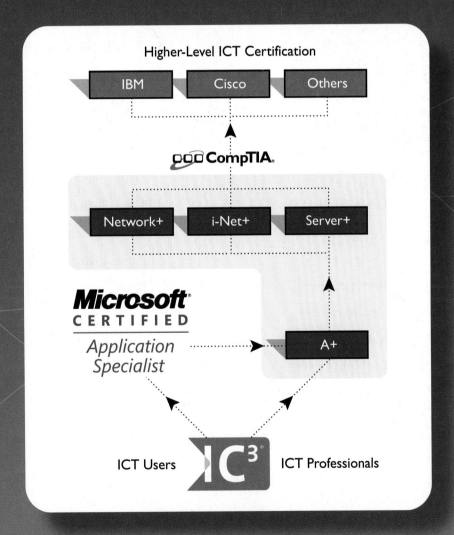

Higher-Level ICT Certification

IBM | Cisco | Others

CompTIA.

Network+ | i-Net+ | Server+

Microsoft
C E R T I F I E D

Application Specialist

A+

ICT Users | IC³ | ICT Professionals

Dedication

We have been working as a collaborative team since 1996. Our many years of friendship have been the glue holding this project together. We would like to dedicate this book to that unique camaraderie.

Acknowledgments

Our thanks go to Michael Payne for asking us to write this book. We appreciate the careful tech edits from Jan Snyder, Elizabeth Lockley, Janet Pickard, and June West, who paid attention to all the little details, and offered helpful suggestions for improvement. We also appreciate the contributions of Melissa Arlio and Eileen Calabro of Pearson Education.

Additionally, we would like to thank the following people for their valuable contributions to this book:

Shelley Allen	Elizabeth Lockley
Michelle August	Thomas McKenzie
Linda Bird	Lawrence Metzelaar
Lynn Bowen	Keith Mulbery
Julie Boyles	Phyllis Pace
Peter Casey	Ralph Phillips
Linda Collins	Janet Pickard
Lew Cousineau	Jennifer Pickle
Doug Cross	Anita P. Ricker
Annette Duvall	Steven Rubin
Denise Farley	Rafaat Saade
Marianne Fox	Cheryl L. Slavik
Anthony Garner	Jan Snyder
Laurie Grosik	Barbara Taylor
Carson Haury	Pam Toliver
Christine Held	Philip Vavalides
Bill Holmes	June West
Cheryl Jordan	

About the Authors

John Preston is an Associate Professor at Eastern Michigan University in the College of Technology in the Technology Management program. He has been teaching, writing, and designing computer courses since the advent of PCs, and has authored and co-authored more than 60 books on computer applications and the relationship between technology and society. He teaches courses in global technologies, managing information systems, project management, and quantitative reasoning. He served as program coordinator of the Energy Management program and has trained commercial energy auditors for all of the major utilities in Michigan. Prior to his tenure at EMU, he was a partner in an energy management consulting firm.

Sally Preston teaches computing in a variety of settings, which provides her with ample opportunity to observe how people learn, what works best, and what challenges are present when learning a new software program. This diverse experience provides a complementary set of skills and knowledge that is blended into her writing. Sally has been writing computer textbooks for nearly 10 years and has authored books for the *GO! Series,* the *Learn Series,* and for the *Essentials Series.* Sally has an MBA from Eastern Michigan University. When she is away from her computer, she is often found planting flowers in her garden.

Robert L. Ferrett recently retired as Director of the Center for Instructional Computing at Eastern Michigan University, where he provided computer training and support to faculty. He has authored or co-authored more than 80 books on Access, PowerPoint, Excel, Publisher, WordPerfect, Windows Vista, and Word. He has been designing, developing, and delivering computer workshops for nearly two decades. Bob has written for the *GO! Series,* and was a series editor for the *Learn 97, Learn 2000,* and *Learn XP* books. He has a BA in Psychology, an MS in Geography, and an MS in Interdisciplinary Technology from Eastern Michigan University. His doctoral studies are in Instructional Technology at Wayne State University. As a sidelight, Bob teaches a four-week Computers and Genealogy class, and has written genealogy and local history books.

IC³ Series Contents

Contents

chapter
four | Communicating Online   120

chapter
five | Working Online   180

Why We Wrote This Book

"I know how to use a computer"

We've probably all heard this statement at some point from our students and employees and wondered exactly what it meant—or, at least, what it meant to them. To those of us in the business of teaching computer skills, it's not just a matter of semantics. There is, in fact, a great deal of confusion out there about what constitutes computer literacy.

We often hear from administrators that the introductory level computer course will soon disappear at the college level. Because students today have greater exposure to computers by the time they leave high school, the argument goes, they feel comfortable enough to skip formal classes altogether. Yet in my experience teaching computer concepts and applications, I have come across such vast differences in the level of computer proficiency that it is nearly impossible to give the same lesson to any one group of students.

Even the best and most prepared students have significant gaps in their knowledge at the basic level. Some know how to surf the Internet, but have only a vague idea of how it works. Others, returning to school as adults, might know a few isolated applications but lack the concepts to learn software more thoroughly. All would benefit from a foundation course that teaches computers in the real world context that students must master in order to succeed—in college and in their careers.

This is where IC^3 comes in. The philosophy behind IC^3 certification helps define the concepts all students must know in order to be considered computer literate. Even if they never take the certification tests, this "common baseline" approach will give your students the confidence to say, "I know how to use a computer" and know exactly what that means.

Why IC^3?

Not just applications

- Unlike other certifications, IC^3 offers a well-rounded approach to computer literacy that covers basic computer concepts, applications, and the Internet.

Software is not vendor specific

- Although we wrote the applications section using Microsoft Office because it is the industry standard, students will learn about other operating systems such as Linux and Mac OS and other applications suites like OpenOffice.org.

Flexibility

- Because of the division of topics into three major areas—Computing Fundamentals, Key Applications, and Living Online—students can choose to focus on areas where they need more work. Faculty have the freedom to be creative while working within IC^3's defined framework. There are also two versions of *Unit 2: Using Productivity Software* allowing for even more flexibility; the traditional version written to Microsoft Office and a new version written to OpenOffice.org that is available through our Custom PHIT Database program.

Why Computer Literacy for IC³?

Comprehensive coverage of objectives
- Each of the IC³ objectives is covered comprehensively so you can be assured that your students are learning everything necessary to meet the standard.

Extensive end-of-project material
- Several levels of reinforcement exercises to choose from at the end of chapter—including **Assess Your Progress, On the Job,** and **On Your Own**—offer a range of choices.

Skills based, hands-on instruction
- Students grasp the material quickly and easily with clearly numbered, bold, step-by-step instructions within these hands-on tutorials.

Typeface Conventions Used in This Book

Computer Literacy for IC³ uses the following typeface conventions to make it easier for you to understand the material.

Monospace type appears frequently and `looks like this`. It is used to indicate text that you are instructed to key in.

Italic text indicates text that appears onscreen as (1) warnings, confirmation, or general information; (2) the name of a file to be used in a lesson or exercise; and (3) text from a menu or dialog box that is referenced within a sentence, when that sentence might appear awkward if it were not set off.

Hotkeys are indicated by underline. Hotkeys are the underlined letters in menus, toolbars, and dialog boxes that activate commands and options, and are a quick way to choose frequently used commands and options. Hotkeys look like this: <u>F</u>ile, <u>S</u>ave.

Student Resources

Companion Website (www.pearsonhighered.com/ic3).   This text-specific Website provides students with additional information and exercises to reinforce their learning. Features include: additional end-of-project reinforcement material; online Study Guide; easy access to *all* chapter data files; and much, much more!

Accessing Student Data Files.   The data files that students need to work through the chapters can be downloaded from the Companion Website (www.pearsonhighered.com/ic3). Data files are provided for each chapter. The filenames correspond to the filenames called for in this book. The filename indicates the unit, chapter, and topic. For example, where U2 is the unit number, Ch01 indicates the chapter number within that unit, which is followed by a descriptive name. After you open the file, you will save it with the same name followed by your name to identify the file as yours.

Instructor's Resources

The Instructor's Resource Center on CD-ROM is an interactive library of assets and links. The Instructor's Resource Center on CD-ROM writes custom "index" pages that can be used as the foundation of a class presentation or online lecture. By navigating through the CD-ROM, you can collect the materials that are most relevant to your interests, edit them to create powerful class lectures, copy them to your own computer's hard drive, and/or upload them to an online course management system. The new and improved Prentice Hall Instructor's Resource Center on CD-ROM includes tools you expect from a Prentice Hall text:

- The Instructor's Manual in Word and PDF formats—includes solutions to all questions and exercises from the book and Companion Website

- Multiple, customizable PowerPoint slide presentations for each chapter

- Data and Solution Files

- Complete Test Bank

- TestGen Software

- TestGen is a test generator that lets you view and easily edit test bank questions, transfer them to tests, and print in a variety of formats suitable to your teaching situation. The program also offers many options for organizing and displaying test banks and tests. A built-in random number and text generator makes it ideal for creating multiple versions of tests that involve calculations and provides more possible test items than test bank questions. Powerful search and sort functions let you easily locate questions and arrange them in the order you prefer.

CourseSmart

CourseSmart is an exciting new choice for students looking to save money. As an alternative to purchasing the print textbook, students can purchase an electronic version of the same content and save up to 50% off the suggested list price of the print text. With a CourseSmart etextbook, students can search the text, make notes online, print out reading assignments that incorporate lecture notes, and bookmark important passages for later review. For more information, or to purchase access to the CourseSmart eTextbook, visit www.coursesmart.com.

Companion Website @ www.pearsonhighered.com/ic3

This text is accompanied by a Companion Website at www.pearsonhighered.com/ic3. Features of this new site include an interactive study guide, downloadable supplements, additional practice projects, Web resources links. All links to Internet exercises will be constantly updated to ensure accuracy for students.

COMPUTER LITERACY FOR IC3™
Visual Walk-Through

From cover to cover, *Computer Literacy for IC3* makes it easier for you to teach the course you want. In addition to breaking each IC3 unit out into its own separate text, *Computer Literacy for IC3* contains many features that help students learn the material, effectively preparing them for each new lesson.

Know where IC3 standards are targeted within each lesson and direct student focus throughout, with the **Learning Outcomes** feature that closely matches the titles of the step-by-step tutorials.

Lesson	Learning Outcomes	Code	Related IC3 Objectives
1	Create a new document	2.01	1.2.1
1	Display the ruler	2.02	2.1.3
2	Create and modify a bulleted list	2.03	2.1.7, 2.1.16
3	Format text	2.04	1.3.6
3	Change text alignment	2.05	1.3.6
3	Indent text	2.06	2.12
4	Create a title with WordArt	2.07	1.3.7
4	Modify WordArt	2.08	1.3.7
5	Insert, resize and move clip art	2.09	1.3.7
6	Insert, move, and crop pictures	2.10	1.3.7
7	Create a table	2.11	2.1.13, 2.1.16
7	Insert and edit data in a table	2.12	2.1.13, 2.1.16
7	Modify table structure	2.13	2.1.14
7	Insert and delete cells, rows, and columns	2.14	2.1.14
7	Change column width and row height	2.15	2.1.14, 2.1.16
7	Convert text to a table or table to text	2.16	2.1.13
8	Format tables with table styles	2.17	2.1.15
8	Modify table formats using command buttons	2.18	2.1.15
8	Align table cell contents	2.19	2.1.15
8	Merge cells	2.20	2.1.15
8	Add, modify, and remove table and shading	2.21	2.1.15
8	Split cells in a table	2.22	2.1.14
8	Split tables	2.23	2.1.14
8	Sort data in a table	2.26	2.1.15
9	Insert and modify a footer	2.24	2.1.10
10	Use a document template	2.25	1.2.1
Advanced Skills	Use overtype	2.27	1.3.3
Advanced Skills	Transmit documents in electronic format	2.28	1.4.6, 1.4.7

Instructions throughout the lessons are based on the Vista operating system, running Microsoft Office 2007.

? *Why* Would I Do This?

Documents can be based on already existing files or written from scratch to create a new file. In addition, several preformatted and designed documents can be used for specific purposes such as memos or fax cover letters.

Formatting text helps the reader see the organization of the document and identify important information or ideas. Font selection conveys the tone of a document from serious to fun. Simple formatting tools enable you to change font, font size, or text alignment. You can emphasize text to make it stand out from the surrounding text by using bold, italic, underline, color, or special character effects.

Graphics add visual components to your documents that help draw the reader's attention or highlight an important idea or fact. Images should be related to the topic and provide visual interest or information. This can be done with pictures that are stored in a digital format, shapes used to create a drawing, borders and shading to draw attention to information, or electronic images provided with your software. Graphic elements can be resized and repositioned. Adding graphics creates excitement and visual appeal.

Tables are lists that display data in a column-and-row format. They organize and present parallel lists of information and can be used in a variety of circumstances.

Why Would I Do This? effectively explains why each task and procedure is important so that students will be able to apply them in real life scenarios.

Earth Day Tour

April 22

Tour behind the scenes to see how your campus is using energy responsibly:

- Discover how ice storage units in the dining commons are used to cool the building.
- See the co-generation unit that provides steam heat and electricity to campus buildings.
- Visiting the campus recycling center and learn how you can make a difference.
- Stop at the computerized energy control center which helps reduce energy use.

TOPIC	LOCATION	TIME
Cooling with Ice	North Dining Commons	1:00 to 1:30
Green Building Features	Student Activity Center	1:45 to 2:15
Co-Generation	Heating Plant	2:30 to 3:15
Energy Distribution	Physical Plant	3:30 to 4:00
Where Trash Goes	Recycling Center	4:15 to 4:45

Sponsored by Campus Committee for Responsible Energy Use (CCREU)

U2Ch02EarthDayStudentName   Last Name 11/6/2010

Make sure your students see the big picture with the **Visual Summary**, a graphical presentation of the concepts and features in each chapter that also includes the final results of the completed project.

visual **summary**

In this chapter, you will create a new document that is a flyer announcing an upcoming Earth Day tour at a local university, and then you will use a preformatted fax cover sheet to distribute the file electronically to the campus community. The documents created are shown in Figure 2.1.

---

4 Click the Page Layout tab. In the Paragraph group, under Spacing, in the After box, be sure that 10 pt displays. If 10 pt does not display, click in the After box, type 10 and then press ↵Enter. *Spacing after* adds space between paragraphs, which occurs when you press ↵Enter to begin a new paragraph. Recall that a paragraph can be a single line of text. The default spacing following a paragraph in Word 2007 is 10 pt, which creates white space between paragraphs.

5 Click the Home tab, and in the Paragraph group, click the Line Spacing button, and then click 1.0 to set the line spacing to single-space. The default *line spacing*—the spacing between lines of text in a paragraph—is 1.15 in Word 2007. When text is *single-spaced*—1.0—there is no additional space between lines of text in a paragraph.

6 Type Earth Day Tour press ↵Enter, and then type April 22 Notice that there is space between these two lines of text because of the spacing after feature that is set to 10 pt.

7 Press ↵Enter. Type Tour behind the scenes to see how your campus is using energy responsibly: and then press ↵Enter.

8 On the Quick Access Toolbar, click the Save button to display the Save As dialog box. If you have not previously saved your file, the Save As dialog box will display when you click the Save button.

Provide students with the "learn by doing" **Step-by-Step Tutorials**, a feature that uses one-at-a-time instructions in a clear numbered and bolded format.

---

to extend **your knowledge...**

CHANGING FONT SIZE

Another way to change font size is to use the Grow Font or Shrink Font buttons that are in the Font group, just to the right of the Font Size box. Each time you click one of these buttons, the font size is increased with the Grow Font button or decreased with the Shrink Font button.

Show your students alternative ways to complete a process, give them special hints about using the software, and provide them with extra tips and shortcuts with the **To Extend Your Knowledge** feature.

Capture teachable moments with **Good Design**, a Unit 2 feature that introduces design tips in the most applicable section of the material. This feature is assessed in the **Fix It**, **On the Job**, and **On Your Own** end-of-chapter exercises.

good **design...**

USING LISTS TO ORGANIZE DATA

Lists of data can be presented using several different techniques. It is important to select the best option for the data to be listed. Use bullet lists when there is no particular order to the items listed, and use numbered lists when there is an order, such as steps in a process, order of importance, or chronological order.

Help students anticipate or solve common problems quickly and effectively with **If You Have Problems**, a feature that provides short troubleshooting notes.

fix *it*

One way to appreciate the value of good design is to fix a file that is not designed well. In this exercise, you open a file that has several errors and design flaws and fix it according to good design elements, using the skills that you practiced in the lessons.

Navigate to the folder with the student files, open **U2Ch02FixIt** and save it as U2Ch02FixItStudentName

Examine this document and format it using the skills you have practiced so that it is a professional, readable flyer that will attract attention and create interest. Make changes to comply with the good design principles that were introduced in this chapter. Here is a list of corrections needed and the design principles introduced in this chapter, along with some tips on how to fix the flyer.

- Create a title for the flyer to attract attention to the topic of energy efficiency.
- Use a clip art that is appropriate to the topic, and position it to break up the opening paragraphs.
- Use a font that is appropriate to the topic, audience, and type of document.
- Use a font size that is easy to read quickly.
- Adjust the alignment and/or indents to create a balanced document.
- Where it is appropriate, convert text to a table, and insert a row with column headings.
- Format the table so that it is clear and easy to read. Center the table on the page.
- Insert the **U2Ch02WDBuilding2** image, which is the building that will be LEED-certified.

Encourage hands-on design practice with **Fix It**. This feature gets students to improve a file containing several errors and design flaws by having them use the skills and good design elements that they practiced in their lessons.

Prepare students to use each lesson outside the classroom with the extensive **end-of-chapter exercises**. These exercises include: **Check Your Work**, **Assessing Learning Outcomes**, **Skill Drill**, **On the Job**, **On Your Own**, and **Assess Your Progress**.

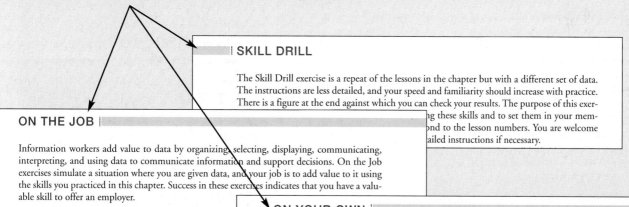

SKILL DRILL

The Skill Drill exercise is a repeat of the lessons in the chapter but with a different set of data. The instructions are less detailed, and your speed and familiarity should increase with practice. There is a figure at the end against which you can check your results. The purpose of this exer-
~~g these skills and to set them in your mem-~~
~~nd to the lesson numbers. You are welcome~~
~~ailed instructions if necessary.~~

ON THE JOB

Information workers add value to data by organizing, selecting, displaying, communicating, interpreting, and using data to communicate information and support decisions. On the Job exercises simulate a situation where you are given data, and your job is to add value to it using the skills you practiced in this chapter. Success in these exercises indicates that you have a valuable skill to offer an employer.

ON YOUR OWN

Once you are comfortable with the skills in this chapter, you can apply them to new situations of your own choosing. In this section, you choose data that you have in your possession or that you can find elsewhere. To successfully complete this assignment, you must apply good design practices and demonstrate mastery of the skills that were practiced. Refer to the list of skills and design practices in the Fix It exercise.

chapter one

Understanding the Internet

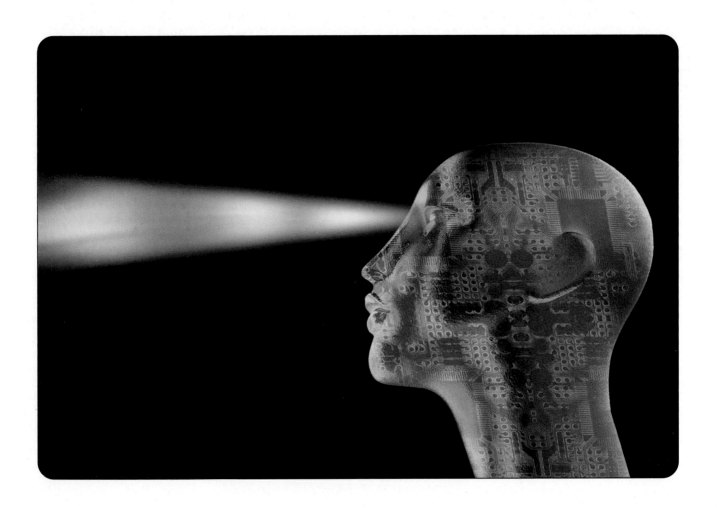

Lesson	Learning Outcomes	Code	Related IC3 Objectives
1	Identify how traditional telephone systems work	1.01	1.1.1
1	Identify why the Internet was created	1.02	1.1.2
1	Identify how packets are labeled	1.03	-
1	Identify how packet switching works	1.04	-
2	Identify relationships between computers in a Local Area Network	1.05	1.1.1, 1.1.2, 1.1.3
2	Identify how computers are connected	1.06	1.1.6
2	Identify characteristics of a Wide Area Network	1.07	1.1.5
2	Identify types of cables and their characteristics	1.08	-
2	Identify how networks are connected to make super networks	1.09	3.1.1
2	Identify the parts of an Internet address	1.10	3.1.1, 3.1.2
2	Search online for available domain names	1.11	3.1.2
2	Identify the role of a domain name server	1.12	2.1.3
2	Identify functions of computers on the Internet as hosts, gateways, and routers	1.13	3.1.4
2	Identify the benefits and risks of networking	1.14	1.1.2
3	Identify the relationship between the Internet and the World Wide Web	1.15	3.1.1
4	Identify the functions of a gateway and an Internet Service Provider	1.16	3.1.2
4	Identify measurements used to describe transmission rates	1.17	1.1.6
4	Identify methods of connecting to the Internet via a telephone company	1.18	1.1.6
4	Identify methods of connecting to the Internet via a cable television company	1.19	1.1.6
4	Identify methods of connecting to the Internet via a wireless radio or satellite company	1.20	1.1.6
5	Identify the organization that coordinates domain names	1.21	-
6	Identify elements of the code of ethical conduct of system administrators	1.22	3.2.6
6	Identify the characteristics of strong passwords	1.23	4.2.3
6	Identify the function of a firewall	1.24	1.1.7

Why **Would I Do This?**

One of the reasons the Internet was created was to provide a communication system that would still work if significant parts of the system failed. It grew and changed into a worldwide communication system that has changed the way we live. This network of computers handles a majority of our personal communications and an increasing amount of commercial communication. In this chapter, you study how it is managed, who controls it, and how we should behave when we use it.

visual summary |

In these lessons, you will study the relationships between computers and the functions that they perform to move data across a network of computers. You will find out how this global system came about and how to connect to it. You will learn who controls it, how people make money from its use, and how you can protect your security and privacy while behaving ethically.

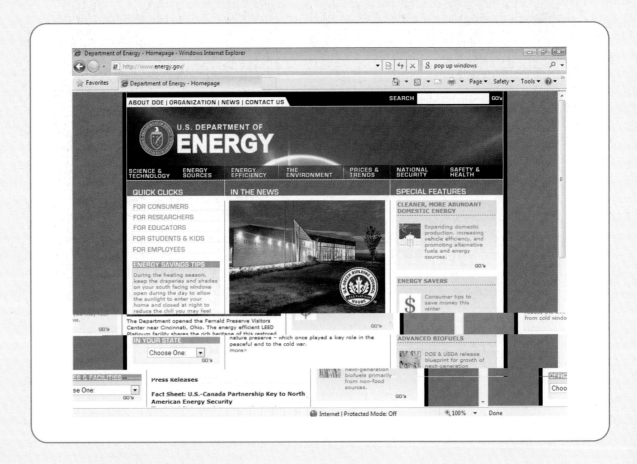

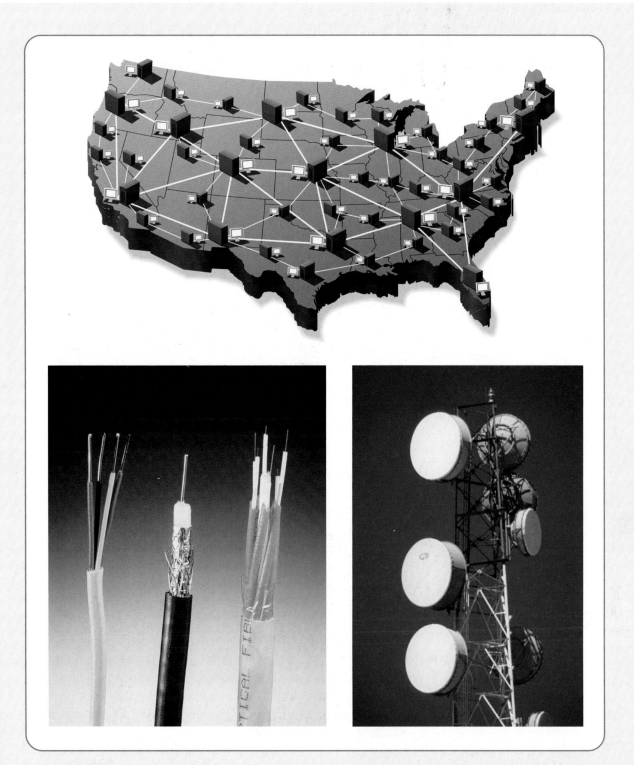

FIGURE 1.1
Computers are connected by wires and wireless systems.

List of Student and Solution Files

In most cases, you will create files using text or pictures found on Web pages. You will add your name to the file names and save them on your computer or portable memory device. Table 1.1 lists the files you start with and the names you give them when you save the files.

ASSIGNMENT	STUDENT SOURCE FILE:	SAVE AS:
Lessons 1–6	none	U3Ch01DomainStudentName U3Ch01SenateStudentName U3Ch01HTMLStudentName U3Ch01SpeedStudentName U3Ch01BackboneStudentName
Skill Drill	none	U3Ch01RegisterStudentName U3Ch01IPStudentName U3Ch01TitleStudentName
Explore and Share	none	U3Ch01IPLocationStudentName U3Ch01TraceStudentName U3Ch01MyDomainStudentName U3Ch01MyHostStudentName
In Your Life	none	none
Related Skills	none	U3Ch01PasswordStudentName U3Ch01PrenhallStudentName U3Ch01FirewallStudentName
Discover	none	none
Assess Your Progress	U3Ch01Assess	U3Ch01AssessStudentName

TABLE 1.1

▶▶▶ *lesson*
one | Creating Faster, More Reliable Communications

The need to coordinate strategic military forces and to improve the coordination between military research facilities led the U.S. government to adapt the telephone system, using a new method of communication that was less vulnerable to disruption. The new system eventually became the Internet that we know today that assists creation of online communities by enabling one-to-one and one-to-many communications. People are able to collaborate online by sharing documents and other resources such as audio and video files. Computers are used at work, home, or school to collect, organize, and evaluate information to increase productivity. People use them to solve real-world problems, support critical thinking and creativity, and to facilitate learning and daily functions such as entertainment, buying and selling, and interacting with government agencies.

The Internet does more than connect traditional desktop and laptop computers. It is used behind the scenes to connect automatic bank teller machines, point-of-sale terminals, and to approve credit card purchases. It is used to coordinate automated industrial processes and natural disaster recovery, and to communicate with sensors in automobiles, appliances, and security systems. Manufacturers use network communications to coordinate robots to increase efficiency.

How Traditional Telephone Systems Work

When you place a telephone call on a traditional phone system, the call uses wires that lead back to a central office, where your wires are connected to other wires leading to the recipient's phone. This method is called *circuit switching*. All the wires in a particular area are connected to the central office. This type of configuration is called a *star*. When a group of devices is arranged so they can be connected to each other, the group and its connection devices is called a *network*.

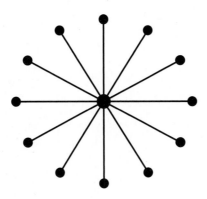

FIGURE 1.2
Star network.

If you want to make a call to a neighboring city, your local phone system uses another set of wires that connect its central office to the central telephone office in the other city, and then that central office connects your call to the wires that lead to the local recipient of the call.

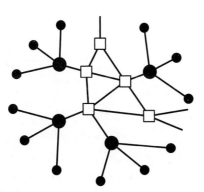

FIGURE 1.3
Star networks linked together.

The farther apart the two parties are from each other, the more cities and wires are used. A single long distance call can use many sets of wires that are not available for use by other people, which is why long distance calls cost more than local calls. If one of the wires in this series of connections is broken, the call is interrupted.

The connection between circuits was originally made by a person called the ***switchboard operator***, who physically lifted a plug at the end of one wire and pushed it into a socket that was connected to a different wire, as shown in Figure 1.4.

FIGURE 1.4
Switchboard and operator.

The act of connecting circuits was later automated with ***relays*** that consist of an electromagnet that pulls a set of contacts together, as shown in Figure 1.5.

FIGURE 1.5
Relays connect circuits.

Need for a System That Could Survive Major Losses

In 1962, the United States had several research facilities around the country that used computers. Government leaders wanted to speed up research by connecting the labs so their computers could exchange data. In August 1962, J. C. R. Licklider of the Massachusetts Institute of Technology (MIT) wrote a series of memos in which he described his concept of a "Galactic Network," which consisted of a globally interconnected set of computers that could quickly access data and programs from each other. Licklider was the first head of a government agency named the ***Advanced Research Projects Agency (ARPA)***, where he was able to implement his ideas and create a small network of connected computers called ***ARPANET***. The new system would use computers to manage connections between computers. At that time, computers failed frequently, so a reliable method of transmitting data in spite of numerous failures had to be developed.

The key to this new method of communication was the recognition of the following facts:

- A telephone system is a network of networks, where each central office is connected to several other offices and there are many possible pathways from one location to another.

- Only one pathway out of many has to survive for a message to get through.

- Computers can perform millions of operations each second. If you divide up a normal telephone conversation into very short time segments and examine them, most of the slices of time are unused. Just in the time it takes a person to breathe in before they start their next sentence, a computer could transmit the text of a small book.

- Computers can be used to connect circuits very rapidly, using electronic switches that have no moving parts.

Transmission Control Protocol/Internet Protocol (TCP/IP)

To allow computers to transfer data reliably in spite of equipment failure, a new method was devised in which the data was divided into small packages that could be transmitted independently, checked for errors, and replaced if lost. The data used by computers consists of zeros and ones, called ***bits (b)***, and each character in the alphabet was assigned an eight-bit number called a ***byte (B)***. For example, the number for the capital letter A was 01000001. A message or data file is divided up into small groups called ***packets*** that are about 1,000 bytes long. Part of each packet is used for labeling, and the label includes:

- the address of the recipient,
- the address of the sender,
- the sequence number of the packet, and
- a ***checksum***—the sum of numbers in the packet.

Because all of the packets have the destination address and a sequence number, shown in Figure 1.6, they can travel different routes across the network to get to the same destination, where they are reassembled into the final message or data file.

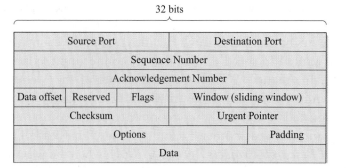

32 bits

Source Port		Destination Port	
Sequence Number			
Acknowledgement Number			
Data offset	Reserved	Flags	Window (sliding window)
Checksum		Urgent Pointer	
Options			Padding
Data			

FIGURE 1.6
Packet addressing.

Groups of rules used to manage data exchange are called **protocols**. Protocols are standards that may be adopted to allow networks to communicate even if they use equipment from different manufacturers or different types of devices. The two major protocols for transmitting the packets across the Internet are usually referred to together as **Transmission Control Protocol/Internet Protocol (TCP/IP)**. The packets can be sent to the local telephone system's central office, where a computer examines all of its connections to other central offices and chooses the connections that are not currently in use. For example, it might send some of the packets out on a telephone line while someone is speaking on it but has paused between words. To the computer, that pause is unused capacity. By rapidly examining every connection for unused capacity and sending the packets out on whatever line is available at the moment, the computer makes very efficient use of its circuits. This lowers the cost of sending messages because circuits are not dedicated to one call at a time.

When the packets arrive at the next computer on the network, it first checks to see if any of the numbers in the packet were lost or changed in transit. The computer adds up the numbers in each packet it receives and compares the result to the checksum on the packet. If they do not match, the computer determines that the packet is flawed, and it sends a request back to the computer that originated the message to send it again. When the computer is satisfied that the packet is undamaged, it examines the destination address and chooses an available circuit that would take the packet closer to its destination. The process is shown in Figure 1.7.

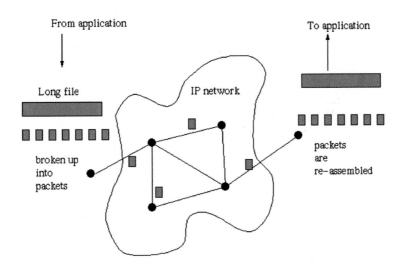

FIGURE 1.7
Data transmitted as packets.

Eventually, all the packets arrive at the destination computer, which reassembles them using the packets' sequence numbers. With this method, messages get through accurately even if large parts of the network are destroyed and some of the packets are lost or damaged. Both circuit switching and packet switching use the same wires, but if a computer does the switching, it can use packet switching with TCP/IP, which makes much more efficient use of the lines. The military adopted TCP/IP as its communication standard in 1980 because of its efficient use of transmission circuits and its reliability when parts of the system fail.

Birth of the Internet

In the early days, ARPANET enabled people to exchange data and to run programs on computers from distant parts of the country. Two popular protocols that are included in TCP/IP are *File Transfer Protocol (FTP)*, which enables users to transfer files between computers, and *Telnet*, which enables a user to log in to a remote computer as if he or she were at the facility. In 1972, ARPANET was demonstrated to the public with a new application—electronic mail or *e-mail*. E-mail permitted people to communicate directly with each other with text messages. Because many of the military research centers were at large universities, researchers and university students who were working on these projects began using e-mail to communicate, and the network became a mode of interpersonal communication.

▶▶▶ *lesson*
tWO | Networks of Computers

Computers on the Internet are connected to each other in a variety of ways. In this lesson, you study the roles and relationships between computers in a network.

Relationships Between Computers

Computers that are close to each other can be connected in a group called a ***Local Area Network (LAN)***. Each element of a network is called a ***node***. A computer can be a node and so can a printer. Computers that provide services to the other computers are called ***servers***. In a server-based LAN, the computers are connected to a ***network server*** that manages the flow of data between the computers, as shown in Figure 1.8.

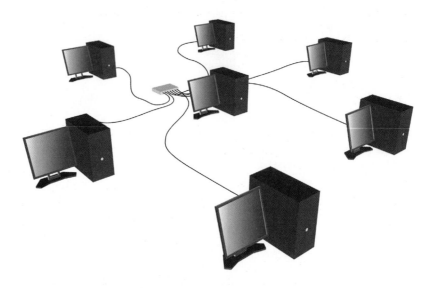

FIGURE 1.8
Server-based network.

If the computers are connected so that they can communicate directly with each other, the relationship is called a ***peer-to-peer*** network. See Figure 1.9.

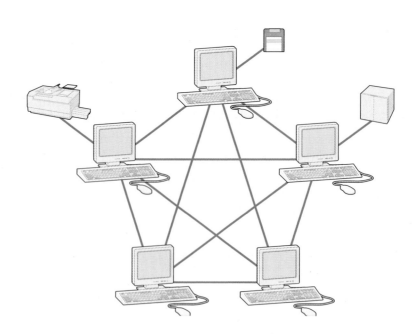

FIGURE 1.9
Peer-to-peer network.

In LANs, where there are dozens or even hundreds of computers, it is more efficient to provide often-used services from a server. Some common functions that are performed by a server on a network are:

- storing and retrieving files—*file server*
- coordinating use of a shared printer—*print server*
- storing and providing Web pages—*Web server*
- interpreting requests and retrieving data from a database—*database server*
- managing electronic mail—*mail server*

Client-Server Relationship

A function—such as retrieving customer information—can be divided into two parts called *client* and *server*. For example, the client software gathers information from the user, such as the customer identification number. The client software makes a service request to the database server for the customer's purchase history. The server software finds the customer's purchase history on the database and sends it back to the client. The relationship between the two computers and the software that runs on them is called a client-server relationship. The server provides services at the request of the client. To provide services to many other computers on the network quickly, the computers that are used as servers often have faster processors and more memory than computers used by individuals. Manufacturers offer lines of powerful computers that are designed to work as servers such as Dell's PowerEdge series.

Computers that are used as clients can be individual desktop computers, laptops, handheld devices, or even game systems.

Methods of Connection

The nodes of a network can be connected by any means that provides a method of sending data between the nodes. The nodes can be connected by wires, by radio, or by *infrared (IR)*—light that is invisible due to its longer wavelength. The most common methods of connection are:

- copper wires, called *twisted pair*, that are insulated and twisted around each other inside an outer coating of insulation (Figure 1.10). The twisting reduces electrical interference.
- a copper wire surrounded by a layer of insulation and then surrounded by a metal sheath, as shown in Figure 1.10. The centerline of the wire and the metal sheath have the same linear axis, and this type of wire is called *coaxial cable* or just *coax*.
- radio signals—usually referred to as *wireless*.
- invisible light in the infrared range of the spectrum.
- thin, flexible, glass fibers inside of a protective covering—called *fiber optic cable* or just *fiber*, as shown in Figure 1.10.

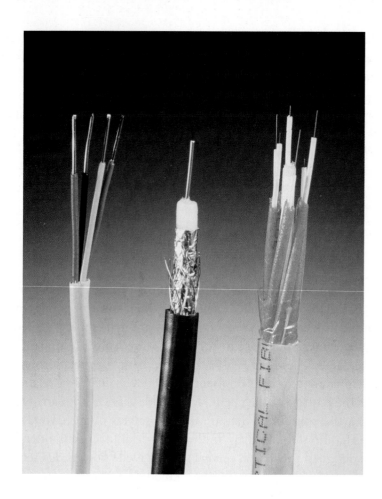

FIGURE 1.10
Twisted pairs, coax, and optical cables.

Each type of connection method has its advantages and disadvantages. The factors to consider are cost, maximum distance between nodes, security, and speed. The relative advantages and disadvantages are summarized in Table 1.2.

TYPE	COST	DISTANCE BETWEEN NODES	SECURITY	SPEED
Twisted pair	Lowest	<100 meters	Good	Good
Coax	Medium	100–500 m	Good	Good
Radio (wireless)	Low	Up to miles	Poor*	Fair
Infrared	Low	Short and line of sight	Excellent	Excellent
Fiber optic	High	Many miles	Excellent	Excellent

TABLE 1.2
*Radio waves can be detected outside the intended area of use. The security can be improved by encoding the signal.

Most networks use a star configuration with twisted pairs of wires. At the center of the star is the **router**. The router identifies and selects the route the data should take to reach its intended destination. LAN connections can transmit millions of bits of data per second (abbreviated *mbps*). The most common standard used to specify the connections between computers in a network using wires or cables is the **Ethernet** standard. The Ethernet standard uses a code to describe the type of wire or cable. For example, a twisted pair that transfers data at 10 million bits per second and is only used for data is labeled 10BASE-T, where 10 is the speed in mbps, BASE means that it is only used for data, and T stands for twisted pair. Nodes on a LAN that are connected by twisted pair and coaxial cable have to be relatively close to the router. Refer to Table 1.3.

CODE	DESCRIPTION	MAXIMUM LENGTH (METERS)	SPEED (MBPS)
10BASE-T	Twisted pair	100	10
100BASE-T4	Four twisted pairs	100	100
1000BASE-T	Four twisted pairs	100	1,000
10BASE-2	Thin coax	185	10
10BASE-5	Thickwire coax	500	10

TABLE 1.3

Wide Area Networks (WAN)

If nodes on the network have to be farther apart than a few hundred meters, it is often called a **Wide Area Network (WAN)**. A bank that has branch banks in the same city is an example of WAN. Connections between nodes of a WAN are usually a mixture of twisted pair for short distances and **broadband coax**, **fiber optic**, or **radio** for intermediate distances. Refer to Table 1.4.

CODE	DESCRIPTION	MAXIMUM LENGTH (METERS)	SPEED (MBPS)
10BASE-36	Broadband coax	3,600	10
10BASE-F	Fiber optic	2,000	10
	Microwave radio	Line of sight	100

TABLE 1.4

Microwave radio uses shaped antennas to direct the waves as shown in Figure 1.11.

FIGURE 1.11
Microwave radio antennas.

Connections Between Networks

When several networks are connected that use the same protocols, a ***bridge*** can be used to send and receive messages. If the connected networks are not similar, a ***gateway***—which can consist of hardware, software, or a combination of both—handles the communications by changing the data from one network to a format the other network can understand. The Internet is a network of networks that are connected by gateways and routers. The gateway and router functions are usually combined in the same device.

Routers send messages along from one network to another until they reach their destination by choosing the best route. The term *router* can be used in two different situations. It applies to a computer at the center of a LAN that routes messages to the appropriate computer, printer, or other device. The term is also used to describe a computer at a node that connects to other networks and chooses the path that packets should take on the next leg of their journey.

Addresses on the Internet

An addressing system was devised that could provide each resource on the Internet with a unique address. The system is called the **Uniform Resource Locator (URL)**. It is similar to the method one uses to address an envelope, except that the portions of the address are separated by periods.

Some URLs end with a code that identifies the country called the **country code top-level domain (ccTLD)**. For example, here is the address of the home Web page of the Australian government:

http://www.australia.gov.**au**

The country is denoted by a two-letter code as emphasized in bold above. Refer to Table 1.5 for a partial list of country codes and notice that the abbreviation for Australia is *au*. Country codes can be part of the address but are not required.

CODE	COUNTRY	CODE	COUNTRY
.ac	Ascension Island	.ir	Iran, Islamic Republic of
.ae	United Arab Emirates	.it	Italy
.af	Afghanistan	.jm	Jamaica
.aq	Antarctica	.jp	Japan
.au	Australia	.ke	Kenya
.bb	Barbados	.kp	Korea, Democratic People's Republic of
.bm	Bermuda	.kr	Korea, Republic of
.ca	Canada	.mx	Mexico
.cg	Congo, Republic of	.ng	Nigeria
.cn	China	.nz	New Zealand
.cu	Cuba	.pk	Pakistan
.de	Germany	.th	Thailand
.eg	Egypt	.to	Tonga
.es	Spain	.tv	Tuvalu
.fi	Finland	.tw	Taiwan
.fj	Fiji	.uk	United Kingdom
.il	Israel	.us	United States
.in	India	.va	Holy See (City; Vatican State)
.iq	Iraq	.ve	Venezuela

TABLE 1.5

The next level of address is the class of domain—**generic top-level domain (gTLD)**. This part of the address is an abbreviation that describes a general category to which the address belongs.

http://www.australia.**gov**.au

The generic top-level domain code in this example is .gov as emphasized in bold above. Refer to Table 1.6 for a partial list of generic top-level domain names.

TYPE OF ORGANIZATION	CODE	RESTRICTIONS
Air transportation	.aero	Air travel related
Asia-Pacific	.asia	Companies, organizations, or individuals based in Asia
Business	.biz	Open—intended for business
Catalan language	.cat	Websites or cultural sites in Catalan
Commercial	.com	Open
Cooperatives	.coop	Cooperative organizations
Education	.edu	Schools
Government	.gov	Government agencies
Information	.info	Open
International	.int	Groups created by treaty between countries
Companies	.jobs	Companies with jobs to offer
Military	.mil	U.S. Military
Mobile	.mobi	Mobile devices
Museums	.museum	Legitimate museums
Individuals	.name	Individual people
General	.net	Open
Noncommercial (open to all)	.org	Open
Credentialed professionals (pending)	.pro	Licensed doctors, attorneys, CPAs
Internet communication services	.tel	
Travel	.travel	Travel and tourism
Television	.tv	Related to television

TABLE 1.6

The next part of the address is the ***domain name***.

http://www.**australia**.gov.au

The domain name can be any combination of letters, numbers, and a few other characters such as a hyphen, but it cannot be the same as any other domain name of the same type. For example, australia.gov and australia.org are two different domains. In general, the combination of the domain name and the top-level domain are referred to as the *domain name*. The combination must be unique.

http://**www.**australia.gov.au

The section before the domain name is the name of the computer that serves the Web pages or files for that domain name. If the address is of a Web page, most Web servers are simply named *www*. This portion is often left off or assumed but it is required by some servers.

http://www.australia.gov.au

The beginning of the address describes the protocol used to transfer the file. In this example, the *Hypertext Transfer Protocol (HTTP)* is specified. This is the protocol used to transfer Web pages across the Internet. This portion is assumed by most browser programs if it is left off. If a network uses Web page servers and the same protocols as the Internet but it is private, it is called an *intranet*.

Available Domain Names

If you can think of a domain name that no one else is already using, you can register it for your own use. Most registration services offer a free service that checks to see if the domain name you want is available. This exercise assumes that your computer is connected to the Internet and that you have a Web browser program.

to check for an available domain name

1 **Start a Web browser such as Internet Explorer, Firefox, or Safari.** Web browsers are programs that request Web pages from Web servers on the Internet.

2 **In the Address box near the top of the Web browser screen, type** `http://www.networksolutions.com` **and then press** `⏎Enter`. The NetworkSolutions homepage displays.

3 **Under *Find a domain*, click in the empty box and type any name you would like to check.**

4 **Below the name, confirm that the boxes next to .com and .net are checked.** Your choice of domain name is ready to check, as shown in Figure 1.12.

FIGURE 1.12
Checking a domain name.

5   **Below the name, click the Search button.** The results are shown and you can see what combinations of names and types are still available.

6   **Click the Start button, click All Programs, click the Accessories folder, and then in the list of programs, click Snipping Tool.**

7   **In the Snipping Tool dialog box, click the New Snip button arrow** ✂, **and then click Window Snip. Point anywhere in the NetworkSolutions window, and then click one time.**

8   **On the Snipping Tool dialog box menu bar, click the Save Snip button** 💾. **In the Save As dialog box, navigate to the folder where you store your files. In the File name box, type** `U3Ch01DomainStudentName` **substituting your name as indicated, and then click Save.**

··

if you have problems

NO SNIPPING TOOL...

The Snipping Tool is available in Windows Vista. If you are using Windows XP, you can use the PrtScn button to capture the screen and paste it into a word processing document.

··

9   **In the upper right corner of each open dialog box or window, click the Close button** ⊠ .

10   **Submit your snip as directed by your instructor.**

The Role of the Domain Name System

Each domain name is assigned to a computer that provides the service of delivering Web pages or files. This computer is called the ***host*** or *Web server*. Computers work best with numbers, and the address of each host computer is a number called its ***Internet Protocol (IP) address***. For example, the address of the official U.S. Senate Web page is http://www.senate.gov. The computer that hosts this Web page has an IP address of 156.33.195.33. One computer can be the host of several different domain names. This combination of domain name and IP number is the ***Domain Name System (DNS)***. A computer that provides a current list of the domain names and the IP addresses of their host computers is a ***domain name server***. The group that coordinates the naming system to be sure there are no duplicate IP addresses or domain names in the entire world is the ***Internet Corporation for Assigned Names and Numbers (ICANN)***.

to use an IP address

1 **Start a Web browser such as Internet Explorer, Firefox, or Safari.**

2 **In the Address box near the top of the Web browser screen, type** `http://156.33.195.33` **and then press** `⏎Enter`**.** The homepage for the United States Senate displays, as shown in Figure 1.13.

FIGURE 1.13
Checking a domain name.

3 **Use the skills you practiced previously to start the Snip program and snip the homepage of the U.S. Senate. Save a copy of this Web page to the folder where you store your files. Name the file** `U3Ch01SenateStudentName` **substituting your name as indicated.**

4 **In the Web browser window, point to the Close button** [X] **in the upper right corner, and then click the left mouse button.** The browser window closes.

If a computer hosts more than one domain name, you usually get a welcome screen that is provided by the hosting service when you enter its IP address.

Hosts, Registries, and the Domain Name System

One company or group—called a *registry*—is responsible for each top-level domain. If you register to use a domain name that ends with their top-level domain—such as .org—you still need to make arrangements with a company that has a host computer with its own IP address on the Internet. This type of company is called an *Internet Service Provider (ISP)*. It has a computer that can communicate with other computers on the Internet using TCP/IP standards, and its computer has an IP address. If you want to display Web pages using your domain name, the host computer stores and serves the Web pages for you. The combination of a domain name that can be understood by humans—like senate.gov—and the IP address of a computer that can be easily used by computers—such as 156.33.195.33—is the *domain name system (DNS)*.

Each registry keeps a master list of all the domain names it has created that end with its top-level domain name. The list also contains the IP address of the computer that is hosting that domain name. If you choose to change hosting services for your domain name, this master list must be updated. When a computer on the Internet receives a request for a Web page, the computer can send a request to the registry for the IP address of the host computer and then route the request to it.

Backbone

Recall that the Internet is a network of networks. The connections between networks often carry large amounts of data. In the early days of the Internet, the government paid for the computers that provided the switching and routing and the main connections between the networks. The metaphor used to describe this arrangement is the spine of an animal that connects the head, ribs, pelvis, and legs together, and this is called the *backbone*. Extremely transparent fiber optic cable was developed that could transmit flashes of light for about 100,000 meters between nodes. This cable is laid on the ocean floor to connect the countries of the world with fast internet connections (Figure 1.14).

Benefits and Risks of Networked Computers

There are several benefits to connecting computers in a network:

- Specialized equipment such as printers and copiers can be shared
- People can share documents and collaborate on projects
- There is centralized control of computing resources to reduce costs and to increase security
- Productivity is increased when people can access the information they need quickly.

Unfortunately, there are risks that arise when computers are connected on a network:

- Each person has less control over the configuration and operation of his or her computer
- Others might use the network connection to invade the user's privacy or to cause damage to the software or data on the computer through the spread of malicious programs or through unauthorized access
- Failure of centralized systems could stop work for many people at once

In general, the benefits outweigh the risks because networking increases individual productivity and group collaboration while reducing costs.

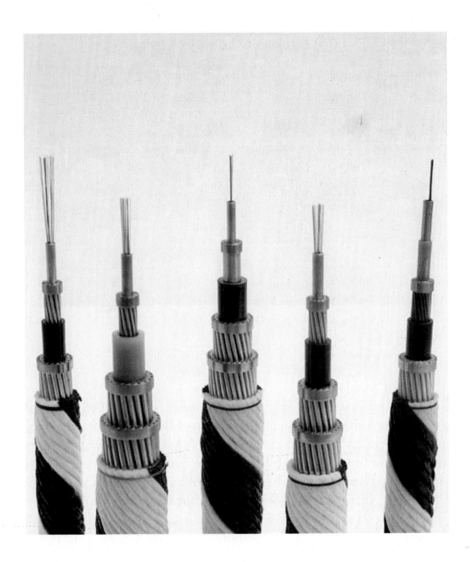

FIGURE 1.14
Undersea fiber optic cables.

▶▶▶ *lesson*
three | Birth of the World Wide Web

In 1990, Tim Berners-Lee (see Figure 1.15), a programmer at the CERN (Conseil Europeen pour la Recherche Nucleaire) physics research facility in Switzerland, developed a way for computers to share text documents. The documents were placed on computers that acted as servers, and other computers were able to run programs called *clients* that could retrieve and display the documents. He used a ***browser***—a program that requests and displays Web pages—to display documents. He envisioned a network of connected computers forming a ***World Wide Web*** of documents that were interlinked. He named his browser ***WorldWideWeb***. The browser was provided free to anyone on the Internet who wanted to use it.

FIGURE 1.15
Tim Berners-Lee.

In 1992, Marc Andreessen and several other students at the University of Illinois at Urbana-Champaign took the World Wide Web design of Berners-Lee and added the ability to embed graphical elements. They called their browser *Mosaic*. It was available as a free download from servers on the Internet, and by 1993 more than one million people were using it. The Mosaic browser was easy to use by the general public and was available in versions that ran on personal computers that used Windows and Macintosh operating systems. Students who worked on Mosaic were instrumental in developing the next generation of Web browser: *Netscape*. Netscape added secure communications that made it possible to conduct business on the Internet, and at one time it had ninety percent of the browser market. The three most common Web browser programs currently in use are Microsoft's *Internet Explorer*, Mozilla Corporation's *Mozilla Firefox*, and Apple's *Safari*.

Web browser programs use *Hypertext Markup Language*, or *HTML*, to describe how text and figures should be displayed. A document that is written in HTML and displayed by a browser is a *Web page*. For example, when you download a Web page, the text you see on the screen is embedded between codes that tell the browser how to display the text. If a word like *hello* is displayed in bold, the word is preceded by <b> and followed by </b>, as in this example: <b>hello</b>. The browser works with your computer's internal graphics system to display the word **hello** in bold. Recall that the method used to transfer Web pages is written in HTML which is the hypertext transfer protocol (http). This is why the Web address of a Web page begins with *http://*—to specify what protocol to use. Web pages can contain links to other Web pages, which are called *hyperlinks*. The links are typically identified with a different color font and underlining. They may also be attached to graphics. Hyperlinks are usually activated by a mouse click.

to view the HTML code of a Web page

1 **Start a Web browser such as Internet Explorer, Firefox, or Safari.** The following instructions are written for Internet Explorer.

2 **In the Address box near the top of the Web browser screen, type** `http://www.senate.gov` **and then press** ⏎Enter**.** The homepage for the United States Senate displays.

3 **In the Web browser window, on the menu bar, click View, and then click Source.** A window opens and displays the HTML code (Figure 1.16). The code is complicated, but you can see how <> and </> symbols are used to mark the beginning and end of sections of the code.

FIGURE 1.16
HTML source code for Senate homepage.

4 **Use the skills you practiced previously to start the Snip program and snip the page that displays the HTML code for the homepage of the U.S. Senate. Save a copy of this window to the folder where you store your files. Name the file** `U3Ch01HTMLStudentName` **substituting your name as indicated.**

5 **In the browser window, point to the Close button** ❎ **in the upper right corner, and then click the left mouse button.** The browser window closes.

Relationship Between the Internet and the World Wide Web

The Internet is the network of networks that can be used for a variety of purposes, including the original functions of transferring files and remote login. The World Wide Web is a subset of the Internet that uses Hypertext Transfer Protocol to exchange Web pages written in HTML.

▶▶▶ *lesson*
four | Connecting to the Internet

If you belong to a large organization, it probably has a connection to the Internet, and you might be given an e-mail address that consists of your username followed by their domain name. In this lesson, you study ways to get connected to the Internet, even if you are a single individual and not a part of a large organization with full-time technical assistants.

Internet Service Providers (ISP)

A company or organization that sells the service of its gateway is called an *Internet Service Provider (ISP)*. This company could be the same one that provides your telephone or television service, but they are two separate functions. For example, if your telephone company has an Internet connection service, you can still buy that service from another provider that uses the same telephone lines. The other provider pays the telephone company a fee for using its lines. An ISP can offer other services such as hosting your domain name, hosting Web pages using their domain name, or electronic mail. When you contract with an ISP, you choose from a menu of services and pay accordingly.

Measures of Connection Speed

The rate of data transfer can vary widely, depending on various factors. The speed can make a big difference in how long you have to wait for a Web page to display or for a large file to transfer. Recall that data is measured in bits (b) and bytes (B), where a byte consists of eight bits. Data transfer rates are measured in thousands or millions of bits per second (bps) or bytes per second (Bps). Because a byte is eight times larger than a bit, it is important to distinguish between the two measurements.

Connecting Through Dial-Up Telephone Service

The zeros and ones in a computer are represented by voltages that vary up or down by a few volts. Telephone lines that are normally used for voice communications are designed to transmit audible sounds. A device called a *modem*, shown in Figure 1.17, converts the high and low voltages into two different tones that are suitable for transmission over telephone lines. If you listen to a computer sending data over a telephone line, you can hear the tone switching rapidly back and forth between two pitches. The modem can perform this service in reverse by converting tones on telephone lines into voltages that go up and down to indicate zeros and ones. Because it uses normal voice connections, this type of service is known as *dial-up*. When the computer is transmitting or receiving tones, the line is unusable for normal conversations.

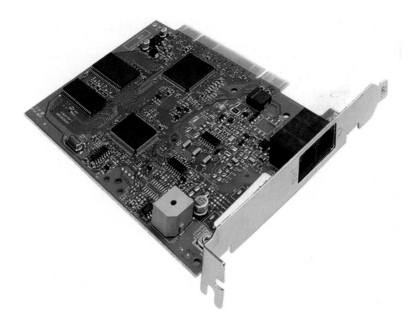

FIGURE 1.17
Dial-up modem.

The copper lines used for voice transmission are designed to carry voices and tones the necessary distance to reach the central switching computer. Modems that use these pitches are limited to the rate at which they can switch between them and keep them as distinguishable separate pitches, which limits the rate of data transfer to about 56,000 bits per second—written *56kbs* or just *56k*. The pitch of the tone is determined by its ***frequency***—the number of variations of the signal per second. Recall that it takes eight bits to make a byte and one byte is used for each character in the alphabet, so this means that a telephone modem is limited to about 7,000 characters per second. For sending pages of ordinary text, this is adequate. When we include pictures in our Web pages that are hundreds of thousands of bytes in size, it takes much longer for the Web page to display.

Connecting Through DSL Telephone Service

There is another option for connecting to the Internet using telephone lines. It is possible to use the same lines to transmit tones that are too high-pitched—high frequency—for humans to hear. Because the tones are higher frequency, the switch between the two tones can be made faster without blending together, so the transmission rates are higher. Several different pairs of high-pitch tones can be used on the same line to increase the transmission rates. Sending several signals over the same medium using different frequencies is called ***broadband***, where each narrow range of pitches is a *band*. This type of connection is a ***digital subscriber line (DSL)***. The high-pitch tones do not interfere with normal conversations using the same lines. A special DSL modem handles the conversion between the low-voltage differences of a computer to the high-pitched tones used on the phone lines, as shown in Figure 1.18.

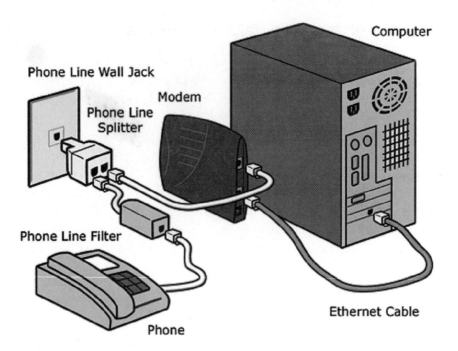

FIGURE 1.18
Phone line used for voice and data.

Phone lines were not originally designed to carry these high-pitch tones the full distance from the farthest customers to the central switching computer. Only customers who are within a few miles of the nearest computerized telephone switch can use this service. Internet service providers usually choose to provide faster download service than upload, because most customers spend much more time receiving Web pages than they do sending data or requests for new pages. Download speeds—from the Internet to the individual computer—vary greatly depending on how close you are to the nearest switch and what service you buy. Download speeds on DSL lines can vary from 256 kbps up to 24,000 kbps, so it is important to test the speed of a DSL connection so you know what to expect.

The maximum speed depends upon the distance from the central switch, but the circuit is not shared with other users, so the speed is not dependent on how many people are using the service.

56K dial up   *256K DSL*
                  Not affected
                  by many users

1.5 mbps Cable-IPS
the more using the
slower it gets

Connecting Through T1 Telephone Service

Telephone companies offer higher-speed connections that are commonly used by businesses to connect their LAN to the Internet. Copper twisted pairs of telephone lines come in bundles of 24 called **T1** or **DS-1** lines. These cables are being replaced by fiber optic cables, but the term *T1* is still in use to indicate 24 channels of data. If a company wanted to pay for all 24 pairs of circuits, they would have 1.5 mbps of data transmission. The European standard is the **E1**, which is 30 channels and is used in most of the world except North America, Japan, and South Korea, where the T1 standard is used.

Connecting Through the Cable Television Service

Cable television systems typically use coaxial cable to deliver television signals to the home. The cable companies are replacing coaxial cable with fiber optic cable wherever it is cost effective. The cable can be used to transmit Internet data in addition to television signals, so most cable television providers also act as ISPs to provide Internet service. Users share connections, and speed varies depending on how many people are using the service at the same time. Speeds are typically about 1.5 million bits per second (1.5 mbps) download and 512 thousand bits per second (512 bps) upload. The speed depends on the number of users on a local line and can be slower during periods of heavy use. Some systems are much faster, with speeds ranging from 2 mbps up to 50 mbps for business service. Service is usually limited to areas with enough population concentration to warrant installation of the relatively expensive coaxial or fiber optic cable. The data is separated from the television signals by a *cable modem*.

Connecting to an ISP by Radio (Wireless)

Internet service can be provided over a wide area by radio transmitters. This type of service is typically called *wireless* because it uses radio transmission and is often confused with wireless connection in a LAN. The typical wireless LAN connection uses a low-power radio signal that only travels a few hundred feet, while a wireless ISP uses a higher-power signal that can travel several miles. Obstructions such as buildings and mountains can create zones without service within the normal range of the radio transmitter. A wireless Internet connection provides mobility within the service area close to the transmitter. Near the edge of the transmission area, a directional antenna is used that points toward the central transmission antenna. Transmission speeds are about 1.2 million bits per second (1.2 mbps) download. Actual download and upload speeds vary depending on the number of users within the range of the antenna.

Connecting Through a Satellite

Television signals are provided by direct link with a satellite. The satellite is about 25,000 miles above the earth, where its orbital period of 24 hours matches the rotation of the earth, so it appears to stay in one spot in the sky. A directional antenna is carefully positioned to point at the satellite to receive its signal (Figure 1.19). The same antenna can be used to transmit signals back to the satellite, where they can be relayed back to earth and the company's office can connect them to the Internet. Because of the distances involved, the speeds are lower than cable or DSL but still faster than dial-up. Download speed is about 1,200 kbps, and upload is much lower at 50 to 150 thousand bits per second (150 kbps). The biggest advantage of a satellite connection is that it is available in rural areas, but due to higher equipment costs and fewer users, the cost is usually much higher. Higher speeds are possible by spending more on larger antennas and special service.

FIGURE 1.19
Satellite dish antenna.

Actual connection speeds depend on several factors and are often much less than the maximums that are possible with each type of connection. There are several sites on the Internet that will test your connection speed—usually with the intent of selling you a faster service—and it is a good idea to test your connection speed at more than one site.

to determine your connection speed

1 **Start a Web browser such as Internet Explorer, Firefox, or Safari.**

2 **In the Address box near the top of the Web browser screen, type** `http://reviews.cnet.com/internet-speed-test/` **and then press** ⏎Enter**. The CNET Bandwidth Meter speed test page displays.**

3 **Fill out the form on the left part of the screen, and then click the Go button.**
After a few moments, results are displayed that compare your connection speed with other types of connections, as shown in Figure 1.20.

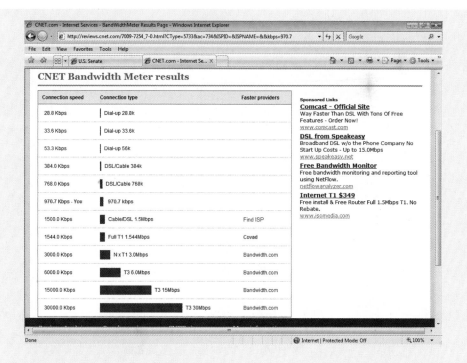

FIGURE 1.20
Checking the speed of an Internet connection.

4 **In the Address box near the top of the Web browser screen, carefully type**
`http://www.digitallanding.com/high-speed-internet/article_`
`display.cfm/article_id/4458` **and then press** Enter. Be sure to type the
underscore characters instead of spaces. The Digital Landing speed test page displays.
This site tests the download and upload speeds. Alternatively, use the Google search
engine to search for *digital landing speed test*.

5 **In the center of the screen, below the dial, click Begin Test.** Watch while the program tests your download and upload speeds and then compares your download
speed to the average in your state and in the U.S., as shown in Figure 1.21. Your
speeds will differ from those in the figure. You might observe that the two tests
resulted in different speed estimates. There are many factors that determine the speed
of a download between two points, which is why it is a good idea to use more than
one test.

FIGURE 1.21
Your download and upload speeds.

6 Use the skills you practiced previously to start the Snip program and snip the window that displays the result of your speed test. Save a copy of this window to the folder where you store your files. Name the file U3Ch01SpeedStudentName substituting your name as indicated.

7 Close the browser window.

▶▶▶ *lesson*
five | Financing and Controlling the Internet

In this lesson, you learn about how the Internet is controlled and who pays for it.

Government Startup and Transfer to Private Industry

At the beginning of the Internet, the U.S. government invested in computerized switches and high-speed data connections across the country to connect military installations and research centers that were often at major universities. With the advent of direct personal communications using e-mail and Web browsing, the Internet became popular with millions of people who were not involved in the military or with universities. In 1988, the government banned commercial use of its network to encourage companies to create a commercial version of the Internet and to pay for further development of backbone connection and computerized switches at privately owned companies. In 1995, the government stopped paying for the backbone transmission lines and the Internet became self-supporting.

to see maps of private providers of backbone services

1 **Start a Web browser such as Internet Explorer, Firefox, or Safari.**

2 **In the Address box near the top of the Web browser screen, type** `http://www.nthelp.com/maps.htm` **and then press** ⏎Enter. A list displays of links to maps of backbone connections provided by more than twenty companies.

3 **Click the Sprint link.** View the map of major data connections in the Sprint system (Figure 1.22).

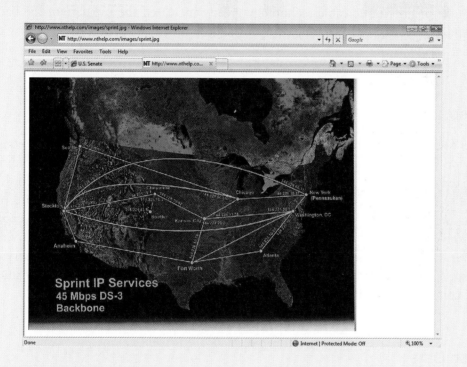

FIGURE 1.22
Sprint backbone.

4 **At the top of your browser window, click the Back button** 🔙. The previous screen displays.

5 **Repeat this process to view a few of the other maps.** Notice that there are several options for sending messages long distances.

6 **Use the skills you practiced previously to start the Snip program and snip one of the windows that displays a map of a backbone. Save a copy of this window to the folder where you store your files. Name the file** `U3Ch01BackboneStudentName` **substituting your name as indicated.**

7 **Close the browser window.**

Paying for the Backbone Services

Telephone companies receive money by charging traditional telephone users a monthly connection fee and additional fees for calls beyond the local network. They also charge ISPs for access to their backbone connections. This model is based on the old circuit-switched system, and it does not reflect how people use the Internet. For example, someone could use a dial-up modem to call an ISP. If the call is a local call, the telephone company would not receive any additional payment, but the person could stay connected all day while sending and receiving Web pages, e-mail, and other files across the Internet that uses the telephone company's backbone.

Because people could not use the same telephone line for dial-up Internet access and for normal conversations, many people paid for a second telephone line. This practice provided additional income to the phone company that offset the additional expense of providing more capacity on long-distance connections.

Advances in fiber optic cable technology greatly increased the capacity of the backbone, which kept costs down so that phone companies did not have to change the way they charged for use.

Increase in Use

New uses for the Internet have increased traffic and reduced income for telephone companies. It is now possible to use the Internet as a telephone service over your broadband Internet connection, and many people no longer pay for traditional telephone connections or for long distance calls. Viewing video online and sharing music have become much more popular. Pictures and video are large files that require much more transmission capacity—*bandwidth*—than e-mail or other text files. In some cases, companies that sell video and music over the Internet also own a portion of the backbone. They have plans to reserve part of the transmission capacity for their own customers, while either charging extra for similar use by other companies or limiting the amount of use for transferring large files.

Caps on Data

The packet-switching method of transferring data was so much more efficient than normal telephone service that adding Internet traffic to the existing telephone system did not increase the company's costs very much in the early days of the Internet. That has changed with the advent of using the Internet to watch video. Video files are much larger than text or audio files. Major companies that provide Internet service are considering placing caps on the amount of data that can be transmitted each month and then charging extra if the maximum is exceeded, using a pricing structure that is similar to charging for cell phone minutes. For example, a contract for Internet service might include a monthly cap of 5 gigabytes. A *gigabyte* is a billion bytes or 1,000,000,000 bytes. Streaming video of a rerun of a popular television show that is shown in relatively low quality would use about 0.2 gigabytes, while a higher-quality version would use 0.5 gigabytes. A high-definition television program would take about 1 gigabyte, and a DVD-quality movie rented online could use up to 5 gigabytes. Online telephone and video calls would also contribute to the total bytes transmitted per month.

Coordination of Domain Names

The Internet was developed in the United States, and for many years the large majority of users were in the U.S. The group that controls creation of top-level domain names such as .com and .net is the Internet Corporation for Assigned Names and Numbers (ICANN) (Figure 1.23). This group was created by the U.S. government and was controlled by it. This caused friction with other countries that had concerns about censorship and allocation of IP addresses. ICANN is attempting to balance these concerns and to become independent of U.S. government control. Countries such as China that are not satisfied with ICANN have threatened to set up their own domain names and services. If the practice of assigning unique domain names and IP addresses becomes fragmented, the Internet may break up into isolated regions that do not communicate easily with each other.

FIGURE 1.23
ICANN homepage.

▶▶▶ *lesson*
SIX | Security and Ethics

When computers are connected in networks, the information they contain must be protected. Access to the network must be limited to authorized users, and the people who control the computers must behave ethically.

User Names and Passwords

To gain access to a particular network, you must identify yourself. This is usually done by requiring each person to enter a ***user name*** and a ***password***. The user name is a unique name on that network. It is not secret and it often includes part of the person's name. Passwords are secret and they consist of letters and numbers. They should be easy to remember but hard to guess. Good choices for passwords consist of a mix of numbers, lowercase letters, and uppercase letters. Avoid numbers that are easy to guess, such your birthday. Instead, use a number like the street address of your childhood home, combined with the first letter of each word of a saying. For example, a password like *Iutla1245HL* would be easy to remember because it stands for *I used to live at 1245 Harmony Lane*. Change passwords periodically, just in case. Some networks use devices that can measure or detect parts of a person's body such as fingerprints, hand shape, and eye coloring. The practice of analyzing body characteristics for identification is called ***biometrics.***

Network Administrators' Ethical Code

The people who issue the user names and decide what services and files users can access are called ***system administrators***. They can install or remove programs, and they can add new users to the network or remove them. They can read most of the mail that passes through mail servers, and they can read most of the files on the computers for which they are responsible. The people who use the network rely on the ethical behavior of the system administrators.

System administrators often belong to professional groups that certify their skills. Those groups usually have a code of ethical behavior that their members agree to abide by. An example is the League of Professional System Administrators (LOPSA). A typical code of ethics for a system administrator has the following elements:

- professional behavior—personal feelings or beliefs will not result in unfair treatment
- personal integrity—be honest and avoid conflicts of interest
- privacy—will only view private information as necessary and not divulge it to others
- laws and policies—make an effort to keep up on current laws and regulations
- communication—communicate on matters of mutual interest with management and users
- system integrity—strive to maintain reliability and availability of the system
- education—keep learning and stay up-to-date on technical information
- responsibility—build a safe and productive workplace that respects privacy

Firewall and Proxy Server

One of the responsibilities of the system administrator is to maintain the system's reliability and availability. To do this, system administrators must protect their networks and their users from threats that come from outside the network. A ***firewall***—a program that blocks unwanted or unsafe data—works with the network's gateway and router to examine packets of data to determine if they should be allowed to enter or leave the network. This slows down the data transmission rate. The system administrator can speed up the process by choosing domain names that are trusted and by allowing data to pass through from those sites without checking. Alternatively, the system administrator can block all data coming from certain domain names without checking the content. Firewalls are often set to block certain types of programs such as file transfer software. The firewall software can be installed on individual computers, network servers, or on dedicated computers. For maximum security, the firewall software is placed on a dedicated computer that is between the gateway and the rest of the Internet, as shown in Figure 1.24. If you need to use a site or software that is blocked by the firewall, you can contact the system administrator and request that the settings be changed for your use. If you are using a home computer on which you are the system administrator and your computer has firewall software, you can make those choices yourself. A ***proxy server*** is a function that is usually included with the gateway that hides the IP address of the user's computer. It sends requests for Web pages using its own IP address so people outside the network do not see the internal addresses used on the network for individual computers.

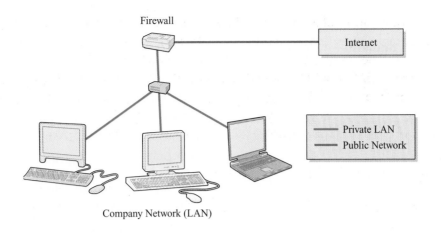

Firewall

Internet

Private LAN
Public Network

Company Network (LAN)

FIGURE 1.24
Firewall.

SUMMARY

In this chapter, you learned about the birth of the Internet and the World Wide Web and how computers are connected in networks. You learned how to gain access to the Internet and about issues that face the Internet, such as control and financing. Finally, you learned about the issues of security, safety, privacy, and ethics as they relate to network administration and use.

You can extend your learning by reviewing concepts and terms and by practicing variations of skills presented in the lessons.

KEY TERMS

Advanced Research Projects Agency (ARPA)

ARPANET

backbone

bandwidth

biometric

bit (b)

bridge

broadband

broadband coax

browser

byte (B)

cable modem

checksum

circuit switching

client

coaxial cable

country code top-level domain (ccTLD)

database server

dial-up

Digital Subscriber Line (DSL)

domain name

domain name server

Domain Name System (DNS)

E1

e-mail

Ethernet

fiber optic cable

file server

File Transfer Protocol (FTP)

firewall

frequency

gateway	modem	star
generic top-level domain (gTLD)	Mosaic	switchboard operator
	Mozilla Firefox	system administrator
gigabyte	Netscape	T1
host	network	Telnet
hyperlink	network server	top-level domain (TLD)
Hypertext Markup Language (HTML)	node	Transmission Control Protocol/Internet Protocol (TCP/IP)
Hypertext Transfer Protocol (HTTP)	packet	
	password	
Infrared (IR)	peer-to-peer	twisted pair
intranet	print server	Uniform Resource Locator (URL)
Internet Corporation for Assigned Names and Numbers (ICANN)	protocol	user name
	proxy server	Web page
Internet Protocol (IP) address	radio	Web server
	registry	Wide Area Network (WAN)
Internet Service Provider (ISP)	relay	wireless
	router	World Wide Web
Local Area Network (LAN)	Safari	WorldWideWeb
mail server	server	

CHECKING CONCEPTS AND TERMS

MULTIPLE CHOICE

Circle the letter of the correct answer for each of the following.

1. What was one of the original reasons the government had for creating the Internet? [L1]

   a. to promote buying and selling online to raise tax revenues

   b. to find a use for excess transmission capacity created by the technology investment bubble

   c. to employ more federal regulators

   d. to create a way to exchange data between research computers

2. Which of the following is **not** an advantage of a packet-switched network over circuit circuit-switching? [L2]

   a. only one continuous circuit is used per call

   b. data is sent on whatever line is available at the moment

   c. packets can be checked for errors using the checksum

   d. failure of several central telephone offices would not keep the message from getting to its destination

3. If a computer has a program that makes a request for service from a program on another computer, the relationship is: [L2]

   a. peer-to-peer

   b. client-server

   c. host-node

   d. file server-client

4. The difference between a WAN and a LAN is _____. [L2]

   a. the computers in a WAN are closer together than in a LAN

   b. a WAN is operated by the government and a LAN is operated by private companies

   c. you have to use a password to gain access to a LAN

   d. the computers are closer together in a LAN

5. What does a domain name server do? [L2]

   a. provides a directory that relates domain names to the servers that host them

   b. provides the alias of a domain name when you provide the IP address

   c. assigns unused domain names to users who log in without one

   d. tracks the number of times a person accesses each Web page

6. What is the difference between the Internet and the World Wide Web (WWW)? [L3]

   a. WWW is the default name of the Web page server, and the Internet is the super network of networks.

   b. The Internet is the network of networks that use TCP/IP to transfer data, while the WWW uses the Internet to transfer Web pages.

   c. The Internet was invented at a Swiss research center and the WWW was created by DARPA.

   d. The Internet is a subset of the WWW.

7. What type of transmission medium is used by wireless communication? [L4]

   a. radio waves

   b. optical fiber

   c. coax

   d. twisted pair

8. What is the relationship between a byte and a bit? [L1]

   a. A byte is 128 bits.

   b. A byte is two bits long, either of which may be a 0 or a 1.

   c. A bit is eight bytes.

   d. A byte is eight bits long.

9. Which group coordinates creation of domain names and IP addresses? [L5]

   a. DARPA

   b. FCC

   c. ICANN

   d. FTC

10. What is **not** a desirable characteristic of a password? [L6]

    a. easy to remember

    b. hard to guess

    c. has a mixture of numbers and letters

    d. is a date like a birthday

MATCHING

Match each term in the second column with its correct definition in the first column by writing the letter of the term on the blank line in front of the definition.

D __C__ 1. Method of using high-pitch tones to send data over phone lines

__F__ 2. Glass strands that transmit data as flashes of light

__A__ 3. Main connections between networks in different parts of the country or world

__E__ 4. Connection with as much capacity as 24 telephone lines

__I__ 5. Millions of bits per second

__J__ 6. Device that chooses the best path through the network

C __D__ 7. Connection to the Internet over normal telephone lines that uses audible tones

__H__ 8. Provides access to the Internet for individuals

__G__ 9. Connects networks that use different software

__B__ 10. Total of the numbers that represent data in a packet

A. Backbone

B. Checksum

C. Dial-up

D. DSL

E. T1

F. Fiber

G. Gateway

H. ISP

I. Mbps

J. Router

SKILL DRILL

Skill Drill exercises reinforce chapter skills. Each skill reinforced is the same, or nearly the same, as a skill presented in the chapter. Detailed instructions are provided in a step-by-step format.

Each exercise is independent of the others, so you can do the exercises in any order.

1. Find a domain name

There are several companies that will help you register a domain name. To use Register.com, follow these steps:

1. Start a Web browser program such as Internet Explorer, Firefox, or Safari.

2. In the **Address** box, type `http://www.register.com` and then press `⏎Enter`.

3. In the box above the **Search for a Name** button, type `basicstudies`

4. Confirm that .com is the top-level domain name.

5. Click the **Search For a Name** button. The screen explains that this domain is not available, but it displays several options and their prices.

6. Click the **Start** button, click **All Programs**, click the **Accessories** folder, and then in the list of programs, click the **Snipping Tool.**

7. In the **Snipping Tool** dialog box, click the **New Snip** button arrow, and then click **Window Snip.** Point anywhere in the **Register.com** window, and then click one time.

8. Near the top of the **Snipping Tool** dialog box, click the **Save Snip** button. In the **Save As** dialog box, navigate to the folder where you store your files. In the **File name** box, type U3Ch01RegisterStudentName substituting your name as indicated, and then click **Save.**

9. Close the browser and Snipping Tool dialog box.

10. Submit your snip as directed by your instructor.

2. Look up an IP Address

You can find out the IP address of the computer that hosts a given domain name, using a service that is available online.

To find the IP address of a host computer, follow these steps:

1. Start a Web browser program such as Internet Explorer, Firefox, or Safari.

2. In the **Address** box, type http://www.whatismyipaddress.com and then press ⏎Enter. When the Web page comes up, it displays the IP address of the computer that is your gateway to the Internet.

3. Along the toolbar near the top of the screen, click **IP Tools.**

4. On the **IP Tools** page, scroll down to **Hostname to IP Lookup** heading. Under this heading, click the **Hostname to IP address** hyperlink.

5. In the box, type prenhall.com and then click the **Lookup IP Address** button. It will notify you that the IP address of the computer that serves the prenhall.com domain is 165.193.123.253.

6. Try it again with a domain name of your choice.

7. Click the **Start** button, click **All Programs,** click the **Accessories** folder, and then in the list of programs, click the **Snipping Tool.**

8. In the **Snipping Tool** dialog box, click the **New Snip** button arrow, and then click **Window Snip.** Point anywhere in the **WhatIsMyIPAddress.com** window, and then click one time to capture the hostname you chose and its IP address.

9. Near the top of the **Snipping Tool** dialog box, click the **Save Snip** button. In the **Save As** dialog box, navigate to the folder where you store your files. In the **File name** box, type U3Ch01IPStudentName substituting your name as indicated, and then click **Save.**

10. In the upper right corner of each open dialog box or window, click the **Close** button.

11. Submit your snip as directed by your instructor.

3. View Source Code of Library of Congress Site

View the source code of the Library of Congress to see how the title is identified using HTML codes.

To see the source code, follow these steps:

1. Start Internet Explorer.

2. In the **Address** box, type `http://www.loc.gov` and then press ⏎Enter. This is the homepage of the Library of Congress.

3. On the browser toolbar, click **View,** and then on the menu, click **View Source.** A text editor window opens that displays the source code. In Windows, this editor is probably Notepad.

4. In the source code, scan the first few lines to find the title **Library of Congress.** Notice the HTML code <title> before the words and </title> after them.

5. Click the **Start** button, click **All Programs,** click the **Accessories** folder, and then in the list of programs, click the **Snipping Tool.**

6. In the **Snipping Tool** dialog box, click the **New Snip** button arrow, and then click **Window Snip.** Point anywhere in the window that displays the HTML text, and then click one time.

7. Near the top of the **Snipping Tool** dialog box, click the **Save Snip** button. In the **Save As** dialog box, navigate to the folder where you store your files. In the **File name** box, type `U3Ch01TitleStudentName` substituting your name as indicated, and then click **Save.**

8. In the upper right corner of each open dialog box or window, click the **Close** button.

9. Submit your snip as directed by your instructor.

EXPLORE AND SHARE

Explore and Share questions are intended for discussion in class or online. Look for information that is related to the learning outcomes for this chapter, as directed. Submit your answers as directed by your instructor.

1. Find out where a Web page server is located. Start a Web browser program such as Internet Explorer. Go to **http://www.whatismyipaddress.com.** On the toolbar, click **IP Tools.** Scroll down and click **Hostname to IP Address.** In the **Hostname to IP Address Lookup** box, type a domain name of a popular website. Write down or copy the IP address. On the toolbar, click **IP Tools.** Under **IP Location, Map, and Details** click **Lookup IP.** In the **Lookup IP Address** box, type or paste the IP address. Click the **Lookup IP Address** button. Scroll down to display the IP address and the map. Use the **Snipping Tool** to copy the window and save it as `U3Ch01IPLocationStudentName` Prepare to share what you learned about the location of your gateway. Submit your answer and the file as directed by your instructor. [L2]

2. Trace the route of a message across the Internet. Start a Web browser program such as Internet Explorer. Go to **http://www.whatismyipaddress.com.** Notice the IP address of the computer that is your gateway to the Internet displays. On the toolbar, click **IP Tools.** Scroll down and click **Traceroute.** In the **Traceroute** box, notice that the IP address of your gateway computer is inserted. Click the **Lookup IP Address** button. Scroll down to display the route that a message takes from the whatismyaddress domain server to your gateway. Use the **Snipping Tool** to copy the window and save it as U3Ch01TraceStudentName Examine the list of computers that route a message from the WhatIsMyIPAddress computer to your gateway computer. Prepare to share what you learned about the location of your gateway. Submit your answer and the file as directed by your instructor. [L2]

3. Find a domain name that is available, and determine how much it would cost to have your own domain name. Start a Web browser and then go to **http://www.networksolutions.com.** Search for different domain names until you find one you like that is available. Click the **Get It Now** button. Proceed through the process far enough to find out what the charge would be to own this domain name for a year. Do not complete the purchase. Use the **Snipping Tool** to copy a window that shows the domain name you found and the price, and then save it as U3Ch01MyDomainStudentName Prepare to share what you learned about the cost of owning a domain name. Submit your answer and the file as directed by your instructor. [L2]

4. Find out what it would cost to have a service host your domain name and provide Web page and e-mail service. Start a Web browser, and then go to **http://www.10-cheapwebhosting.com.** Examine the options, and make a list of the services offered by one of the sites and the cost for one year. Do not complete the purchase. Use the **Snipping Tool** to copy a window that shows the features offered and the price, and then save it as U3Ch01MyHostStudentName Prepare to share what you learned about the cost of hosting a domain name. Submit your answer and the file as directed by your instructor. [L4]

IN YOUR LIFE

In Your Life questions are intended for discussion in class or online where you can share your personal experience. Restrict your answers to the topics described in each exercise. Submit your answers as directed by your instructor.

1. How is a home computer with which you are familiar connected to the Internet? A complete answer will include the connecting medium (dial-up, DSL, cable, wireless, or satellite), the name of the ISP, the domain name they provide for electronic mail, and the approximate cost per month. [L6]

2. If ISPs institute a charge for data that is similar to charging for cell phone minutes, do you think it would affect what you do on the Internet? Refer to the type of activities described in Lesson 5 to estimate whether or not you would use more than 5 gigabytes per month, and use this information in your answer. [L5]

3. How do you feel about the fact that network administrators can read your e-mail messages? Do you think it is important that your network administrator belong to a professional group that has a code of ethics for network administrators? Explain your reasons. [L6]

| RELATED SKILLS

Related Skills exercises expand on or are related to skills presented in the lessons. The exercises provide a brief narrative introduction, followed by instructions in a numbered-step format that are not as detailed as those in the Skill Drill section.

1. Check the Strength of a Password

Using passwords that are hard to guess but easy to remember will make it more difficult for unauthorized people to gain access to the network. You can practice creating passwords at the Password checker site.

To practice creating strong passwords, follow these steps:

1. Open a Web browser such as Internet Explorer.

2. In the Address box, type `http://www.microsoft.com/protect/yourself/ password/checker.mspx` and then press `↵Enter`. Alternatively, go to Google and search for *password test*.

3. On the **Password checker** Web page, in the **Password** box, type `10272008` Notice that entering a date is rated as Weak on the strength bar.

4. Clear the Password box. Type the example from Lesson 6: `Iutla1245HL` Notice that this password is strong but not the strongest possible.

5. On the **Password checker** Web page, under *Do you use strong passwords?* click **Strong passwords: How to create and use them**. Read this page.

6. Under **Create a strong, memorable password in 6 steps**, skip step 2. Do not use spaces as part of the password. Many computers on the Internet do not support spaces in passwords.

7. On the browser window, click the arrow that points to the left to return to the previous page. In the **Password** box, type a password that receives a score of **Best**.

8. Use the **Snipping Tool** to capture the **Password Checker** window that displays the **Best** rating for a password. Save the file as U3Ch01PasswordStudentName

9. **Close** all open windows without saving any changes. Submit the file as directed by your instructor.

2. Find Out Who is the Registered Owner of a Domain Name

If the person or group that owns the use of a domain name chooses to make their ownership public, you can find out who owns the domain name.

To look up the owners of a domain name, follow these steps:

1. Open a Web browser such as Internet Explorer.

2. In the Address box, type `http://whois.domaintools.com` and then press `↵Enter`.

3. On the **Whois Source** Web page, in the **Enter a Domain Name to Lookup** box, type `prenhall.com` and then click the **Lookup** button.

4. Scroll down to display the **Registry Data** section. Use the **Snipping Tool** to capture the window that displays the registry data for this domain name. Save the file as `U3Ch01PrenhallStudentName`

5. **Close** all open windows without saving any changes. Submit the file as directed by your instructor.

3. Firewall Settings in Windows

Firewall programs are often located in gateway computers, but firewall software is also available as part of Windows Vista and Windows XP. You can change the settings to allow or block content. The following directions are for use in Windows Vista. The steps are similar in Windows XP. This exercise assumes that you have administrative rights to the computer you are using. If you do not have administrative rights on the computer you are using, you might not see the Control Panel or the Security options.

To review and change firewall settings in Windows Vista, follow these steps:

1. Click **Start,** and then click **Control Panel.**

2. In the Control Panel dialog box, under Security, click **Allow a program through Windows Firewall.**

3. In the **Windows Firewall Settings** dialog box, click the **General** tab. Notice whether or not the Windows firewall is active on your computer.

4. In the **Windows Firewall Settings** dialog box, click the **Exceptions** tab. Review the list of programs that are allowed to communicate through the firewall.

5. Use the **Snipping Tool** to capture the window that displays the list of exceptions on your computer. Save the file as `U3Ch01FirewallStudentName`

6. **Close** all open windows without saving any changes. Submit the file as directed by your instructor.

DISCOVER

Discover exercises give students general directions for exploring and discovering more advanced skills and information. Each exercise is independent of the others, so you may complete the exercises in any order.

1. Finding Out How Small the World Is on the Internet

The backbone of the Internet extends to all of the major countries of the world. The far side of the world is less than a second away on the Internet. To find out how long it takes a packet of data to make a round trip from your computer to the far side of the world and back, you can use a basic program named **Ping**. Click **Start**, point to **All Programs,** point to **Accessories,** and then click **Command Prompt.** In the **Command Prompt** window, type `ping www.usyd.edu.au` and then press ⏎Enter. The program will send a packet of data from your computer to the server at the University of Sydney in Australia. That computer will respond by sending the packet back. The program will repeat the process four times. Each time, it will report the results, including the time to make the round trip in milliseconds or one-thousandth of a second. For example, it might take 240 ms to make the round trip, which is 240/1000 seconds or about a quarter of a second. Some organizations block the use of programs like Ping. If the program does not work, try it from a computer at home or at another location. Try this again with a domain name that is probably hosted in the United States or near your current location. See how much difference the physical distance makes in the time. Write down what you learned and what you think about what you have discovered. When you are finished, **Close** the **Command Prompt** window. Submit the document as directed.

2. Check for Reverse DNS

When you send a request for information over the network, the domain name server provides the IP address of your server in order for the message to be returned. Some servers also provide the domain name from which the request originated. Other computers on the Internet do not need to know this. You can test your system by asking an outside agency if it can see the domain name from which you made your request. This is called the *reverse DNS*. Start a Web browser and go to http://www.grc.com. Click the words **ShieldsUP!!**, scroll down the page to **Hot Spots,** and then click **ShieldsUP!!** Scroll to the middle of the page. A text box informs you of the IP address of the gateway server you are using and whether or not it can see your domain name. Write down what you learned and submit the document as directed.

ASSESS YOUR PROGRESS

At this point, you should have a set of skills and concepts that are valuable to an employer and to you. You may not realize how much you've learned unless you take a few minutes to assess your progress.

1. From the student files, open **U3Ch01Assess.** Save it as `Ch01AssessStudentName`

2. Read each question in column A.

3. In column B, answer Yes or No.

4. If you identify a skill or design concept that you don't know, refer to the learning objective code next to the question and the table at the beginning of the chapter to find the skill and review it.

5. Print the worksheet if your instructor requires it. The file name is already in the header, so it will display your name as part of the file name.

6. All of these skills and concepts have been identified as important by surveying hundreds of individuals working at over 200 companies worldwide. If you cannot answer all of the questions affirmatively even after reviewing the relevant lesson, seek additional help from your instructor.

chapter **two**

Searching for Information

Lesson	Learning Outcomes	Code	Related IC3 Objectives
1	Identify elements of a Web browser	2.01	3.1.3
1	Identify elements of a Web page	2.02	3.1.3
1	Identify the elements of a Web address	2.03	3.1.3
1	Identify the use of a cache and when to use Refresh	2.04	3.1.2, 3.1.6
1	Locate the history of Web pages visited	2.05	3.1.7
1	Identify the functions of plug-in programs	2.06	3.1.14
1	Modify browser settings	2.07	3.1.13
1	Identify typical browser problems	2.08	3.1.14
2	Identify the functions of Web crawlers and search engines	2.09	3.2.2
2	Identify classification strategies used by search engines	2.10	3.2.2
2	Identify keyword search strategies	2.11	3.2.3
2	Refine searches using Boolean logic	2.12	3.2.3
2	Find words or phrases on a Web page using the Find feature	2.13	3.1.8
3	Use bookmarks to return to favorite websites	2.14	3.1.9
3	Copy text and pictures from a website	2.15	3.1.10
3	Download a Web page and save to the computer	2.16	3.1.11
4	Use MS Word to create a Web page	2.17	3.2.1
4	View HTML source code of a Web page	2.18	-
4	Identify Web page design software	2.19	3.2.1
4	Identify use of FTP software to transfer Web pages to host	2.20	-
5	Identify standards for citing sources	2.21	3.2.6
5	Identify issues affecting quality of information	2.22	3.2.5
5	Identify ethical issues regarding ranking of Web pages in search engines	2.23	-
5	Protecting from unwanted content by blocking websites and pop-ups	2.24	-
5	Using the Internet ethically	2.25	3.2.6

Why Would I Do This?

Thomas Friedman, in his book *The World is Flat*, explained that the Internet has empowered individuals, and one of those empowerments is the ability to become informed. The Internet is a vast storehouse of knowledge that is readily accessible if you know how to use search engines to find information and how to assess the quality of the information.

visual summary

In these lessons, you will study the use of a Web browser and search engine to find information on the Internet. The browser used to capture screens is Internet Explorer 8.

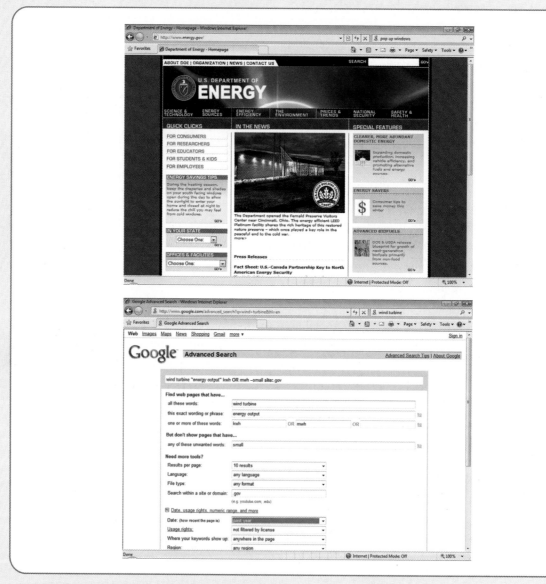

FIGURE 2.1 A, B
Web browser and search engine.

List of Student and Solution Files

In most cases, you will create files using text or pictures found on Web pages. You will add your name to the file names and save them on your computer or portable memory device. Table 2.1 lists the files you start with and the names you give them when you save the files.

ASSIGNMENT	STUDENT SOURCE FILE:	SAVE AS:
Lesson 1	none	U3Ch02WindBillsStudentName U3Ch02HomeStudentName
Lesson 2	none	U3Ch02SearchStudentName
Lesson 3	none	U3Ch02WindMapStudentName U3Ch02DOEStudentName
Lesson 4	none	U3Ch02WebPageStudentName
Skill Drill	none	U3Ch02Home2StudentName U3Ch02AdvancedStudentName U3Ch02ExcelStudentName
Explore and Share	none	none
In Your Life	none	none
Related Skills	none	U3Ch02WindFutureStudentName U3Ch02ElectricCarStudentName
Assess Your Progress	U3Ch02Assess	U3Ch02AssessStudentName

TABLE 2.1

▶▶▶ *lesson*
One | Using a Web Browser

A Web browser enables you to navigate within a website and move from site to site. It also enables you to update information on pages that change constantly. Currently, the most popular browsers are Microsoft Internet Explorer and Firefox on computers that use the Windows operating system and Safari on Macintosh computers. Chrome is a browser from Google that is integrated with Google's other services. Internet Explorer will be used throughout this project, but numerous references to other browsers are included. The Windows Vista Snipping Tool is used to capture and save example screens. Users of Windows XP can press the Print Screen (PrtScn) button on the keyboard and paste the captured screen into a word processing document. Users of Macintosh computers can press Command + Control + Shift + 3 to capture a screen image to the clipboard and then paste the captured screen into a word processing document.

Functions of a Web Browser

A Web browser is a program designed to retrieve Web pages from servers on the Internet. The browser communicates with a domain name server to find the IP address of the computer that hosts the pages, and then it sends a request for the pages to the Web server at that address. The server sends the requested pages to the browser for display. The Web page provided by the Web server is written in Hypertext Markup Language (HTML), and it might include text, graphics, links to other Web pages, buttons, menus, or checkboxes.

to navigate the Web using a browser

1 **At the left edge of the Windows taskbar, click the Start button. Locate and click Internet Explorer.** The Internet Explorer window opens to a preselected Web page called the *home page*—the main page of the website that contains links to the other pages is the site's home page. The address of the home page displays near the top of the browser in the address box. To request a different Web page, you can type its address in the address box. The Internet is used to provide public services to the community.

2 **If necessary, in the title bar, click the Maximize button** 🔲 **. In the Address box, type** `http://www.thomas.gov` **and then press** ⏎Enter. This is the address of a Web page that helps visitors find information about the United States Congress, as shown in Figure 2.2. From this page, you can connect to several other pages. A group of related Web pages is a *website*.

Link to related webpage   Address box   Graphic object   Text

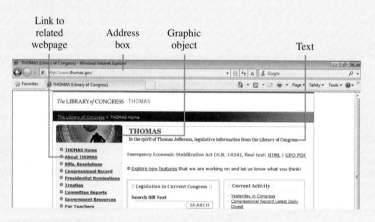

FIGURE 2.2
Thomas home page.

3 **At the left side of the Web page, click the underlined phrase *About THOMAS*.** The *About THOMAS* page displays, as shown in Figure 2.3. Underlining usually indicates the word or phrase is a *hyperlink* that contains the Web address of another

File name

FIGURE 2.3
Address of a file on a Web site.

Web page. Notice that the Web page address in the address box is *http://www.thomas.gov/home/abt_thom.html*. This Web page is in a folder named *home*. The file name is *abt_thom*, and the file extension—.html—indicates that the file is written in HTML, the language of Web pages. The combination of domain name, folder name, and file name is the ***Uniform Resource Locator (URL)*** address of that file on the Internet.

··

if you have problems

CHANGING WEB PAGES

Web pages are constantly changing. Your screen may not look exactly like the one in the figure. This is true throughout all projects. If necessary, examine the screen closely to find substitute links or, if necessary, try different links.

··

4 **At the left side of the Web page, click the underlined phrase *Bills, Resolutions*.** Notice that the address of this Web page is *http://www.thomas.gov/home/bills_res.html*, which indicates that this file—bills_res.html—is also in the home folder. Recall that a group of related Web pages like those listed at the left side of the Web page is a website.

5 **On the Address bar, at the left end, click the Back button** ⬅ **to go back to the About THOMAS page.** The Back button takes you back to the previous page you visited.

to extend your knowledge

TEMPORARY STORAGE OF WEB PAGES

Each time you request a Web page, your browser program saves the page in a temporary storage area called a *cache*. The Back and Forward buttons enable you to move back and forward through a sequence of Web pages you have already downloaded and stored in the cache. The pages display quickly because your browser retrieves them from the folder on your computer instead of requesting a new copy from the Web server.

---

6 **On the browser's Address bar, click the Refresh button** [⟳]. The Web page displays again but might take noticeably longer than using the Back button, because the *refresh* process forces the browser to ask for a new copy of the page from the Web server instead of recalling the copy it stored previously on your computer.

7 **On the Address bar, at the left end, click the Forward button** [→] **to return to the *Bills, Resolutions* page.** The Back and Forward buttons provide a way to review previously viewed Web pages and then return to the most recently viewed page. Notice that the Forward button becomes gray because this is the most recently downloaded Web page.

8 **On the Address bar, click the Back button** [←] **two times.** The Thomas home page displays, as shown in Figure 2.4. Notice the search options in the middle of the page. The home page of many websites often has an option for searching just the Web pages that comprise its site.

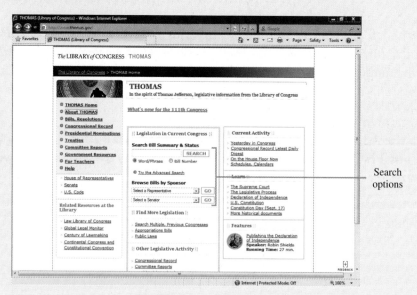

FIGURE 2.4
Searching within a Web site.

9 In the *Search Bill Summary & Status* box, type Energy Notice that the *option button* next to *Word/Phrase* is selected and the one next to *Bill Number* is deselected. Option buttons can be selected or deselected to specify criteria to use during a search.

10 Below *Browse Bills by Sponsor*, click the *Select a Representative* **arrow.** A menu of representatives displays. Menus are often attached to boxes to provide a list of choices. An arrow on the box indicates the presence of a menu.

11 Click the arrow again to close the list without selecting a particular name.

12 To the right of the *Search Bill Summary & Status* box, click the Search button. The results of the search display the bills that have been introduced related to wind energy in the current or most recent Congress.

13 Click the Start button, click All Programs, click the Accessories folder, and then in the list of programs, click the Snipping Tool.

14 In the Snipping Tool dialog box, click the New Snip button arrow 📷, and then click Window Snip. Point anywhere in the Thomas window, and then click one time.

15 Near the top of the Snipping Tool dialog box, click the Save Snip button 💾. In the Save As dialog box, navigate to the folder where you store your files. In the File name box, substituting your name as indicated, type U3Ch02WindBillsStudentName and then click Save.

16 In the upper right corner of each open dialog box or window, click the Close button 🗙.

17 Submit your snip as directed by your instructor.

to extend your knowledge

TEMPORARY STORAGE OF WEB PAGES

If you think the Web page you are viewing should have more current information, it is possible that your browser is displaying the page from the folder on your computer instead of getting a more recent version from the Web server. If you suspect this might be a problem, or if it is important to be sure a Web page displays the most current information, use the Refresh button to force the browser to get the most recent version of the page.

Browser Address AutoComplete Feature

When you type an address into the Address box of a browser, it stores the address in a list. If the **AutoComplete** feature is turned on, the next time you begin to type the address, a list of addresses appears below the address box, as shown in Figure 2.5. The AutoComplete feature

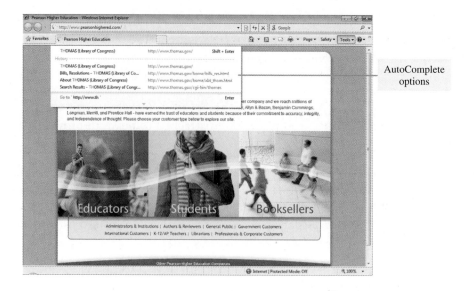

AutoComplete
options

FIGURE 2.5
AutoComplete aids Web page navigation.

displays a list of addresses you have typed before that begin with the letters you have typed so far. As you type more of the address, the list of possible matches gets shorter. At any point in the process, you can use a down arrow on the keyboard or a mouse click to choose the complete address from the list.

History of Web Pages

The browser keeps a list of Web pages you have requested. The list is displayed by clicking the Recent Pages arrow ▼ to the right of the Back and Forward buttons, as shown in Figure 2.6.

Recent pages

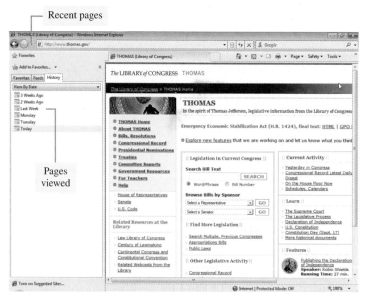

Pages
viewed

FIGURE 2.6
History of Web pages.

This feature is useful if you do not recall the address of a Web page but you know approximately when you found it. The number of days included in the history is an option that can be set by the user.

Adding Functionality to the Browser

A Web browser displays and manages Web pages. Some Web pages contain additional content beyond the basics. To use those functions, the browser program needs to be supplemented with small accessory programs called ***plug-ins***. The name implies a standardized way of connecting the programs to the browser so that different programs can be connected in the same way. They are also called ***add-on*** programs because they extend the capabilities of an existing application. Examples of additional functionality that plug-in or add-on programs provide are:

- display special graphics files such as *portable document format (PDF)*
- display video
- connect remote sensors to monitor a home
- privacy software to encode electronic mail messages

   Most of these programs are free downloads from a provider's website. Some of them make attempts to place extra toolbars on your browser or try to become the default choice for handling a particular type of file. When you are installing the plug-in program, you have the option to refuse these choices. In some cases, these choices are only available in the Custom installation option. If you choose the Express installation option, the choices regarding extra toolbars and defaults are made for you.

Modifying Browser Settings

There are many choices a browser must make to handle the wide variety of Web pages. Those decisions concern convenience, security, privacy, and the content. An example of such a decision is which Web page to display as the home page when the browser is started. The right to change the settings might not be available if you are using a computer in a laboratory that does not allow it. Many organizations compete for users by providing a Web page that contains several types of useful information plus links to other sites. They would like you to make their site your home page. This type of Web page is called a ***portal***.

to change the home page setting

1. **Start Internet Explorer, if necessary.** The Internet Explorer window opens to the home page. This page can be changed.

2. **On the tool bar, click the Tools arrow.** A menu of options displays, as shown in Figure 2.7.

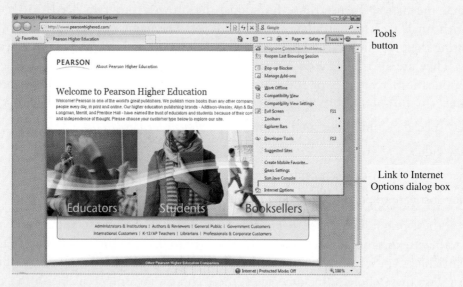

Tools button

Link to Internet Options dialog box

FIGURE 2.7
Tools menu.

3. **At the bottom of the menu, click Internet Options. In the Internet Options dialog box, click the General tab, if necessary, to display the Home Page, Browsing History, Search, Tabs, and Appearance options, as shown in Figure 2.8.**

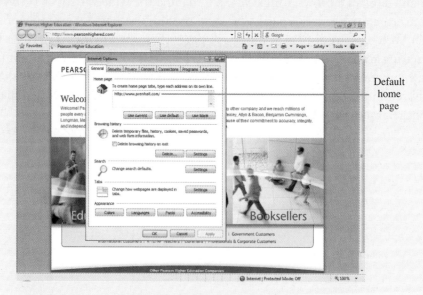

Default home page

FIGURE 2.8
Internet Options dialog box.

4   **Under Home page, notice the address of the default Web page.** Write the address down, if necessary, so you can restore it if you are working on someone else's computer.

5   **Select the Web address, delete it, and then type** `http://www.loc.gov` **At the bottom of the Internet Options dialog box, click OK.** The dialog box closes and the changes are made. The next time the browser is started, it will display the home page of the Library of Congress. The browser's home page can be displayed after the browser is opened by clicking the Home button 🏠.

6   **On the browser title bar, at the right end, click the Close button** ❌ . The Internet Explorer browser program closes.

7   **Start the Internet Explorer browser.** The program starts and displays the home page of the Library of Congress. Notice that the actual address is *http://www.loc.gov/index.html.* The name of the home page for the domain is *index.html.*

8   **Use the skills you practiced previously to start the Snipping Tool program and do a Window Snip of the Internet Options window. Save a copy of this window to the folder where you store your files. Name the file** `U3Ch02HomeStudentName` **substituting your name as indicated.**

9   **In the upper right corner of each open dialog box or window, click the Close button** ❌ .

10   **Submit your snip as directed by your instructor.**

11   **If you are using someone else's computer, use the skills you practiced in steps 2 through 6 to restore the original address.**

Recent versions of Web browsers such as Internet Explorer 7, Firefox 3, and Google Chrome 1 can have several Web pages open at the same time. The Web pages are identified by tabs near the top of the window. Switching between open Web pages is done by clicking the tabs. Web pages can be opened in new tabs by clicking an empty tab, and then entering the Web address. Tabs can be deleted by right-clicking the tab and selecting Delete from the shortcut menu.

Typical Internet Problems

Some Internet problems are fairly common, and you should be aware of them and of what to do about them. Refer to Table 2.2 for a list of common problems and solutions.

DESCRIPTION OF PROBLEM	POSSIBLE EXPLANATIONS	WHAT TO DO
Page Not Found–an error message displays that says it could not find the Web page	1) There is a mistake in the spelling of the Web address or a period is left out or missing. 2) The Web server is offline for maintenance or repair. 3) The entire Web address was not typed and the assumed server name was not accurate. 4) The website was deleted.	1) Check the spelling of the Web address. 2) Try another page in the same website or try again later. 3) Type the entire Web address.
Slow response downloading Web page	1) High traffic on your Internet connection has reduced your share of bandwidth. 2) You have hundreds or even thousands of Web pages stored on your computer and it takes time to index the content. 3) High demand on the Web server or its connection to the Internet is causing a server to place your request on hold.	1) Try again at an off-peak time. 2) Delete stored Web pages in Internet Options or reduce the time they are kept.
Parts of the Web page do not work, such as an animation	1) The plug-in for that animation is not installed or the version is outdated. 2) Your browser does not support that type of program or plug-in.	1) Download a new plug-in and install it. 2) Use another Web browser program.
Part of the Web page is garbled	The Internet connection was interrupted.	1) Try again. 2) If the connection is wireless, move closer to the antenna or try another position where the signal is stronger.

TABLE 2.2

▶▶▶ *lesson*
two | Searching for Information

There are many sites on the Internet that offer free services, such as those sites that help us search for Web pages that contain information, pictures, services, or activities.

One problem in searching the Web is finding so many related Web pages that you cannot examine even a small fraction of them. If you search for a common term, you can often find a million or more Web pages that use the term—far too many to explore. To narrow the list of Web pages that might contain the information you want, you will study how Web pages are indexed and ranked.

Automated Indexing and Ranking

In 1992, Tim Berners-Lee provided a list of all the Web servers on the Internet—all thirty of them. At that time, it was possible to make a directory of the Web pages that were available from the servers, which could be searched with relatively simple tools. In less than two decades, the number of Web pages has grown to more than 1 trillion and it is impossible to review, index, and rank these pages by having humans look at each one. Computer programs called **Web crawlers** or **spiders** search for Web pages, examine the content of pages, and then report their findings back to a central computer that performs the indexing, classifying, and ranking. The combination of these programs is called a **search engine**. The companies that own these programs put up a Web page on which users can make a request for a list of Web pages that contain information related to their request. Examples of popular search engines are Google, Yahoo!, Live Search, Baidu (China), and Guruji (India), as shown in Figure 2.9.

FIGURE 2.9
Guruji home page.

The method used by the Web crawler and the main program that analyzes the data from the Web crawler is different for each search engine. If you enter the same request on competing search engines, you will get a different list of Web pages. The companies compete on which one can deliver a list of Web pages that provides the information you want within the first few items on the list. This makes the issue of ranking the Web pages important.

An early ranking method relies on keywords. Recall from Chapter 1 that the HTML code of Web pages can include a list of keywords. The Web crawler program can record this list and associate it with a page's address. The main program creates an index like the one at the back of a textbook. If you ask for a particular keyword, the program can produce all of the Web pages that include that keyword. The competition between websites to have their address display in the first page of a search engine's results is fierce. Because of this desire to be listed first, the authors of the Web-page code often include hundreds of keywords in hopes that their Web page will come up more often in the search. As a result, the search engines that use this system often display many Web pages that are not closely related to the subject of the search.

Page Ranking

Another method of categorizing Web pages was popularized by Google. Their Web crawler made note of the hyperlinks in a Web page and the addresses to which those hyperlinks referred. Google reasoned that the Web pages that were referred to most by other Web pages with regard to a particular request for information contained the most relevant answers for the most people. This strategy was very successful and made Google the leader in the search engine field. The name of the company has entered the vocabulary as a verb. To *google* something means to use the Google search engine to find information on that subject.

Some companies still try to influence the ranking of their Web page by tricking the Web crawler or indexing programs, while others simply pay to have their Web page displayed on the first or second page of results. The addresses for these sites are usually labeled as *sponsored links*, as shown in Figure 2.10. Selling this space is a significant source of income for the companies that provide the search engine service.

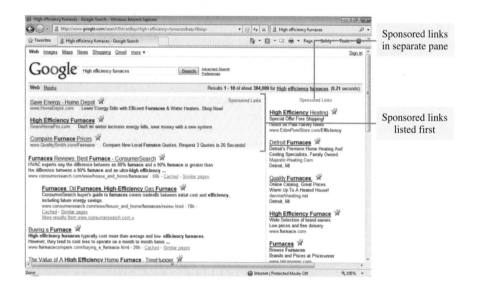

FIGURE 2.10
Sponsored links.

One search strategy does not fit all needs. Other methods of helping users find the information they want are:

- categorizing—providing categories of sites (dir.yahoo.com)
- definitions—dictionaries (Dictionary.com)
- history of words—etymologies (etymonline.com)
- WikiAnswers—posting questions and inviting readers to answer or view previous exchanges (wiki.answers.com)

Search Methods

To find the information you want, you can begin by searching for sites that are related to a few individual words. This method is called a *keyword search*.

Computers use a formal logic system called ***Boolean logic*** for making decisions, developed by George Boole in the 1800s. It uses the operators ***and***, ***or***, and ***not***. Search engines combine Boolean logic with their own proprietary logic to choose which Web pages to display and how to rank them. To demonstrate how a search engine uses a mixture of Boolean and proprietary logic, you will search for recent authoritative information on the energy output of large wind turbines.

to refine a search using logic operators

1   **Start Internet Explorer.** The Internet Explorer window opens to the default Web page.

2   **In the Address box, type** `Google.com` **and then press** `↵Enter`. The Google home page displays. Most browsers will assume that you want to use the hypertext transfer protocol, so you do not have to type it unless the shortened address does not work.

3   **Below the Google logo, in the empty search box, type** `wind turbine`, **and then press** `↵Enter`. The first ten websites are listed on the first page, along with a separate section of links to Web pages whose sponsors paid a fee to have their sites come up on the first page of the search, as shown in Figure 2.11. Google uses a proprietary logic to determine which pages to include. Notice that the logic used by the Google search engine selected millions of Web pages that are related to wind turbines. This is far too many to examine, so the search must be refined.

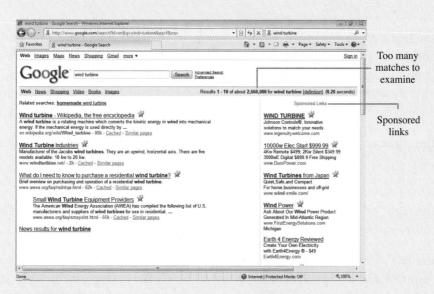

FIGURE 2.11
Google search results.

4 **To the right of the Search button, click *Advanced Search.*** The Advanced Search window displays, as shown in Figure 2.12. Notice that the words used earlier are in the *all these words* box. The Google search engine combines its logic with the Boolean *and* logic to find sites that contain both words—*wind* and *turbine.*

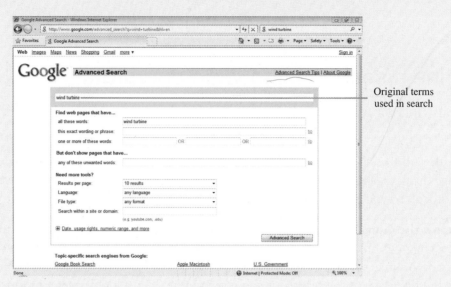

Original terms used in search

FIGURE 2.12
Advanced search criteria.

5 **In the *this exact wording or phrase* box, type** energy output Each of these words is commonly used in many ways. It is the exact combination of them that has meaning in this search.

6 **To the right of *one or more of these words*, in the first box, type** kwh **and, in the second box, type** mwh This is an example of the logical *or* operator. Energy output for large turbines can be measured in kilowatt hours (kwh) or megawatt hours (mwh). By searching for sites that contain either of these measurement terms, the results will be limited to sites that contain data with either of these energy labels.

7 **To the right of *any of these unwanted words*, in the box, type** small This criteria uses the logical *not* operator. This criterion will eliminate sites that describe small wind turbines that are more appropriate to home use.

8 **To the right of *Search within a site or domain*, in the box, type** .gov This will limit the search to government websites.

9 **To the left of *Date, usage rights, numeric range, and more*, click the plus sign. To the right of *Date: (how recent the page is)*, click the arrow on the box, and then click *past year*.** This criterion filters the websites by the date of posting to display only Web pages that have been posted in the last year, as shown in Figure 2.13. Be aware that the page might contain older information.

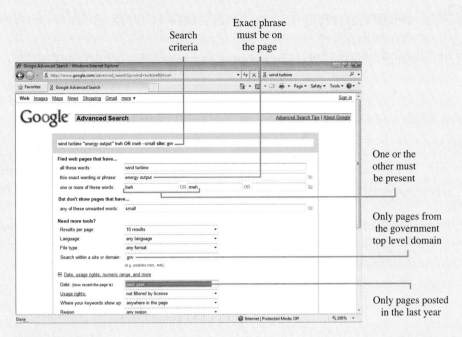

FIGURE 2.13
Advanced search.

10 Use the skills you practiced previously to start the Snipping Tool program and do a Window Snip of the Advanced Search window. Save a copy of this window to the folder where you store your files. Name the file U3Ch02SearchStudentName substituting your name as indicated.

11 Scroll to the bottom of the browser window, if necessary, and click the Advanced Search button. The combination of criteria applied with Boolean and proprietary logic reduces the number of Web pages from millions to a much smaller number. Notice the criteria in the Search box. If you know the codes, you can enter the advanced search criteria directly into the Search box.

12 In the upper right corner of each open dialog box or window, click the Close button [X].

13 Submit your snip as directed by your instructor.

to extend your knowledge

SEARCH FOR WORDS WITHIN A WEB PAGE

Some Web pages or the documents attached to them can be many screens or pages long. To find a particular word or phrase in the displayed page, the browser provides a Find feature that is similar to the one in a word processing program. The Find feature is found on the browser's menu bar in the Edit menu or may be started with Ctrl + F.

▶▶▶ *lesson*
three | Managing Information from a Website

Once you find the information you seek, the next step is to manage the information.

Marking the Web Page for Convenient Retrieval

When you find a site that you know you will want to return to in the future, you can save a link to the site. In Internet Explorer, these links are called ***Favorites***; in Mozilla Firefox, they are called ***Bookmarks***. You can add and delete Favorites at any time, and you can organize your Favorites by topic in folders in much the same way you deal with files in Windows Explorer. If the details of the following steps do not exactly match the browser version you have, they will be similar. Use the browser's Help feature for specific instructions on adding website addresses to a list of favorite sites.

to save links to Web pages

1 **Start Internet Explorer. In the Address box, type** energy.gov **and then press** Enter**.** The home page of the U.S. Department of Energy displays.

2 **On the toolbar, click the Favorites button. On the menu, click Add to Favorites.** The Add a Favorite dialog box displays, and the name of the Web page displays in the Name box. If you are unsatisfied with the default name, you can change it.

3 **To the right of *Create in* at the right of the box, click the arrow.** A list of any existing folders displays.

4 **On the menu at the top, click Favorites to close the menu. In the Add a Favorite dialog box, click the New Folder button.**

5 **In the Folder Name box, type** Energy **and then click the Create button.** A link to the Department of Energy home page will be saved in a folder named *Energy*, as shown in Figure 2.14.

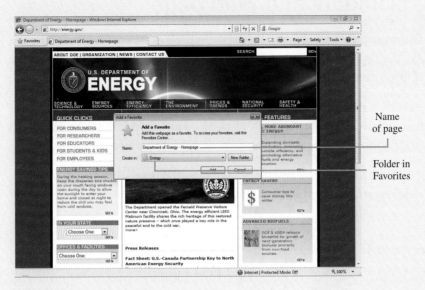

FIGURE 2.14
Link stored in a folder under Favorites.

6 **In the *Add a Favorite* dialog box, click the Add button.** The link is stored.

7 **On the browser's toolbar, click the Home button** 🏠. The default home page displays.

8 **On the toolbar, click the Favorites button. At the top of the menu, click the Favorites button. On the menu, click to the Energy folder.** A subfolder displays that includes the link to the Department of Energy.

9 **Click the link to the Department of Energy home page.** The Department of Energy home page displays.

10 **Close** ❌ **the browser.**

Copying Information from a Website

You can copy text and graphics from websites and use them for other purposes, such as reports or presentations. You can copy content and paste it into other documents or you can save the entire Web page. The legal and ethical use of copied material is discussed in Lesson 5.

Managing Bookmarks or Favorites

Lists of favorite Web site addresses take time to accumulate and are a valuable resource. These lists can be shared between different types of browsers or exchanged between users as e-mail attachments or postings on social networking sites. The list of browsers can be exported or imported in Internet Explorer by using the *File, Import or Export* menu options.

to copy elements of a Web page

1 **Start Internet Explorer. In the Address box, type** `energy.gov` **and then press** `⏎Enter`**.** The home page of the U.S. Department of Energy (DOE) displays. This is a Federal government site, and copying is permitted if appropriate credit is given.

2 **In the DOE home page, in the Search box, type** `wind powering America` **and then, to the right of the box, click the Go button.** The Search results page displays, showing the pages that contain the phrase *wind powering America*.

3 **Click the link titled** *Wind and Hydropower Technologies Program: Wind Powering America*. The home page for Wind Powering America displays.

·····

if you have problems

Remember that websites change frequently. Although you will find a page on wind power, it may not look like the one in Figure 2.15. If you do not see this page, find a similar page with text and a picture.

·····

4 **Move the pointer to the beginning of the first full text paragraph and drag the paragraph to select it, as shown in Figure 2.15.**

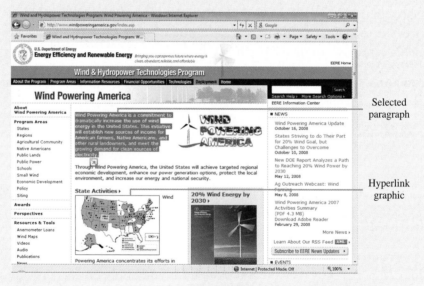

FIGURE 2.15
Copying part of a Web page.

5 **Hold down** `Ctrl` **and press** `C` **to copy the selected paragraph.**

6 **From the Start menu, open Microsoft Office Word, and then choose to open a blank document. In the blank document, type** `Excerpts from Wind Powering America` **and then press** `⏎Enter`**.** Alternatively, from the Start menu, click All Programs, click Accessories, click WordPad, and then type the title.

7 On the Home tab, in the Clipboard group, click the Paste button. The text is pasted at the insertion point. Alternatively, you can press Ctrl + V. If you are using WordPad, on the menu bar, click Edit, and then click Paste.

8 Click the Internet Explorer icon on the taskbar to return to the DOE website.

9 Click anywhere on the page to deselect the text. Move your pointer to the map of state activities. Position the pointer on an empty portion of the map, and then right-click. From the shortcut menu, click Copy. The picture is placed in the clipboard.

10 On the taskbar, click the Microsoft Word icon to return to the Word document.

11 Press ↵Enter to move the insertion point to a new line. On the Home tab, in the Clipboard group, click the Paste button. Alternatively, press Ctrl + V.

if you have problems

MAP DID NOT COPY CORRECTLY...
If the map was not successfully transferred to the Clipboard, the previous content of the Clipboard will be pasted. Click the Undo button ↺ to remove the extra content, and try again. This map contains hyperlinks to other pages, so it is important to right-click on an empty part of the map and not on one of the embedded hyperlinks. If that still doesn't work, choose the Save As option from the shortcut menu and save the map to your computer. Then use the Word menu options to insert the picture into the document.

12 In the upper left corner of the Word window, click the Office button 🏢, and then click Save As. Navigate to the folder where you save your files and save the document as U3Ch02WindMapStudentName Alternatively, in WordPad, on the menu bar, click File, and then click Save As. Save in *.txt* format.

13 Close Word and close the browser window.

Mapping software is often included in Web sites to help users find locations. Some Web sites are dedicated to providing maps such as Google Maps or Yahoo! Maps.

to extend your knowledge

PRINT SELECTED AREAS OF WEB PAGES
You can print a portion of a Web page. Begin by selecting the text you want to print. On the browser's menu bar, click File, and then click Print. In the Print dialog box, in the Print Range section, click Selection, and then click the Print button. Selecting long sections can be problematic because dragging might include unwanted elements of the Web page. If you want to print a long section of a Web page, begin by selecting the first word in the text, scroll to the end of the text, press ⇧Shift, click the end of the desired text, and then print the selection. Avoid selecting unwanted portions of the page, if possible.

Downloading a Web Page

You can also save entire Web pages to your hard disk and view them with the browser. This enables you to look at the saved pages even when you do not have an Internet connection. This is useful if you plan to show a Web page at a presentation and you are not sure whether you will have an Internet connection.

to save and view a Web page

1 **Start Internet Explorer. In the Address box, type** energy.gov **and then press** ⏎Enter**. The home page of the U.S. Department of Energy (DOE) displays.**

2 **If the menu bar is not displayed, right-click the toolbar and click the Menu Bar option to display it. On the menu bar, click File, and then on the menu, click Save As.**

3 **Navigate to the folder where you save your files.**

4 **Change the file name to** U3Ch02DOEStudentName

5 **In the** *Save as type* **box, notice that the default file type is** *Web Archive, single file,* **as shown in Figure 2.16.** Web pages are a combination of text and graphics elements that are often assembled from different folders before they are provided by the Web server. The ***Web Archive*** file type is used by Microsoft's Internet Explorer to create a single file that might not display in Firefox or Safari. Alternatively, use the *Save as type* options to save the file as a complete Web page.

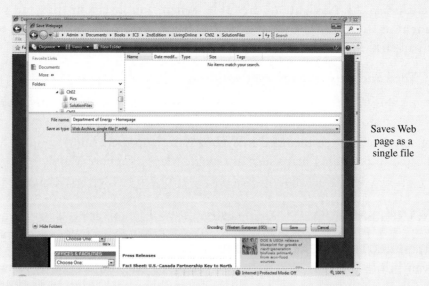

Saves Web page as a single file

FIGURE 2.16
Save a Web page.

6 **With** *Web Archive, single file* **selected as the type of file, in the Save Webpage dialog box, click the Save button.** The text and graphics that make up the Web page are stored as a single file.

if you have problems

SINGLE FILE WEB PAGE NOT SUPPORTED...
The Web Archive, single file format might not be supported in another browser. Most other browsers have a choice to save a Web page as a collection of files. There is a file written in HTML, plus a folder of related files by the same name. Care must be taken to store the file and the folder together and not change the name of the file or the folder.

7 **On the browser's menu bar, click File, and then click Open.** The Open dialog box displays.

8 **In the Open dialog box, click the Browse button. Navigate to the folder in which you stored the Web page. Click the file name—**U3Ch02DOEStudentName.

9 **In the dialog box, click Open. In the Open dialog box, click OK.** The Web page displays from the folder on your computer. This page is now available even if you are not connected to the Internet. Submit the file as directed by your instructor.

10 **Close the browser window.**

▶▶▶ *lesson*
four | Creating and Hosting Web Pages

A Web page is written in HTML code. If you know the rules for writing HTML code, you can create a Web page using a text-editing program such as Notepad. This takes time to learn and is not necessary for most purposes if you use other programs to write the code for you.

Creating Web Pages with Word, Excel, or PowerPoint

The ability to save documents as Web pages that are written in HTML is included in Microsoft Office. You can save a Word, Excel, or PowerPoint file as a Web page and the program will write the appropriate code for you. Web pages can do more than display documents from MS Office. If you want to include more sophisticated features, you can use a program that is dedicated to writing Web pages.

to create a Web page using Microsoft Word 2007

1 **From the Start menu, open Microsoft Office Word.** The program displays a blank document.

2 **On the first line of the document, type** `Wind Energy` **and then press** Enter.

3 **On the Insert tab, in the Illustrations group, click Clip Art.**

4 **In the Clip Art pane, in the Search for box, type** `wind energy` **and then click the Go button to search for a picture or clip art related to wind energy.**

5 **In the Clip Art pane, click one of the pictures that results from your search.** The picture is placed in the document, as shown in Figure 2.17.

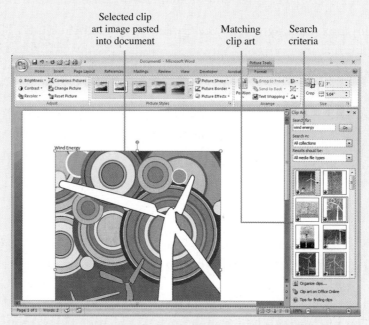

FIGURE 2.17
Copying pictures from Web pages.

6 **In the upper left corner, click the Office button** , **and then click Save As.**

7 **In the Save As dialog box, at the right end of the** *Save As Type* **box, click the arrow. On the menu, click** *Single File Web Page*.

8 **Navigate to the folder where you save your files and save the document as** `U3Ch02WebPageStudentName` **Close Word.**

9 **Start Internet Explorer. Use the skills you practiced in the previous lesson to open and view the Web page, U3Ch02WebPageStudentName, from the folder on your computer.**

10 **In Internet Explorer, on the menu bar, click View. On the menu, click Source.** A basic text-editing program opens that displays the HTML code. Notice that there is a lot of code for just two words and a single graphic. The code written by MS Office includes a great deal of information about features that are not used in this Web page.

11 **Close the text editing window. On the right of the menu bar, right click. On the menu, click Menu Bar to deselect it, and close the menu bar. Close the browser.** The Web pages created by MS Office are not what a knowledgeable Web designer would create, but they can be useful for creating Web versions of flyers or financial statements and for sharing a PowerPoint presentation, for example, with people who are unable to attend a meeting.

Web Page Design Software

To design more sophisticated Web pages and websites that allow interaction with users requires software programs that are designed for that purpose. Examples range from expensive professional programs, such as Adobe Dreamweaver and Microsoft Expression Web, to free programs like HTML Kit. Several Web pages can be connected by hyperlinks to form a website. The principle Web page is called the home page or *index*, and the other pages are linked to it. Dedicated design software manages the hyperlinks between the home page and other pages of a website.

Hosting Web Pages

Once the Web pages are created, they must be transferred to a Web server that has an IP address on the Internet. On the Web server, the files are stored in a folder that can be related to a particular domain name. Recall from Chapter 1 that you can buy the right to use a domain name and then pay an Internet Service Provider (ISP) to host the domain name. The domain name servers (DNS) on the Internet maintain a directory of domain names and the IP addresses of the host computers. When someone requests a Web page by using a domain name, the request is routed to the host computer and it locates the home page for the domain name.

If you create Web pages on your computer, you need to transfer those files from your computer to the host computer. This process is one of the original uses of the Internet and uses a set of rules for moving files called the *File Transfer Protocol (FTP)*. You can use an FTP program or this feature might be included with the browser software. An example of a free, open-source FTP program is FileZilla, seen in Figure 2.18. The host computer usually requires a password to gain access. If you belong to an organization that owns a Web server, you might have permission to use it or be able to get permission without additional charge.

If you create a Web page that can be viewed anywhere in the world, you have a responsibility to respect the privacy of other people and to avoid using your Web page to bully or harass someone. You should treat other people's opinions with respect and be sure that your own opinions are based on verifiable, accurate facts. If you use an informal style, be sure that it is appropriate for your intended audience.

if you have problems

FILE TRANSFER BLOCKED...

If you cannot transfer files from a local computer to the Web server, the use of FTP software might be blocked by firewall software on your computer or at the gateway between your LAN and the Internet. Check those two locations to see if the use of FTP software is allowed or if you can get permission to use it while you are uploading files.

FIGURE 2.18
FileZilla home page.

▶▶▶ *lesson*
five|Security, Privacy, and Ethics

In this lesson, ethics, security and privacy are discussed as they pertain to using a Web browser and search engine on the Internet.

Citing Sources

You can copy text and graphics from websites and use them for other purposes, such as reports or presentations. Before you copy anything from a website, you need to consider who owns the copyright to the material. A ***copyright*** is ownership of intelectual property and the exclusive right to use it or to choose who else uses it. Unauthorized copying is prohibited in most cases. There are copyright-free sites on the Web from which you can reproduce information and pictures; for example, the National Aeronautics and Space Administration (NASA), the National Oceanic and Atmospheric Administration (NOAA), and the U.S. Fish and Wildlife Service (FWS). Some pictures may have copyright notices indicating that the image is being used with permission from a copyright holder. You can also, under some circumstances, use copyrighted materials for education purposes. Regardless of whether the information is copyrighted, you must let the reader know what thoughts are yours and what has been copied from someone else.

When you see the term *copyright* or the copyright symbol (©), it means the author is reminding people that they should not use this material without permission. A copyright exists even if the author does not use the symbol. Copyrighted materials may be used without paying royalties for purposes of research, criticism, comment, news reporting, and teaching under the name of ***fair use***. Specific information on U.S. copyright laws and rules is available from the Library of Congress at copyright.gov. Other protections of creative works include a ***trademark***—a word or symbol that indicates ownership of a product or service and its use is reserved for the owner. A ***patent*** provides protection for the idea behind an invention.

In formal research papers, there are specific rules for ***citing***—referencing—the source of someone else's text, pictures, or other work that is the result of a creative process. One of the important functions of a good citation is that it enables the reader to check the source material to see if it was taken out of context or misrepresented. When citing a Web page from which you have copied text or pictures, you need to provide enough information for someone else to find the same text or picture that you did.

The standards for citation that are commonly used in education in the U.S. are administered by the Modern Language Association (MLA) and the American Psychological Association (APA). Refer to Table 2.3 for a list of reference styles.

STYLE	WHERE IT IS USED
APA	Research papers in the social sciences
Chicago	Publishing
GB7714	China
GOST	Russia and former Soviet-bloc countries
ISO-690	International standard used in industry, manufacturing, and patent applications
MLA	English studies
SISTO2	Japan
Turabian	Academic research, particularly in musicology, history, and theology—based on Chicago style

TABLE 2.3

Citing Web pages poses problems that are different from citing traditionally published articles and books. The types of information in Web pages changes as new technologies are used, and some Web pages are assembled from pieces upon request and are not stored. Guidelines for citing references according to a particular standard are usually found at the organization's website where the standard is defined or in official organization publications.

There are electronic aids to help students create citations that meet most style requirements. Microsoft Word 2007 includes a feature that lets you fill in a form and, when you specify the reference style, provides a list of references and citations in that style. Third-party software like EndNote assists researchers to manage references. There are websites that perform similar services for free, such as Son of Citation Machine and Knight Cite.

Evaluating Quality Web Page Content

The ease with which anyone can publish a Web page means that there is little quality control. To determine the quality of the content of a website that appears as the result of a search, ask yourself the following questions:

- Is the content relevant to the topic I searched for?

- What does the Web address tell me? Look at the top-level domain to determine the type of domain (government, military, nonprofit) and if the domain name is hosted in a different country. Does the page come from a source that has an established reputation for accuracy and reliability or is it from an ISP like AOL that hosts sites posted by individuals?

- Is the source likely to be biased on this topic? For example, how does the issue affect the income of the site's sponsors or authors? Look for links such as *About Us*, *Philosophy*, or *Staff Biographies* that would provide an indication of bias on the topic. Is the author of the content qualified to provide an informed opinion?

- Is the information current? Old news stories can be recirculated in summaries where the summary has a recent date but the original article is old.

- Does the site contain references to authoritative sources? Look for hyperlinks to the sources the author uses as background for the article.

- Does the information go into enough detail and is it original? If the text is mostly someone else's ideas, follow the links back to the source and use that instead.

- Search for other articles by the same author or comments about the author, using a search engine like Google. Enclose the author's full name in quotation marks and include another word that describes the author's specialty to restrict the search.

If you have questions about a site, you can contact the site's creators if they provide a *Contact* link or an electronic mail address. It can be helpful to consider the ranking the search engine gave the site as an indication of how popular it is.

Unethical Search Engine Practices

The ranking of websites on a search engine has considerable value. Commercial sites whose Web pages come up on the first page of a popular search engine are likely to have many more people visit their sites than if they appeared on the second page. This value can lead to unethical practices by the operators of search engines and by the authors of Web pages.

Because placement of a link on the first page of search results is valuable, some Web page sponsors simply pay the search engine company to place their link on the first page of results when someone searches for information on certain related topics. The search engine company keeps track of how many people actually click the link and charge the company an additional amount for each **click through** (clicking the link to connect to another website). An ethical search engine company will clearly label the sponsored links so the user can tell which ones are listed because they are appropriate matches for the search criteria and which links have been placed in a prominent location on the page for a fee. An unethical search engine company will not disclose that a sponsored link is at the top of the list because they paid for the location; they simply want to increase the number of click-throughs. Some search engines skirt the issue by shading the sponsored links with a light grey background and labeling them using a small font that users might not notice, as shown in Figure 2.19.

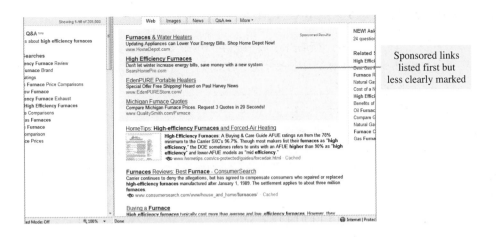

FIGURE 2.19
Sponsored links with lightly shaded background.

Some Web sponsors use practices that are designed to raise their rankings at search engines without paying for special placement. For example, a group of sites might agree to place links on their pages to each of the other sites in the group. Some search engines, like Google, use the number of links on other pages as one of the ranking criteria, so the extra links increase the rankings of all the pages in the group. Another practice is to create programs that repeatedly ask for the same Web page to increase the number of requests per day, which is another ranking criteria used by search engines. In general, practices that are designed to misrepresent a website's ranking in the list of search results are unethical because they are intended to deceive the user of the search engine.

Searching Safely by Blocking Websites

The Internet has a wide variety of content, and because content crosses state and national boundaries easily, it is difficult to monitor and control. If there are categories of websites that you do not want to view, it is possible to block many of them by using the browser's content filter. Examples of these categories are adult and political content. Some countries block access to websites that contain political content that they deem to be subversive.

Another type of unwanted content is ***pop-up*** windows that contain unwanted messages, advertising, or surveys, as shown in Figure 2.20. A pop-up window appears as a result of clicking or even simply moving the pointer over a portion of the Web page. Some sites use pop-up windows for desirable purposes, but most pop-up windows display without the voluntary permission of the user. Display of pop-up windows can be disabled in most browser programs.

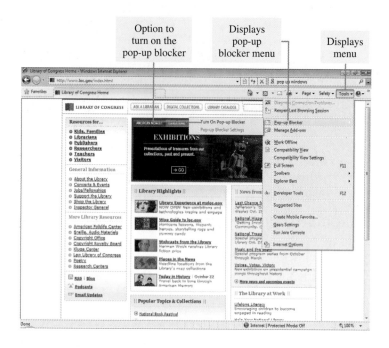

FIGURE 2.20
Pop-up blocker options.

Ethical Behavior on the Web

The basic concept behind ethical behavior is to treat others as you would have them treat you. When you use the Internet, consider the following and use them as guidelines:

- Respect the privacy of others.
- Treat the opinions of others with respect.
- Do not write something about another person or group that is not true.
- Do not use the Internet to harrass someone.
- Do not force offensive material on someone else.
- Respect the right of parents to limit their children's access to adult material.

| SUMMARY

In this chapter, you learned how to use a Web browser and search engine to gather information online and how to manage the information. You learned about creating and hosting Web pages and tips on how to use the Internet safely, ethically, and respectfully.

You can extend your learning by reviewing concepts and terms and by practicing variations of skills presented in the lessons.

| KEY TERMS

add-on	Bookmarks	citation
address box	Boolean logic	click through
and	cache	copyright

fair use	not	spider
Favorites	option button	sponsored links
File Transfer Protocol (FTP)	or	trademark
google	patent	Uniform Resource Locator (URL)
home page	plug-in	Web archive, single file
hyperlink	pop-up	Web crawler
index	portal	website
keyword search	search engine	

CHECKING CONCEPTS AND TERMS

Assessing Learning Outcomes
SCREEN ID
Identify each element of the screen by matching callout numbers shown in Figure 2.21 to a corresponding description. Lessons in which these skills are practiced are shown in brackets.

FIGURE 2.21

_____ **A.** URL

_____ **B.** Back

_____ **C.** Forward

_____ **D.** History

_____ **E.** List of URLs used with AutoComplete

_____ **F.** Links to other pages in the website

_____ **G.** Search restricted to information on website

_____ **H.** Option list

_____ **I.** Refresh

_____ **J.** Link to default Web page

MULTIPLE CHOICE

Circle the letter of the correct answer for each of the following.

1. Why does a Web page appear more rapidly the second time you request it? [L1]

   a. The browser stores the host's IP address so it doesn't have to request it again from the domain server.

   b. The browser stores a copy of the Web page on the computer's hard drive and uses that copy for subsequent requests.

   c. The browser stores the pictures and only requests the text for later requests of the same page.

   d. The image of the first screen of a website is stored in video memory for five minutes and used to display the page if the second request is made soon enough.

2. Which of the following is **not** a typical reason for the browser to return a *Page not found* error? [L1]

   a. The page does not exist at the address given to the browser.

   b. The Internet connection is not working.

   c. The Web server is not working.

   d. The Web browser does not use the same version of HTML code as the Web page.

3. The main purpose of a Web crawler is: [L2]

   a. to locate Web pages on the Internet and record their characteristics.

   b. to analyze and categorize the characteristics of Web pages.

   c. to display Web pages.

   d. to provide a free alternative to Internet Explorer and Firefox.

4. Which of the following combinations of keywords and Boolean logic operators would produce the largest list of matching Web pages? [L2]

   a. wind AND power

   b. wind OR power

   c. wind NOT power

   d. The number of matching pages is not affected by the use of Boolean logic.

5. What is the purpose of a Bookmark or Favorite? [L3]

   a. to save the Web page on the computer's hard disk for quick retrieval

   b. to block access to a website that is offensive

   c. to make it more convenient to remember and retrieve a previously visited site

   d. to mark a word on a Web page to make it easy to find

6. Why would you save a copy of a Web page to the computer's hard disk? [L3]

   a. to compare it to the current version of the Web page to detect changes

   b. to scan it for noncopyrighted material

   c. so it can be retrieved even without an Internet connection

   d. so it can be printed

7. What is the type of program that can transfer files from your computer to a Web server? [L4]

   a. FTP

   b. IP

   c. e-mail

   d. Telnet

8. What type of code is used to write Web pages? [L4]

a. XML

b. TCP/IP

c. FTP

d. HTML

9. What are two common standards for citing references that are used in the U.S.? [L5]

a. FTP and APA

b. APA and MLA

c. Chicago and FTP

d. MLA and GOST

10. Which of the following is **not** an ethical practice? [L5]

a. placing a well-labeled, sponsored site at the top of a list of matches in a search result

b. respecting the privacy of others

c. using the Internet to force ideas on people for their own good

d. treating the opinions of others with respect

MATCHING

Match each term in the second column with its correct definition in the first column by writing the letter of the term on the blank line in front of the definition.

_____ 1. To seek information about someone using a popular search engine

_____ 2. Type of software used to move files between computers over the Internet

_____ 3. Connection to another Web page or to an element on the same page

_____ 4. Supplementary program that adds functionality

_____ 5. Program that displays links to selected Web pages based on search criteria

_____ 6. Protected symbol associated with a product or brand

_____ 7. Web address

_____ 8. Address and connection for a fee to a website that is ranked highly

_____ 9. Protection for an inventor

_____ 10. Permission to use copyrighted material for a limited set of purposes

A. FTP

B. Search engine

C. Trademark

D. Patent

E. Google

F. Fair use

G. Sponsored link

H. Hyperlink

I. URL

J. Plug-in

SKILL DRILL

Skill Drill exercises reinforce chapter skills. Each skill reinforced is the same, or nearly the same, as a skill presented in the chapter. Detailed instructions are provided in a step-by-step format.

Each exercise is independent of the others, so you can do the exercises in any order.

1. Change the default Web page

Change the Web page that displays by default.

To choose your own default Web page or to restore the original Web address:

1. Start Internet Explorer. On the toolbar, click **Tools**. At the bottom of the menu, click **Internet Options**.

2. On the **General** tab, in the **Home Page** section, select the address and delete it. Type a Web page address of your choice.

3. Use the skills you practiced previously to start the Snipping Tool program and do a Window Snip of the Internet Options window. Save a copy of this window to the folder where you store your files. Name the file U3Ch02Home2StudentName substituting your name as indicated.

4. In the upper right corner of the **Snipping Tool** window, click the **Close** button.

5. In the **Internet Options** dialog box, click **OK**.

6. On the **Address** bar, click the **Home** button. The new default page displays.

7. Use the skills you have practiced to restore the original home page Web address. Close the browser. Submit your snip as directed by your instructor.

2. Search for Web Pages Using Advanced Options

Search, using Boolean operators, for government websites that have information on the power output of solar photovoltaic cells (not including small or home installations).

To perform an advanced search using Boolean operators, follow these steps:

1. Start a Web browser program such as Internet Explorer and go to the **Google.com** Web page.

2. Click the **Advanced Search** link.

3. On the **Advanced Search** page, in the *all these words* box, type solar photovoltaic cells

4. In the *this exact wording or phrase* box, type power output

5. In the first box to the right of *one or more of these words*, type kwh and in the next box, type mwh

6. In the box to the right of *any of these unwanted words*, type small home

7. In the box to the right of *Search within a site or domain*, type .gov

8. To the left of *Date, usage rights, numeric range, and more*, click the plus (+) sign.

9. In the box to the right of *Date (how recent the page is)*, click the arrow, and then click **past year**. Scroll down, and then click the **Advanced Search** button. A short list of qualifying sites displays.

10. Use the skills you practiced previously to start the Snipping Tool program and do a Window Snip of the Internet Explorer window. Save a copy of this window to the folder where you store your files. Name the file U3Ch02AdvancedStudentName substituting your name as indicated.

11. In the upper right corner of each open dialog box or window, click the **Close** button.

12. Submit your snip as directed by your instructor.

3. Create a Web Page Using Excel

You can create Web pages using Microsoft Office programs like Word, Excel, PowerPoint, and Access.

To create a Web page from Excel, follow these steps:

1. Start Microsoft Excel.

2. In cell **A1**, type Open to Public

3. In cell **A3** type Days and in cell **B3** type Hours

4. In cells **A4** through **A10**, type Monday, Tuesday, Wednesday, Thursday, Friday, Saturday, and Sunday Widen column A as needed.

5. In cells **B4** through **B10** type Closed, Closed, Open, Open, Open, Open, and Open

6. In the upper left corner, click the **Office** button. On the menu, click **Save As**.

7. Change the file type to **Single File Web Page**. Save the file in the folder where you store your files and name it **U3Ch02ExcelStudentName** If asked about losing functionality, click **Yes**.

8. Close **Excel**. Start Internet Explorer. On the toolbar, right click and choose the Menu bar, if necessary, to display the Menu bar. On the Menu bar, click **File**, and then click **Open**. Alternatively, press Ctrl + O to display the Open dialog box.

9. In the **Open** dialog box, navigate to the folder in which you saved the Excel file as a single-file Web page. Click the file name, and then click the **Open** button. In the **Open** dialog box, click **OK**. The worksheet displays as a Web page.

10. Close the browser window. Submit your file as directed by your instructor.

EXPLORE AND SHARE

Explore and Share questions are intended for discussion in class or online. Look for information that is related to the learning outcomes for this chapter, as directed. Submit your answers as directed by your instructor.

1. Learn about the search engine used in China. Open your Web browser and go to **http://www.baidu.com**. This is the home page of the Baidu search engine. Click the *About Baidu* link. Read *The Baidu Story*. Next, go to **http://www.google.com**. On the Google home page, click the *About Google* link. On the *About Google* page, click the *Corporate Info* link. Read the *Company Overview* and *What's a Google* sections. Prepare to discuss the similarities and differences between the two companies by noting specific information that you can quote. [L2]

2. Your computer may use more plug-in programs than you realize. Start your favorite Web browser and examine the list of plug-ins or add-ons. Choose one of the following sets of instructions, depending on the browser you use most often. [L1]
   - In Internet Explorer, on the Tools menu, click Internet Options. In the Internet Options dialog box, click the Programs tab. In the Manage add-ons, click the *Manage add-ons* button.
   - In Firefox, on the Tools menu, click Add-ons.
   - In Safari, on the title bar, click Help. On the Help menu, click *Installed Plug-ins*.

   Review the list of add-on or plug-in programs your computer uses and prepare to summarize the types of functions they support and give examples.

3. The most authoritative sources are articles that have been reviewed and approved by experts. These articles appear in scholarly journals where each article is reviewed by other knowledgeable persons. These articles include reports of research discoveries. Many college libraries provide access to these articles for their students. Many of the same articles can be found online through Google Scholar. Start a browser program and go to **http://scholar.google.com**. One of the problems with solar photocells is that they are not very efficient at converting solar energy into electrical energy. Use this search engine to look for articles on photovoltaic cell efficiency to see what scientists have reported in the last two years in engineering and physics journals (Tip: Use the Advanced Scholar Search.) Prepare to report examples of discoveries that are improving photocell efficiency or lowering costs and examples of how the Advanced Scholar Search differs from the normal Advanced Search option. [L2]

4. Most photos are copyrighted by the photographer or studio. If you want to use a photo you see on a website that is copyrighted, you cannot do so without the owner's permission, which often involves paying a royalty. There are sites that provide photos that are preapproved for use, where you do not have to pay royalties or seek additional permission as long as they are used for purposes that are listed at the site. Start your Web browser and go to your favorite search engine and search for *royalty free photos*. Prepare to share the results of your search—including Web addresses—and describe the categories and quality of the photos you find. [L5]

IN YOUR LIFE

In Your Life questions are intended for discussion in class or online where you can share your personal experience. Restrict your answers to the topics described in each exercise. Submit your answers as directed by your instructor.

1. Find out what *fair use* means. Start a browser and read section #107 of the U.S. Copyright Law at **http://www.copyright.gov/title17/92chap1.html#107** Because teaching is one of the exceptions mentioned in the law, students often observe instructors using copyrighted material in class. Go to **http://www.usg.edu/legal/copyright/** and read the guidelines prepared by the University System of Georgia for its educators—particularly the section on course packs. Be prepared to discuss the following questions: Do you think this practice misleads students into thinking that they can use copyrighted materials outside of class without permission or payment? How can teachers avoid this misunderstanding? What is an example of an educational use that

would violate the copyright law in spite of the exception? Have you observed teachers exceeding the privileges of the fair use exemption, and why do you think so? [L5]

2. Find out what plug-in programs are associated with each file type on your computer. The following directions assume you have Windows Vista and Internet Explorer. In Internet Explorer, click **Tools**, and then click **Internet Options**. In the Internet Options dialog box, click the **Programs** tab. In the Internet Programs section, click the **Set Programs** button. In the next dialog box, click *Associate a file type or protocol with a program*. The next dialog box lists all of the file extensions and the programs associated with them. Click the *Current Default* column header to sort the list by type of program. Review the list and look for plug-in programs like QuickTime Player and Adobe Reader. Prepare to report what you found.

3. Your browsing habits are not a secret if someone else can look back at the history of Web pages you have visited. You can erase this history. In Internet Explorer, to the right of the Back and Forward buttons, click the **Recent Pages** arrow. On the menu, click **History**. Click the folders for **Last Week** and **Today** to see a list of Web pages this browser has viewed. In the Internet Explorer window, click **Tools**, and then click **Internet Options**. In the Internet Options dialog box, on the **General** tab, in the **Browsing History** section, click the **Delete** button. In the **Delete Browsing History** dialog box, in Internet Explorer 8, remove the check marks from all the boxes except **History**, and then click the **Delete** button. In the browser, attempt to display the history. It should be empty. Prepare to answer the following questions: When would you use the ability to delete the history? Would you be tempted to look at the history of someone else's use of a Web browser? Is it acceptable for parents to use this to see what sites their children have visited? [L5]

RELATED SKILLS

Related Skills exercises expand on or are related to skills presented in the lessons. The exercises provide a brief narrative introduction, followed by instructions in a numbered-step format that are not as detailed as those in the Skill Drill section.

1. Citation Help in Word 2007

If you copy content from a Web page into a text document, you should document your source using a standard style. To copy text into a Word 2007 document and create a reference in APA and MLA styles, follow these steps:

1. Start Internet Explorer. Go to **http://news.cnet.com/8301-11128_3-10023553-54.html**. Alternatively, go to **news.cnet.com** and search for *GE reshapes the future*. Examine the article by Martin LaMonica titled *GE reshapes the future of wind power*.

2. Start **Microsoft Word 2007** and open a blank document. In the first line, type Thoughts on the Future of Wind Power and then press ⏎Enter.

3. Switch back to **Internet Explorer**. Select the fourth paragraph that begins with *So instead...*, and then press Ctrl + C to copy the paragraph into the Clipboard.

4. Switch to the **Word** window. Press Ctrl + V to paste the paragraph.

5. In **Word** 2007, on the **References** tab, in the **Citations & Bibliography** group, click the **Style box** arrow. On the menu, click **MLA**.

6. In the **Citations & Bibliography** group, click **Insert Citation**. On the menu, click **Add New Source**. Using the **Type of Source** menu, select **website**. In the **Author** box, type Martin LaMonica

7. In the **Name of Web Page** box, type GE reshapes the future of wind power

8. In the **Year**, **Month**, and **Day** boxes, type 2008, August, and 28

9. In the **Year Accessed**, **Month Accessed**, and **Day Accessed** boxes, type the current year, name of month, and day.

10. Switch to the **Internet Explorer** window. In the **Address** box, select the Web address. Press Ctrl + C to copy the address.

11. Switch to the **Word** window. Click the **URL** box. Press Ctrl + V to paste the Web address.

12. In the **Create Source** dialog box, click **OK**. The author's name is cited after his work and placed within parentheses.

13. In the **Citations & Bibliography** group, click **Bibliography**. On the menu, click **Insert Bibliography**. The full reference is inserted.

14. In the **Citations & Bibliography** group, click the **Style box** arrow. On the menu click **APA**. Notice the citation and the reference are changed to match the APA style.

15. Repeat the process used in step 14 to see the references in different styles. Make **MLA** your last choice.

16. Click the **Office** button. On the menu, click **Save As**. Navigate to the folder where you save your files and save the file as U3Ch02WindFutureStudentName

17. **Close** all open windows without saving any changes.

2. Search for Images

Some of the search engines will search for images. This makes it convenient to find pictures on the Internet. It is possible to copy the pictures, but you should not use them if your purpose violates the fair use provision. In this case, you are doing an exercise for educational purposes and it will not harm the commercial value of the image, so it would be allowed under the fair use provision.

To locate a picture and paste it into a document, follow these steps:

1. Start Internet Explorer. Go to **Google.com**. Near the top of the window, click **Images**. The Google Image Search screen displays.

2. In the Search Images box, type Electric Automobiles of the Future and then click the **Search Images** button. A list of images is displayed where each image is a small version of a full-size image.

3. Choose an image and click it. The Web page on which the image is located displays. Examine the picture for a copyright notice. The picture may not be used without permission except under the fair use provision, unless otherwise stated. Because you will use it for educational purposes and its use will not damage its market value, using it for this exercise is permitted under the fair use provision.

4. Near the top of the window, click **See full-size image**. The image is displayed by itself.

5. Right-click the image. On the menu, click **Copy**.

6. Start **Microsoft Word** or another word processing program and open a blank document. In the first line, type Electric car of the future and then press ↵Enter. On the **Home** tab, in the **Clipboard** group, click the **Paste** button, and then press ↵Enter. Alternatively, press Ctrl + V to paste the image.

7. Switch back to the **Google** window. Click the **Back** button. Near the top of the page, locate the line that begins with *Below is the image in its original context on the page:* and is followed by a link to the Web page where the image is located. Click the link to that page. The Web page displays.

8. In the **Address** box, select the **URL**. Press Ctrl + C to copy the URL.

9. Switch back to the word processing document. Type Retrieved from and then press Ctrl + V to paste the URL.

10. Click the **Office** button. On the menu, click **Save As**. Navigate to the folder where you save your files and save the file as U3Ch02ElectricCarStudentName

11. **Close** all open windows. Submit the file as directed by your instructor.

DISCOVER

Discover exercises give students general directions for exploring and discovering more advanced skills and information. Each exercise is independent of the others, so you may complete the exercises in any order.

1. Search for Information on Wind Energy

Some answers are surprisingly difficult to find. For example, let's say that your local government is debating investing in a wind turbine. You know from the sales literature that it has a rated output of 1,000 kilowatts (1 megawatt) at a wind speed of 30 miles per hour. You also know from your own experience that the wind in your area does not blow at that speed constantly, so you've looked through the sales literature to find out how much energy in kilowatt hours (kwh) or megawatt hours (mwh) to expect from the unit in a year. That information is not in the literature provided, so you decide to find out on your own by looking for reports from owners of 1 mw wind turbines that have been in service for more than a year to see how much they actually generated in a year.

In order to assess the quality of the answers you find, you decide to estimate the upper limit of possible answers first. For example, if the wind was steady at 30 mph constantly for a year, the most you could expect from the unit would be the product of its rated power times the number of hours in a year (1 mw * 24 hr/day * 365 days/year = 8,760 mwh/year), so you expect an answer of less than 8,760 mwh or 8,760,000 kwh.

For this exercise, use what you have learned about search engines to find an authoritative source that will give you an approximate idea of how much energy to expect from a 1 mw wind turbine in a typical year. Make a log of what you try and how you refine your search. Describe the best answers you obtain, including the Web addresses of sites with the information. Do not be surprised if your early efforts are not successful. Refine your search and try to think of criteria that will yield better results. If you find it difficult to find the answer to this basic question about wind power, speculate on the reasons why this information is not readily available.

2. Use Translation Software to Browse in a Foreign Language

In the past, the large majority of Internet users were in the United States. That is no longer true, and many Web pages are available in foreign languages. Some search engine providers include a translation service that provides a translation that is generated by a computer. The translation is not exact, but it might be good enough for your purposes. Go to Google.com and open the Advanced Search window. In the *this exact wording or phrase* box, type `nuclear power` Click the Language box arrow and choose *Chinese (Simplified)*. In the *Search within a site or domain* box type `.ch` to restrict the search to Chinese domain names. Click the Advanced Search button. Scroll through the list of results and choose one that has the option *Translate this page*. Click *Translate this page*. Repeat this process to view two other pages. Make notes about each page and comment about the accuracy of the translation.

ASSESS YOUR PROGRESS

At this point, you should have a set of skills and concepts that are valuable to an employer and to you. You may not realize how much you've learned unless you take a few minutes to assess your progress.

1. From the student files, open **U3Ch02Assess**. Save it as U3Ch02AssessStudentName

2. Read each question in column A.

3. In column B, answer Yes or No.

4. If you identify a skill or design concept that you don't know, refer to the learning objective code next to the question and the table at the beginning of the chapter to find the skill and review it.

5. Print the worksheet if your instructor requires it. The file name is already in the header, so it will display your name as part of the file name.

6. All of these skills and concepts have been identified as important by surveying hundreds of individuals working at over 200 companies worldwide. If you cannot answer all of the questions affirmatively even after reviewing the relevant lesson, seek additional help from your instructor.

chapter three

Buying, Selling, and Banking Online

Lesson	Learning Outcomes	Code	Related IC3 Objectives
1	Identify that money is an idea that can be represented as digits in a computer	3.01	4.1.3
1	Identify the characteristics of a wire transfer	3.02	4.1.2
1	Identify the definition of an exchange rate	3.03	4.1.2
1	Use an Internet site to calculate equivalent values in different currencies	3.04	4.1.2
1	Identify the characteristics of a direct deposit	3.05	4.1.2
1	Identify the functions of an automatic teller machine	3.06	4.1.2
1	Identify the process of transferring data using symmetric encryption	3.07	3.1.2, 4.2.7
1	Identify the process of transferring data using public key encryption	3.08	3.1.2, 4.2.7
1	Identify the role of a certificate authority In public key encryption	3.09	3.1.2, 4.2.7
1	Identify the functions performed when banking online	3.10	4.1.2
2	Identify the relationships abbreviated as B2B, B2C, and C2C	3.11	4.1.2
2	Identify the advantages of shopping online	3.12	3.1.3
2	Identify the disadvantages of shopping online	3.13	3.1.3
2	Identify the role of Java and ActiveX in storefront Web pages	3.14	3.1.2, 4.1.3
2	Identify the function of cookies	3.15	3.1.13
2	Identify the advantages and disadvantages of paying online	3.16	4.1.2
3	Identify how businesses use EDI for B2B commerce	3.17	-
3	Identify how suppliers connect their LANs as extranets to manufacture LANs	3.18	-
3	Identify how businesses use auctions and reverse auctions to buy and sell between businesses	3.19	-
4	Identify the role of venture capitalists in startup companies	3.20	-
4	Identify how individuals can use intermediary sites to hold auctions	3.21	4.1.3
4	Identify characteristics of online classified advertising	3.22	4.1.3
4	Identify the process of self publishing and print on demand	3.23	-
4	Identify the functions of storefront software	3.24	-
5	Identify fraudulent practices including phishing	3.25	3.1.14
5	Identifying practices that allow companies to send unwanted e-mail and make unwanted telephone calls	3.26	4.2.7
5	Identify characteristics of adware and spyware	3.27	4.2.4
5	Locate and identify browser privacy and security settings	3.28	4.2.8

Why Would I Do This?

Living online includes exchanging goods and services using the Internet, which has fundamentally changed the way we do business with each other and how we handle money. In this chapter, you study how to use the Internet for electronic commerce.

visual summary | In these lessons, you will study how encryption is used to provide secure commercial interactions on the Internet.

FIGURE 3.1 A, B
Shopping and Shipping Online

List of Student and Solution Files

In most cases, you will create files using text or pictures found on Web pages. You will add your name to the file names and save them on your computer or portable memory device. Table 3.1 lists the files you start with and the names you give them when you save the files.

ASSIGNMENT	STUDENT SOURCE FILE:	SAVE AS:
Lessons 1–5	none	U3Ch03ExchangeStudentName U3Ch03DefenderStudentName U3Ch03PrivacyStudentName
Skill Drill	none	U3Ch03WireStudentName U3Ch03CertificateStudentName U3Ch03EDIStudentName
Explore and Share	none	none
In Your Life	none	none
Related Skills	none	U3Ch03PayPalStudentName U3Ch03VeriSignStudentName U3Ch03AdAwareStudentName
Discover	none	none
Assess Your Progress	U3Ch03Assess	U3Ch03AssessStudentName

TABLE 3.1

▶▶▶ *lesson*
one | Online Banking and Making Payments

To do business online, the parties involved must be able to pay for the goods and services that are exchanged.

Money as Digits

Although money can be represented by pieces of paper or metal, its actual value is not in the paper or metal but in what these items represent. They represent a certain amount of value that can be exchanged for services or physical items. Money is essentially an idea rather than physical items, and ideas can be transmitted electronically over the Internet if they can be represented by numbers.

Each country, or group of countries, establishes its own standard unit of value called its *currency*. For example, in the United States, the unit of currency is the U.S. dollar, and in most of Europe it is the *euro*. The value of an item can be described in these units, and euros or dollars can be exchanged as payment for goods and services.

Transferring Funds

The government of a country controls the amount of currency that is available for use by loaning it to banks that can loan it to businesses and individuals. The government does not send out trucks full of paper money to the banks. In place of paper money, they connect their computers with a bank's computers and send messages between them in which they agree to increase the value in the bank's account. This transaction is called a *wire transfer* because it originally used dedicated telephone lines. The wire transfer is still commonly used to transfer money between banks, including banks in different countries. As an individual, if you want to transfer money from your bank account to an account in another country using a wire transfer, you have to physically go to a bank, identify yourself, provide enough information so your bank can look up the other bank's *International Bank Account Number (IBAN)* or *ISO 9362 code*, and then pay a fee to your bank of serveral dollars.

FIGURE 3.2
Money can be transferred as data.

If the two countries use different currencies, the money is converted from one currency to another. The conversion factor used to calculate the value in another currency is the ***exchange rate***. The exhange rate depends on the relative value of each country's currency and changes often. This affects how much you can buy from another country or how much it would cost someone from that country to buy something from you.

to compare currency values online

1 **At the left edge of the Windows taskbar, click the Start button. Locate and click Internet Explorer. In the Address box, type** `finance.yahoo.com/currency` **and then press** ⏎Enter). The currency converter page on Yahoo! displays.

2 **Scroll down to display the *Major Currency Cross Rates* table.** The table shows how much you would get if you exchanged one unit of currency for another, as shown in Figure 3.3. Because these exchange rates change often, the times are indicated.

Major Currency Cross Rates

Currency Last Trade		U.S. $ N/A	Yen 7:26am ET	Euro 7:26am ET	Can $ 7:26am ET	U.K. £ 7:26am ET	AU $ 7:26am ET	Swiss Franc 7:26am ET
1 U.S. $	=	1	96.7900	0.7905	1.2309	0.6632	1.5425	1.2055
1 Yen	=	0.01033	1	0.00817	0.01272	0.00685	0.01594	0.01245
1 Euro	=	1.2650	122.4393	1	1.5571	0.8390	1.9513	1.5249
1 Can $	=	0.8124	78.6335	0.6422	1	0.5388	1.2531	0.9793
1 U.K. £	=	1.5077	145.9331	1.1919	1.8559	1	2.3257	1.8175
1 AU $	=	0.6483	62.7490	0.5125	0.7980	0.4300	1	0.7815
1 Swiss Franc	=	0.8296	80.2937	0.6558	1.0211	0.5502	1.2796	1

FIGURE 3.3
Table of exchange rates.

3 Scroll upward, if necessary, to the *I want to convert* box. Confirm that 1 U.S. Dollar is the default in the first row. Click the *into* box arrow. On the menu, click Chinese Yuan, and then click the Convert button. The program calculates the value of one U.S. dollar in Chinese Yuan, as shown in Figure 3.4

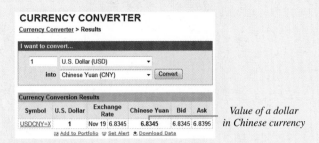

Value of a dollar in Chinese currency

FIGURE 3.4
One dollar in Chinese Yuan.

4 Scroll down to display the chart that shows how the exchange rate has changed in the last year. The currency exchange rate is an indicator of the relative value of each country's currency.

5 Repeat the process you practiced in steps 3 and 4 to find the exchange rate from U.S. Dollars to Indian Rupees.

6 Use the skills you practiced previously to start the Snipping Tool program and do a Window Snip of the window. Save a copy of this Web page to the folder where you store your files. Name the file U3Ch03ExchangeStudentName substituting your name as indicated.

7 Close ☒ the Snip window and the browser. Submit your snip as directed by your instructor.

Automatic Deposit

If a company pays its employees with paper checks, the employee must take the check to another location to deposit it. This exchange of paper results in the numbers in the employer's account decreasing and the numbers in the employee's account increasing, but it involves considerable time and effort by several people. Because the final result is adjusting the two accounts electronically, many employers offer ***direct deposit***, where the employer's bank transfers money to the employee's bank and it is added to the employee's account by computer. The employee might be notified of the transfer by the issuance of a document that looks like a check, or the employer might send an electronic mail message.

Automatic Teller Machines

If an individual wants to get cash from the bank, it can be obtained at an ***automatic teller machine (ATM)***, which is a device that provides many of the functions that were formerly provided by a person, but they are often available 24 hours a day in weatherproof enclosures, as shown in Figure 3.5. Banks provide cash to each other's customers but charge a handling fee for the wire transfer to exchange money between banks.

FIGURE 3.5
Automatic Teller Machine.

Secure Communications on the Internet Using Encryption

Banking on the Internet involves transferring packets of data across the network of routers where it could be intercepted and altered. Because the system used by the Internet is not private, electronic exchange of money depends upon transferring data using packets that are written in code that cannot be read by an unauthorized person or changed without detection.

Keeping communications private that might fall into unauthorized hands is an age-old problem that predates computers. Simple methods used a logical way of altering the content of a message so that if the recipient of the method knew how it was done, they could reconstruct the original message. For example, if you want to send the phrase *My name is John* and you shift your fingers on the keyboard one position to the right, you get *<us ms,r od Kpjm*. The encoded text is called **cipher text**. If the recipient knows this trick, they can reconstitute the original message by typing the coded message with their fingers shifted one key to the left to recreate the original— the **plain text**. Changing a message into a code that is not easily understood by unauthorized people is called *encryption*, and changing it back is called **decryption**. One of the first uses of modern computers was to look for logical patterns in codes that could be used to decrypt them.

During wartime, the encryption of messages is vitally important, so an encryption method was developed that was very hard to break. A person would pick a book and assign a number to each letter in a message that corresponded to a page number, line number, and character number in the book. For example, the first letter *M* in the message above would be replaced by a number sequence, or **code group**, like 142,34,29. The second letter *m* would be replaced by the location of a different letter *m* in the book—for instance, 205,20,15. In this code group, the first number indicates the page number, the second number is the line, and the third number is the number of characters to the right in that line. The book that is used for this type of code is called the **key** because it is used to lock and unlock the message. The person sending the message and the one receiving it must both know what book or key to use. This type of key is called a **symmetric key** because both parties use the same key, as shown in Figure 3.6.

The symmetric key does not have to be a book. It can be a large number that is used to multiply the numeric value of each letter or word. This type of code is almost impossible to break by looking for logical relationships between the code groups. Encrypting or decrypting a message using a key is very laborious for a human but is just the type of task that a computer can do quickly. Computers do not even need a real book. They can just use hundreds of pages of random letters.

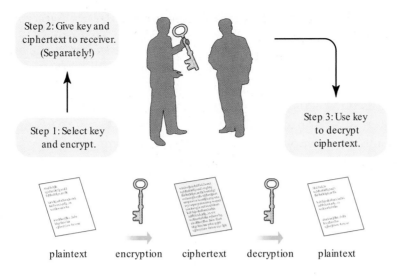

FIGURE 3.6
Symmetric key.

The weakness of the symmetric key method became apparent in the last world war. If an agent was captured and forced to tell what book was used as the key, the messages were no longer secure. Consequently, the parties were forced to change keys often. This presented a different problem: how to tell agents in the field what book to use as the new key.

The answer to this problem is to use a computer to generate two different keys that are related to each other—a ***public key*** and a ***private key***. Either key can be used to encrypt a message, and the recipient has to have the other key to decrypt it, as shown in Figure 3.7. Generating the keys and using them to encrypt and decrypt messages takes many more steps than using a symmetric key.

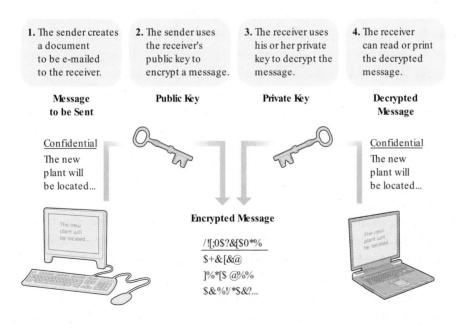

FIGURE 3.7
Public key encryption.

Secure Communications with Web Browsers

To use a Web browser to buy and sell over the Internet with confidence, the browser and Web server must be able to communicate securely, but it must also be done quickly. To have the best of both encryption methods, the public key method is used to securely transmit a symmetric key that is used to encrypt and decrypt the rest of the data. The rules for using this type of encryption were standardized in the **Secure Sockets Layer (SSL)** protocol and later updated to become the **Transport Layer Security (TLS)** protocol. If a Web address uses a secure protocol, the address begins with **https** instead of *http*, to indicate that the protocol is **Hypertext Transfer Protocol over Secure Sockets Layer (HTTPS)**. When you want to exchange data securely with a bank online, the process has several steps:

1. Your browser program uses your computer to generate a long number—usually 64 or 128 bits long—to be used as a symmetric key.
2. Your browser sends the domain name of the bank to a service that specializes in certifying the legitimacy of domain names—called a **certificate authority (CA)**. The CA stores the public keys of companies and banks that are registered with them. It sends the bank's public key to your browser.
3. Your browser uses the bank's public key to encrypt the number that will be used as the symmetric key.
4. Your browser sends the encrypted key to the bank, where its computer uses its private key to decrypt the message and extract the symmetric key.
5. Your browser and the bank's computer use the symmetric key to encrypt the remaining data that is exchanged between the computers. The browser displays a symbol on the status bar, such as a padlock, to indicate a secure exchange is taking place, as shown in Figure 3.8.

FIGURE 3.8
Secure browser session.

6. When you are finished, both computers erase the symmetric key.

Digital Signatures

Websites can include programs that perform functions such as confirming that all the required information is provided on a form. These programs can be identified with a **digital signature** to confirm that they are from the authentic website. A digital signature is created by using a private key to encrypt data that uniquely characterizes the program. The browser can retrieve that program's public key, decrypt the digital signature, and then compare its contents to the program. If they do not match, the browser will not run the program or will ask your permission to do so. Digital signatures are also used to encrypt e-mail messages.

Banking Online

Once secure communications are established, you can use the Internet to interact with a bank to transfer money between accounts, pay bills, or any of the other normal banking functions shown in Figure 3.9.

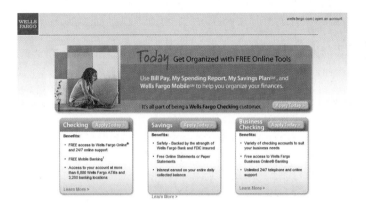

FIGURE 3.9
Bank home page.

▶▶▶ *lesson*
two | Buying from Businesses Online

If you buy something online, secure communications make it possible to pay for it. The development of secure communications made it practical to transact business online. ***Electronic commerce*** can involve several forms of transactions between businesses and consumers that are abbreviated for convenient reference. Business-to-consumer commercial activity is abbreviated as ***B2C***.

Buying Unusual Items Online

A traditional retail store does not have room for every product. The manager has to choose the products that are most popular and that will sell enough in the local market to justify the display space. There are a few people in each area near each store that are not served by this practice. Because the Internet is a global market, a few people from each local area can add up to a sizeable number online. If you are looking for something that is hard to find because of its unusual size, or you have tastes or dietary requirements that are different than those of most people, it is profitable for companies to sell you items online where many people like you can visit their online Web page, as shown in Figure 3.10.

FIGURE 3.10
Specialty store online.

Typical Online Storefront

A Web page that serves as a retail store is designed to help you find what you want among the products they have to offer. A larger site will often have a search engine dedicated to searching its website, pictures, and descriptions of the products. The site will also have a program to keep track of the items you choose to buy—called a ***shopping cart***—as shown in Figure 3.11. The shopping cart is a program that is usually written in ***Java***, a program designed to operate with Web pages under control of the Web browser. Internet Explorer can use programs written in ***Active X*** to add functional features to Web pages. These programs provide simple services like displaying a calendar when you want to pick a date or checking to make sure you filled in an order form completely. The shopping cart program keeps a list of the items you have chosen and presents the total when you are ready to buy.

FIGURE 3.11
Shopping cart.

Taking Orders and Tracking Customers with Cookies

The first time you make a purchase from an online retail store, you must provide enough information to allow for delivery of the item and payment. The company stores this information in its database of customers and assigns a customer code. The Web server sends the code to your browser software, which places the code on your computer along with another code that identifies the store's website and a few other pieces of information. This is a text file—not a program—that is called a ***cookie***. The cookie does not contain the information you provided to the store; that information remains in the store's database. The cookie just contains enough information to identify you to the store's computer so it can look up your file, as shown in Figure 3.12.

FIGURE 3.12
Cookie text file.

The next time you request the store's website, your browser will check to see if it has any cookies for that website. If it does, it will include the information in the cookie with the request. When the request for a Web page arrives at the company's Web server, the cookie is included with your customer identification number. The company's Web server sends a request to its own database server for details about you, including your last purchase and your name. The Web server can customize the Web page to welcome you back by name and suggest items that you might be interested in buying, based on your recent purchases.

Paying for Goods or Services Online

The most common method of paying for goods and services at an online retail store is by credit card. Most credit cards are provided by local banks or credit unions. They provide valuable services to both the retail company and the buyer. The retail company benefits because they do not have to try to collect the money owed to them. The credit card company aggregates the charges made by its customers to that company for a particular month and pays the bill. The retail company gets its money right away, so it can buy more goods to sell. The customer is protected in the transaction. If the goods are not delivered or do not match the description, the customer can refuse payment and the credit card company can withhold payment to the company until the issue is resolved. If the credit card number is stolen and used by an unauthorized person, the legitimate cardholder is usually not required to pay if they notify the credit card company of the incorrect charge when they receive the bill. The credit card company charges the retailer a percentage of the sale for its service—typically between 2% and 3%. Some card companies do not charge the customer if the bill is paid in full and on time each month, but they might charge 18% or more if the payment is late or less than the full amount. An alternative to using credit cards and paying their fees is to use a payment service like PayPal that handles payments between individuals for a fee.

Delivery and Returns

There are several drawbacks to buying goods online. The customer cannot see the exact color, test the fit, or feel the texture of materials when making the purchase decision. Once the purchase decision is made, the customer cannot walk out of the store with the product but must wait for days for it to be delivered. When the product arrives, if it is not satisfactory, arrangements must be made to return the item. Companies that have retail stores often allow customers to return items to the store instead of arranging for return shipping. Similarly, if a retail store does not carry an item that is available at its online website, the customer can order the item from the store online and have it delivered. When you choose to have a package delivered, the company usually charges extra for the delivery service. There are often choices that determine how fast it will be delivered. The large delivery services, including the U.S. Postal Service, assign a code to your package and keep track of it at each transfer point. Delivery services have websites at which you can enter the tracking number and follow the package across the country as it is transferred to your location, as shown in Figure 3.13.

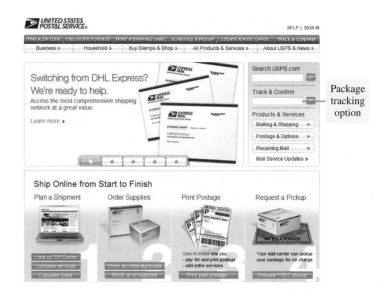

FIGURE 3.13
USPS Tracking website.

Customer Service

If you buy a device that comes with an owner's manual, the manual might be hard to find when the device breaks or needs maintenance years later. Most companies provide user manuals for their products as downloadable documents from their websites. Information can be provided at a website, allowing the humans in the customer service department to concentrate on the unusual situations that require personal attention, instead of answering the same questions repeatedly.

Evaluating Quality

When you are choosing which product to buy, you should consider the quality of the merchandise or service. Companies that have invested in building a reputation for quality are likely to continue to provide quality goods or services to protect that reputation. If you have never heard of a particular retail store or its products, you might do an online search for the company name and its products to see if they are mentioned in news stories or individual postings that would alert you to problems with quality or service.

▶▶▶ *lesson*
three | Businesses Buying from Businesses Online

Commercial activities between businesses are known as ***business-to-business (B2B)*** activities. To produce a product, companies buy directly from other companies. Some companies use the Internet to facilitate these purchases.

Business-to-Business Commerce Without the Internet

Like the banking industry's use of wire transfers, large businesses set up private communication systems between suppliers and manufacturers. This system is known as ***electronic data interchange (EDI)***. EDI is a standard for exchanging data such as invoices, lists of goods transported, and other standard business documents transferred between computers. EDI is widely used for international business-to-business communications.

Connecting Companies Using Virtual Private Networks

Companies can use the Internet to connect their systems by encrypting the data before it is sent over the Internet and then decrypting it at the destination. For example, the network server of a supplier can connect over the Internet to the network server of a manufacturing company, and users on either network can exchange data. The supplier's network is called an ***extranet***.

One of the pioneers of the use of the Internet for B2B data exchange is Dell Computer. Dell set up a Web page for each of its business customers that used an electronic version of the customer's purchase order forms and provided the invoices and other data in a manner that was compatible with the customer's internal accounting system. The customer can browse a customized version of Dell's catalog. At checkout, the system calculates discounted prices for that customer based on the size of the purchase and credit history. Dell integrated this ordering system with its manufacturing to assemble computers to the customer's specifications after the order was received, avoiding the cost of storing unsold computers that quickly become obsolete.

Auctions Online

If a business that makes parts has a surplus, it can hold an ***auction*** online, where manufacturers bid on the parts. In an auction, the objective is to get the highest selling price for the seller. If a manufacturer needs parts, it can hold a ***reverse auction***, taking bids from suppliers who compete for the business of supplying those parts. The purpose of a reverse auction is to get the lowest price on supplies.

Adding Value and Disintermediation

Each step in the process of producing goods or services must increase the value of those goods or services; otherwise, that step is likely to be eliminated if an alternative is available. For example, if a manufacturer of an electronic device—like an aircraft navigation system—needs several different types of integrated circuits, they can send the specifications for the circuits to a distributor. The distributor has a relationship with several suppliers and can arrange the purchase and delivery. In the past, an engineer at a manufacturing plant would not be able to conveniently contact several suppliers, get bids, and arrange delivery. With the advent of online business-to-business reverse auctions and automated ordering systems, however, it is easier for the end user to bypass the distributor. When an intermediate step is eliminated, it is called *disintermediation*. This is one of the ways that doing buisiness online has lowered costs and changed the job market. To stay in business, the distributor must add value to the process. For example, the distributor could get a better price by aggregating orders from several clients and buying a large amount, or the distributor could become more familiar with the quality and characteristics of the products and could advise the end user on which ones to buy for better quality. Many jobs that consisted of just taking orders have been replaced by B2B websites.

▶▶▶ *lesson*
four | Consumers Buying and Selling to Consumers

The Internet has revolutionized commercial activities between individuals by dramatically lowering the cost of doing business so that consumers can buy and sell to each other. In some cases this has resulted in disintermediation, and in others it has created new types of intermediaries who add value. Commercial transactions between consumers are known as *consumer-to-consumer (C2C)* activities.

Online Auctions

One of the first functions to move from the realm of B2B into C2C was the online auction. Instead of a company offering a million dollars' worth of computer chips, an individual could offer a broken laser pointer. The most famous online auction site is eBay, which started as part of the personal Web page of Pierre Omidyar. The first thing he sold was a broken laser pointer that sold for $14.83 to a collector of broken laser pointers! Two years later, Pierre got $5 million in funding from a *venture capitalist*—someone who loans money to startup companies for a share in the ownership of the company. Pierre's company was named Echo Bay Technology Group and he wanted to use the domain name *echobay.com*. This domain name was already taken, so he tried eBay.com, which was available. eBay now has customized sites in more than thirty countries. The eBay story contains several lessons that demonstrate the changes the Internet has made in commerce. They are:

- One person can set up a website.
- The Internet has so many people that there are buyers for almost any product.

- The buyer can find the seller using a search engine.
- An individual can borrow large amounts of money to expand a startup company if they are willing to share ownership.

Classified Advertising Online

Newspapers have large sections of advertising that are classified by category—known as *classified ads*—in which an individual lists something for sale and an individual contacts the person to conclude the sale. The newspaper adds value to the information by distributing the paper to thousands of people in the local area. If an item is too bulky to ship cheaply or the buyer must be able to assess its quality in person, a local advertisement is preferred to an online auction. Some newspapers publish their classified ads online. Sites like KiJiJi.com and Craigslist.org combine the worldwide scope of the Internet with the local market focus of the local newspaper, as shown in Figure 3.14.

FIGURE 3.14
Craigslist.

Self Publishing and Print on Demand

A combination of the Internet and computer-operated laser printers is changing the nature of book publishing. In the past, a quality book had to be printed on an expensive printing press that took hours to set up. New printing technologies combine computer databases with laser printers and automatic binding machines, making it possible to print a single book at an affordable cost. This process is called *print on demand (POD)*. A publisher no longer has to print and store copies of books that might not be sold. Like Dell, they can wait for the orders to come in over the Internet and then produce as many as needed.

Computer software that is designed to create professional-looking book pages and covers—*desktop publishing software*—is available for use on personal computers. An individual can write a book in a word processing program, paste the text into desktop publishing software, create an electronic copy of the book, and sell it directly from their website as an electronic file to be read on a monitor or printed locally on the user's personal laser printer. If you handle the creation and publishing of your own book, it is called *self publishing*.

Storefront Software

If you want to sell a product online directly to consumers without using an intermediary, you can purchase a software package that has the necessary functions—called *storefront software*. This type of software guides you through the process of creating a website that displays your product. It has the ability to take orders and shipping information and receive payments, as shown in Figure 3.15. Most storefront software packages include the following features:

- e-mail link for customer questions
- handles online payment by credit card, debit card, or other services
- transfers customer payments directly to your bank account
- keeps statistics on number of visits, purchases
- keeps a database of customers

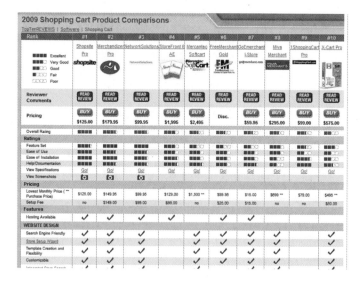

FIGURE 3.15
Online storefront.

Evaluating Quality

When dealing with other individuals online, it is difficult to assess their honesty or reliability if you have never dealt with them before. An intermediary like eBay can monitor the activities of its members and block those who are dishonest. Many intermediary sites provide a rating service where customers are sent a survey and asked to rate the quality of the product and service. The results are summarized in a seller's rating. If you pay with a credit card, the credit card company has influence with a seller to keep his or her side of the bargain in order to continue using the credit card service.

▶▶▶ *lesson*
five | Security, Privacy, and Ethics

Buying, selling, and banking online involve the exchange of money and goods, which attract unethical people who are trying to profit by taking advantage of other people.

Fraud

Fraud is an intentional deception for the purpose of inducing someone to part with something of value, and there are many ways that it can be practiced in online commerce. One form of fraud is to trick someone into providing the user name and password of their online bank or credit card account. Once the theives have this information, they can impersonate you and gain access to your funds, which is called *identity theft*. One method of tricking you into providing private identity information is to send you an e-mail that claims your account has been attacked and that you should check your account for unusual activity. They provide a link to a page that looks like the home page of your bank or credit card company. If you log in using that page, it records your user name and password before it logs you into the real website. The use of such a message to trick you into divulging sensitive or private information is called *phishing*—which is pronounced like the word *fishing*.

Other forms of fraud include offering to sell items that do not exist or buying an item and not paying for it.

Unwanted E-Mail and Telephone Calls

When you buy something online, the purchase is recorded in the company's database. Contact information such as your e-mail address and telephone number are often required to complete the purchase. The company can use this information to send you advertisements, or they might sell the list of their customers and their contact information to advertising groups. Check the privacy statement at the merchant's website when you buy something to see if they agree not to sell your contact information. If you have more than one e-mail address, you can provide one of them to companies when you make purchases and use a different one for personal messages. Companies have the right to call you for up to eighteen months after you transact business with them. They can do this even if you are registered with the U.S. government's *Do Not Call* registry—a list of people who do not want to receive unsolicited calls from telemarketers—as shown in Figure 3.16. To avoid unwanted telephone calls, some people provide a fictional telephone number if the transaction requires one. To avoid sending calls to another person, they use telephone numbers in the range of 555-0100 to 555-0199 that are reserved for fictional use in the U.S.

Customer Profiling

Advertisers use information about customers to choose which products to tell them about. Knowing a customer's previous purchases, age, sex, and interests is very valuable because this information can be used to choose an advertising approach that is likely to be successful. Some companies collect information about people who browse the Internet and make lists of people

Security, Privacy, and Ethics   107   **Chapter 3**

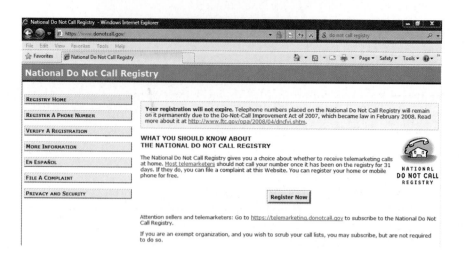

FIGURE 3.16
Do Not Call Registry.

who are most likely to buy certain types of products. They sell these lists to companies that make those types of products so that they can send advertising to the people who are most likely to buy their products. When you buy something from a company online, they are required to provide information about their privacy policy. Most reputable companies disclose whether or not they sell their information to other companies, but be aware that even if they say they do not share data with other companies, a large company can have many divisions with many other brands.

When you visit a commercial website, it might save a cookie on your computer with its name and your customer code number so it can identify you the next time you visit. This is the intended use of cookies, and they can save a lot of time if you do not have to enter the same shipping and credit card information each time you buy something from that website.

A problem of privacy arises when your Web browsing activity is recorded and reported. If you do not read the fine print when you visit a site and buy something or download free programs, you might be agreeing to host a program on your machine that facilitates advertising such as pop-up windows, surveys, toolbars, or logos—***adware***. Another type of program that might become installed on your computer scans your cookies and records your browsing choices. This type of program is called ***spyware***, and it can even send a report back to its host computer with this data. If you visit many websites and shop a lot on the Internet, your computer can have so many of these programs installed and running that it slows down your computer. Special programs can scan your computer and remove the spyware programs.

A program to scan and remove adware and spyware called ***Windows Defender*** is included in Windows Vista. Programs such as Ad-Aware and Spybot that provide this service are available for other operating systems.

to explore Windows Defender

1 At the lower left corner of the screen, click the Start button. On the menu, click Control Panel. On the Control Panel dialog box, locate the Windows Defender icon shown in Figure 3.17.

Click to display individual icons

Windows Defender

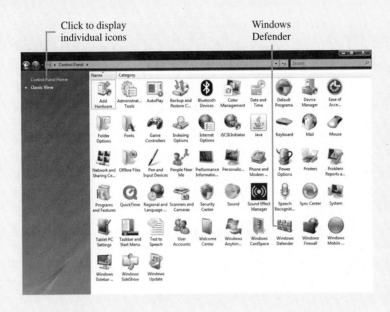

FIGURE 3.17
Windows Defender.

if you have **problems**

CONTROL PANEL VIEW ...
Your control panel might display the Control Panel Home view. If that is the case, click the Security link to display the Windows Defender icon.

2 **Click the Windows Defender icon.** The Windows Defender dialog box displays.

3 **On the toolbar, click the Help button** 🔘**.** The Windows Help and Support dialog box displays.

4 **In the Windows Help and Support dialog box, in the Getting Started section, click** *How to tell if your computer is infected with spyware.* A dialog box with a bulleted list of options displays.

5 **Use the skills you practiced previously to start the Snipping Tool program and do a Window Snip of the Help window. Save a copy of this window to the folder where you store your files. Name the file** `U3Ch03DefenderStudentName` **substituting your name as indicated.**

6 **Close all of the dialog boxes and windows.**

Blocking or Trusting Websites

Web browsers have security settings that can block or allow activities that might pose security risks. If you know the files you download from a certain site are trustworthy, you can add the site's address to a list of trusted sites. Conversely, if there are sites you do not want your browser to communicate with, the sites can be blocked.

to explore Internet Explorer's privacy and security settings

1 Start Internet Explorer. Click the Tools button, and then, on the menu, click Internet Options.

2 In the Internet Options dialog box, click the Security tab. Notice that security settings can be specified for local intranet sites and that some sites can be identified as trusted while others are blocked, as shown in Figure 3.18.

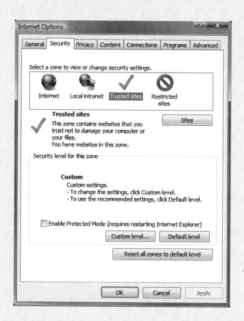

FIGURE 3.18
Internet Options Security options.

3 In the Internet Options dialog box click the Privacy tab. Notice the choices for allowing or blocking pop-up windows, as shown in Figure 3.19.

FIGURE 3.19
Internet Options Privacy options.

4 Use the skills you practiced previously to start the Snipping Tool program and do a Window Snip of the Privacy window. Save a copy of this window to the folder where you store your files. Name the file `U3Ch03PrivacyStudentName` substituting your name as indicated.

5 Close all of the dialog boxes and windows.

SUMMARY

In this chapter, you learned how public and symmetric key encryption is used to make commerce possible online, and how online commerce is conducted between business and individuals.

You can extend your learning by reviewing concepts and terms, and by practicing variations of skills presented in the lessons.

KEY TERMS

ActiveX

adware

auction

automatic teller machine (ATM)

business-to-business (B2B)

business-to-consumer (B2C)

certificate authority (CA)

cipher text

classified ad

code group

consumer-to-consumer (C2C)

cookie

currency

decryption

digital signature

direct deposit	International Bank Account Number (IBAN)	reverse auction
disintermediation		Secure Sockets Layer (SSL)
Do Not Call registry	ISO 6392 code	self publishing
electronic commerce	Java	shopping cart
electronic data interchange (EDI)	key	spyware
	phishing	storefront software
euro	plain text	symmetric key
exchange rate	print on demand (POD)	Transport Layer Security (TLS)
extranet		
fraud	private key	venture capitalist
identity theft	public key	wire transfer

CHECKING CONCEPTS AND TERMS

ASSESSING LEARNING OUTCOMES

MULTIPLE CHOICE

Circle the letter of the correct answer for each of the following.

1. If a public key is used to encode a message, its corresponding _____ key is used to decode the message. [L1]

   a. secret

   b. symmetric

   c. cypher

   d. private

2. Which type of encryption uses the same key to encrypt and decrypt? [L1]

   a. symmetric key

   b. public key

   c. private key

   d. password

3. Where does your browser get the public key and confirm that it is authentic? [L1]

   a. The company's Web server sends it upon request.

   b. The certificate authority provides public keys for sites it has checked.

   c. A list of public keys is published by ICANN each month and stored by the browser.

   d. The domain name servers include the public key for each site when its IP address is requested.

4. A cookie is a(n) _____. [L2]

   a. Java program that provides functionality to Web pages

   b. ActiveX program the provides functionality

   c. text file that can contain an identification code

   d. banner advertisement that contains spyware

5. How is a symmetric key used with public and private keys to transmit data? [L2]

   a. A symmetric key is used for most of the message, but the symmetric key itself is transferred using the public and private keys.

   b. The methods are alternated between each site visit to confuse spyware programs.

   c. The combination of public and private keys is always used for the entire transaction because it is most secure.

   d. The symmetric key is used for the whole transaction because it is fastest.

6. What is an extranet? [L3]

   a. a separate network that is connected to the main network by dedicated telephone lines

   b. a separate network that is connected to the main network over the Internet using encryption to maintain security

   c. a smaller network at the same company that is connected to the main network by a gateway and a firewall

   d. a network that is not connected to the Internet

7. What is an example of a company that provides intermediary services for online auctions? [L4]

   a. Craigslist

   b. CA

   c. eBay

   d. Google

8. How are computers used in print on demand (POD)? [L4]

   a. They serve up music files and collect money for them.

   b. They route messages between extranets and LANs.

   c. They manage the encryption and decryption.

   d. They store files that can be used to print books as they are sold.

9. What is phishing? [L5]

   a. an attempt to trick someone into revealing their user name and password

   b. recording the addresses of websites visited by the user and reporting this

   c. displaying unwanted pop-up ads or other forms of advertising

   d. searching a computer's cookies for credit card numbers

10. What does adware do? [L5]

   a. tries to trick someone into revealing their user name and password

   b. records the addresses of websites visited by the user and reports this

   c. displays unwanted pop-up ads or other forms of advertising

   d. searches a computer's cookies for credit card numbers

MATCHING

Match each term in the second column with its correct definition in the first column by writing the letter of the term on the blank line in front of the definition.

J 1. Offering something for sale to many possible bidders to get the highest price

B 2. Small text file that can contain identification codes

A 3. Bank identification number

D 4. The ability to print a few books at any time

C 5. Offering to buy from the lowest bidder

G 6. Transfer from an employer's bank to an employee's bank account

E 7. Creates a Web page from which you can sell goods and collect money

I 8. Electronic transfer of funds—usually between banks

H 9. Conversion factor used to determine value of one currency in terms of another

F 10. Entity that guarantees the identity of the source of a public key

A. IBAN or ISO 6392

B. Cookie

C. Reverse auction

D. POD

E. Storefront software

F. Certificate authority (CA)

G. Direct deposit

H. Exchange rate

I. Wire transfer

J. Auction

SKILL DRILL

Skill Drill exercises reinforce chapter skills. Each skill reinforced is the same, or nearly the same, as a skill presented in the chapter. Detailed instructions are provided in a step-by-step format.

Each exercise is independent of the others, so you can do the exercises in any order.

1. Wire Money Overseas

The U.S. Department of State will assist in the transfer of funds to a U.S. citizen in a foreign country in an emergency. There are several options, including use of wire transfer. Explore the methods available to send money to someone in another country in an emergency.

To determine the choices for transferring money to someone in another country:

1. Start Internet Explorer. In the address box, type `http://travel.state.gov` and then press ⏎Enter to go to the U.S. Department of State travel site.

2. On the site's menu bar, click the **International Travel** link.

3. At the left of the International Travel page, point at **Tips for Traveling Abroad.** On the menu, click **Travel Brochures.**

4. Under **Consular Affairs Brochures,** click **Sending Money Overseas to a U.S. Citizen in an Emergency.**

5. Scroll down to display the Bankwire option.

6. Use the skills you practiced previously to start the **Snipping Tool** program and do a **Window Snip** of the browser window that displays the Bankwire option.

Save a copy of this window to the folder where you store your files. Name the file U3Ch03WireStudentName substituting your name as indicated.

7. Close the browser. Submit your snip as directed by your instructor.

2. Display the Certificate of a Bank Website

A secure communication over the Internet requires a public key from a certifying authority that guarantees the identity of the source. Instructions are written for Internet Explorer 8. Google Chrome, Apple Safari, or Firefox can also be used.

To view the certificate from a bank, follow these steps:

1. Start Internet Explorer. In the address box, type http://www.nationalcity.com and then press ↵Enter. The NationalCity Web page displays.

2. On the browser's address bar, click the **padlock** icon. In Firefox, the padlock is at the bottom of the screen.

3. On the menu, click **View Certificates.** Notice the name of the certificate authority that issued the certificate.

4. In the **Certificate** dialog box, at the bottom, to the right of *Learn more about*, click the **certificates** link. Another Certificates dialog box displays with a section titled *Certificates Overview*. Review the information on this page. If you use a different browser or the page has changed, locate the screen that describes certificates.

5. Use the skills you practiced previously to start the **Snipping Tool** program and do a **Window Snip** of the Certificates overview dialog box. Save a copy of this window to the folder where you store your files. Name the file U3Ch03CertificatesStudentName substituting your name as indicated.

6. Submit your snip as directed by your instructor. Close the dialog boxes and your browser window.

3. Grocery Store Chain Uses EDI with Suppliers

Businesses that buy from numerous suppliers can require them to use standardized billing and payment methods. If you have a product that you want to sell through the Kroger food chain, you have to use the EDI standard.

To see how Kroger uses EDI, follow these steps:

1. Start Internet Explorer. In the address box, type http://edi.kroger.com and then press ↵Enter. The Kroger EDI Enterprise page displays.

2. At the left of the screen, click the **EDI Compliance** link.

3. Explore this site by clicking the links at the left, such as the FAQs link. Return to the EDI Compliance Requirements page when you have explored other pages on this site.

4. Use the skills you practiced previously to start the **Snipping Tool** program and do a **Window Snip** of the EDI compliance page. Save a copy of this window to the folder where you store your files. Name the file U3Ch03EDIStudentName substituting your name as indicated.

5. Submit your snip as directed by your instructor. Close the dialog boxes and your browser window.

EXPLORE AND SHARE

Explore and Share questions are intended for discussion in class or online. Look for information that is related to the learning outcomes for this chapter as directed. Submit your answers as directed by your instructor.

1. Learn about encrypting your files with PGP. Open your Web browser and go to **http://www.pgp.com.** This is the home page of the PGP Corporation. PGP originally stood for **P**retty **G**ood **Pr**ivacy and was one of the first companies to offer encryption technology to everyday users. Search this site to learn about the products they offer for secure communications. Prepare to discuss the features available for individuals and the difference between a **perpetual license** and a **subscription.** [L1]

2. Learn more about storefront software. Assume you are interested in starting your own retail outlet on the Internet and are searching for appropriate storefront software. Start your favorite Web browser and go to google.com. Use Google to search for **online storefront software** and examine sites that sell this type of software. Choose two software packages and compare their features and prices. Be prepared to provide the Web address of both sites. [L2]

3. Find out about writing your own book at a publish-on-demand (POD) service. Begin by going to wikipedia.org and searching for **self publishing.** Read the first paragraph to familiarize yourself with this concept. Next, in Wikipedia, search for **print on demand** and read the first two paragraphs. Finally, explore two leading services: **Booksurge (booksurge.com)** and **LightningSource (lightningsource.com).** Look for answers to the following questions: [L4]

   - How is the book marketed?

   - What services do they offer?

   - What percentage of the sale price does the author get?

IN YOUR LIFE

In Your Life questions are intended for discussion in class or online where you can share your personal experience. Restrict your answers to the topics described in each exercise. Submit your answers as directed by your instructor.

1. Assume that you have a used item that you want to sell to a friend, but you have no idea how much to ask for it. Go to Craigslist to see what people are asking for similar items. Start your Web browser and go to **craigslist.org** and choose a city near you. Under the **for sale** section, look for the item. Do this for several items to get an idea of what fraction of the original retail price you could get for used items. Make a list of the items you look up, and be prepared to share what you have learned. [L4]

2. Track packages at the U.S. Postal Service. A key component of B2C commerce is prompt and reliable shipping from the business to the customer. Shippers use computers to track packages and record the time and location each time the package is handled so you can track the progress of its delivery. Go to the **United States Postal Service** website at **www.usps.com.** At the top of the screen on the right side, click **Track & Confirm.** In the middle of the page, click each of the three **Learn about**

links. If you have received a package in the last two months or are awaiting delivery of a package, look for the tracking number on your sales information. Go to the shipper's website and look up the details of the route the package took. Write down some of the details of the shipping route and be prepared to share what you found about the package tracking options or how your package was handled. [L2]

3. Find out how many cookies are used when you visit a website. Start Internet Explorer. On the menu bar, click **Tools,** and then, on the menu, click **Internet Options.** In the Internet Options dialog box, click the **Privacy** tab. On the Privacy tab, click the **Advanced** button. In the **Advanced Privacy Settings** dialog box, in the **Cookies** section, next to **Override automatic cookie handling,** click the check box. Under **First-party cookies,** click **Prompt.** Under **Third-party Cookies,** click **Prompt.** Click **OK** in both dialog boxes to close them. Use your browser and go to several different websites. Each time a website tries to place a cookie on your computer, you will have to approve it. Make notes on how many cookies you have to approve at each site you visit. Look for patterns as to which type of site uses more cookies than others, and be prepared to share what you observe. Try government sites, nonprofit organizations, and retail sales sites. Use the skills described in the first part of this exercise to restore automatic cookie handling when you are finished. [L5]

RELATED SKILLS

Related Skills exercises expand on or are related to skills presented in the lessons. The exercise provides a brief narrative introduction, followed by instructions in a numbered-step format that are not as detailed as those in the Skill Drill section.

1. Paying Online or Sending Cash with PayPal

When buying from an unknown individual at a website, you might not want to send them your credit card number. Similarly, if you are selling an item to an unknown individual but you are not set up to accept payment by credit card, you need a way to receive payment from a reliable source before you ship the item. An intermediary service called PayPal provides this service.

To learn more about using PayPal, follow these steps:

1. Start Internet Explorer. Go to **http://www.paypal.com.**

2. On the PayPal home page, under **Pay online,** click **Learn how PayPal works,** and then read the page.

3. On the Web browser, click the **Back** button. Under **Pay Online,** click the **Shop without exposing** link, and then read that page.

4. On the Web browser, click the **Back** button. Under **Get paid online,** click **Accept payments,** and then read that page.

5. Use the skills you practiced previously to start the **Snipping Tool** program and do a **Window Snip** of the **Accept Payments on eBay** window. Save a copy of this window to the folder where you store your files. Name the file U3Ch03PayPalStudentName substituting your name as indicated.

6. **Close** all open windows without saving any changes.

2. Protecting Online Accounts with Public Key Encryption

One way to counteract identity theft is to use your own public key encryption system. To learn about obtaining identity certification for an individual, follow these steps:

1. Start Internet Explorer. Go to **www.verisign.com.** Near the top of the window on the left side, point to **Products & Services,** and then, on the menu, click **Identity and Authentication Services.**

2. On the **Verisign Identity and Authentication Services** page, on the left side, click **Authentication for Individuals.**

3. Under **Featured Products & Services,** click **VIP Credential.**

4. On the **Identity Protection Center** page, under Links, click **Learn More.**

5. Use the skills you practiced previously to start the **Snipping Tool** program and do a **Window Snip** of the **About VeriSign Identity Protection** page window. Save a copy of this window to the folder where you store your files. Name the file U3Ch03VeriSignStudentName substituting your name as indicated.

6. **Close** all open windows. Submit the file as directed by your instructor.

3. Searching for Adware and Spyware with Third-Party Software

If you are not satisfied with the Windows Defender program that comes with Microsoft Windows Vista or you have a computer with an older Windows operating system, you can use programs that are available from other sources, some of which have a free version such as Ad-Aware.

To learn about obtaining identity certification for an individual, follow these steps:

1. Start Internet Explorer. Go to **www.lavasoft.com.** Near the top of the window on the left side, point to **Products,** and then, on the menu, click **Ad-Aware.**

2. Navigate the web site to the **Ad-Aware Free** page, read the overview, and then, in the middle of the page, click **Features** and read this page.

3. Near the middle of the page, click **More feature details.** Scroll downward, if necessary, to display the feature details.

4. Use the skills you practiced previously to start the **Snipping Tool** program and do a **Window Snip** of the **Ad-Aware** page window. Save a copy of this window to the folder where you store your files. Name the file U3Ch03AdAwareStudentName substituting your name as indicated.

5. **Close** all open windows. Submit the file as directed by your instructor.

DISCOVER

Discover exercises give students general directions for exploring and discovering more advanced skills and information. Each exercise is independent of the others, so you may complete the exercises in any order. Report your findings as directed by your instructor.

1. Discover More about Public key Encryption

The use of the Internet for commercial purposes depends on the use of public key encryption. Learn more about how this vital system provides secure communications. Begin by opening a Web browser and going to http://www.howstuffworks.com. In the Search box, type `Public Key Encryption` and then click the **Search** button. Scroll to the area below the sponsored links and click **Introduction to How Encryption Works.** Play the demonstration video. Near the top of the window, click the **Next Page** link. Alternatively, click the links in the **Inside this article** section. Read all six pages. If this link is not available, choose another article that describes public key encryption. In your own words, summarize what you have learned from each of the six pages in the article.

2. View Startup Programs to Locate Adware and Spyware

Adware and spyware programs run at the same time as the other applications on your computer and can slow down their performance. Discover what programs are started and run in the background every time you start your computer. You must have administrative rights on the computer you are using to do this exercise. Click the **Start** button, and then point at **All Programs.** On the programs list, click **Accessories,** and then, on the menu, click **Run.** In the Run dialog box, in the Open box, type `msconfig` and then click **OK.** In the **System Configuration** dialog box, click the **Startup** tab. Drag the line between the column headings to widen the Startup Item and Manufacturer columns to reveal the full names. Make a list of the programs under three headings: those you recognize and know that you want to run, those you do not recognize, and those that you think are unnecessary or unwanted. Explain your choices.

ASSESS YOUR PROGRESS

At this point, you should have a set of skills and concepts that are valuable to an employer and to you. You may not realize how much you've learned unless you take a few minutes to assess your progress.

1. From the student files, open **U3Ch02Assess.** Save it as U3Ch02AssessStudentName

2. Read each question in column A.

3. In column B, answer Yes or No.

4. If you identify a skill or design concept that you don't know, refer to the learning objective code next to the question and the table at the beginning of the chapter to find the skill and review it.

5. Print the worksheet if your instructor requires it. The file name is already in the header, so it will display your name as part of the file name.

6. All of these skills and concepts have been identified as important by surveying hundreds of individuals working at over 200 companies worldwide. If you cannot answer all of the questions affirmatively even after reviewing the relevant lesson, seek additional help from your instructor.

chapter four

Communicating Online

Lesson	Learning Outcomes	Code	Related IC3 Objectives
1	Identify parts of a unique e-mail address	4.01	2.2.1
1	Identify the protocols used for sending and receiving e-mail	4.02	2.1.3
1	Identify the components of an e-mail message	4.03	2.2.2
1	Identify methods of replying and forwarding e-mail	4.04	2.2.3
1	Identify appropriate and inappropriate uses of reply and forward	4.05	2.2.3
1	Identify methods of reading and sending e-mail	4.06	2.2.4
1	Identify how to supplement an e-mail message with attachments, — hyperlinks	4.07	2.2.5
1	Identify the uses of an address book	4.08	2.2.8
1	Identify advantages of using e-mail	4.09	2.3.2
1	Choose appropriate communication technologies	4.10	2.3.1
1	Identify common problems with e-mail and possible solutions —	4.11	2.3.3
1	Identify issues regarding unsolicited e-mail	4.12	2.3.6
2	Identify uses and functions of e-mail lists	4.13	2.1.1
2	Identify uses and functions of message boards	4.14	2.1.1
2	Identify uses and functions of blogs	4.15	2.1.1
2	Identify uses and functions of video sharing, streaming, and podcasting	4.16	2.1.1
2	Identify uses and functions of RSS feeds	4.17	2.1.1
2	Identify uses and functions of file sharing	4.18	2.1.1
3	Identify uses and functions of Internet telephone service using Voice over Internet Protocol (VoIP)	4.19	2.1.1
3	Identify uses and functions of Internet chat	4.20	2.1.1
3	Identify uses and functions of instant messaging (IM)	4.21	2.1.1
3	Identify uses and functions of texting	4.22	2.1.1
4	Identify uses and functions of sites devoted to interest groups	4.23	2.1.1
4	Identify uses and functions of social-networking sites —	4.24	2.1.1
4	Identify the communications technologies used for online education	4.25	2.1.1
4	Identify social networks that work on projects together	4.26	2.1.1
5	Identify threats posed by malware such as worms, and Trojans	4.27	4.2.4
5	Identify threats posed by hoaxes and directory harvest attacks	4.28	4.2.4
5	Identify methods for avoiding hazards online	4.29	4.2.7
5	Identify methods of identifying users	4.30	2.1.2

Why Would I Do This?

The Internet has revolutionized the way people communicate with each other. In this chapter, you study how the Internet is used for communications between people outside of the work environment.

visual summary |

In these lessons, you will study how the Internet is used to communicate using electronic mail, instant messaging, live audio, and live video exchanges. You study how the Internet supports communications between individuals and between members of a group.

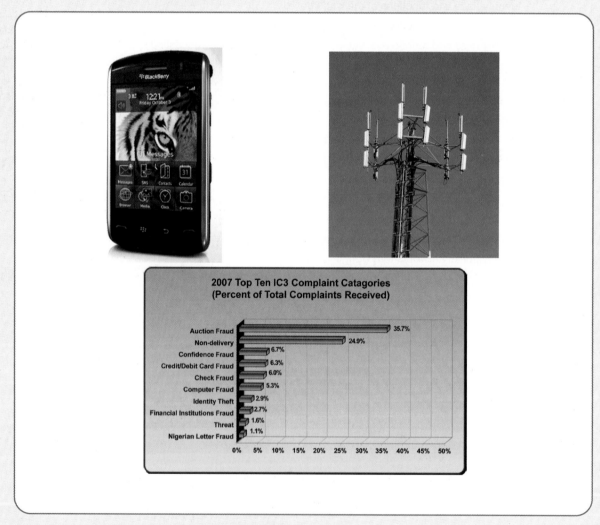

FIGURE 4.1

E-mail, text messaging, instant messaging, and crime.

List of Student and Solution Files

In most cases, you will create files using text or pictures found on Web pages. You will add your name to the file names and save them on your computer or portable memory device. Table 1.1 lists the files you start with and the names you give them when you save the files.

ASSIGNMENT	STUDENT SOURCE FILE:	SAVE AS:
Lessons 1–5	none	U3Ch04ListStudentName U3Ch04MessageStudentName U3Ch04OpenStudentName U3Ch04SupportStudentName U3Ch04FactsStudentName U3Ch04DatingStudentName U3Ch04WikiStudentName U3Ch04IDStudentName
Skill Drill	none	U3Ch04TravelStudentName U3Ch04SecurityStudentName U3Ch04SenatorStudentName
Explore and Share	none	U3Ch04AlexaStudentName U3Ch04TrusteStudentName U3Ch04DegreeStudentName U3Ch04MusicStudentName
In Your Life	none	none
Related Skills	U3Ch04Magnolia	U3Ch04Pic1StudentName U3Ch04Pic2StudentName U3Ch04ArchiveStudentName
Discover	none	U3Ch04OpenStudentName U3Ch04SandboxStudentName
Assess Your Progress	U3Ch04Assess	U3Ch04AssessStudentName

TABLE 4.1

▶▶▶ *lesson*
one | Electronic Mail

In the United States, we send more personal mail via e-mail than through the U.S. Postal Service. In 1997, e-mail messages outnumbered paper mail for the first time. E-mail provides a way for people to stay connected, whether they are employees at distant locations or families and friends in the same town or across the world. Because e-mail has become so pervasive in the work and home lives of so many people, it is necessary to understand its strengths and weaknesses and its potential problems. Microsoft Outlook 2007 will be used to illustrate electronic mail features, but most mail programs have the same basic components.

How E-Mail Works

Electronic mail is usually referred to as *e-mail* or *email*. Sending a message by electronic mail begins by starting an e-mail program and then filling out a form. The form can be provided by a client program that resides on your computer, like Microsoft Outlook, or it can be provided as a Web page by a program that resides on a server, like Google's Gmail. The form consists of two major sections. At the top of the form are boxes in which to enter the electronic mail address of the recipient, the addresses of any people to whom you want to send copies of the message, and a box in which to sumarize the subject of the message. For the **body** of the message, there is a box where you type the text of the message, as shown in Figure 4.2.

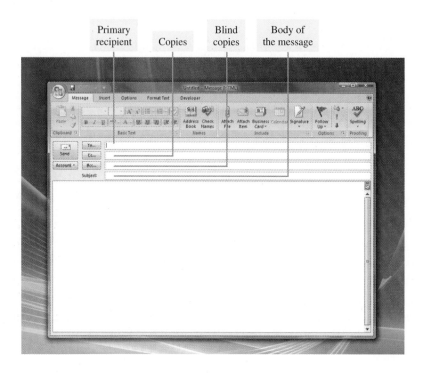

FIGURE 4.2
E-mail form.

An e-mail address is a combination of a user name and a domain name that are separated by the @ symbol. The user name can be a single group of letters and numbers or groups that are separated by periods. For example, Congressperson Dale Kildee's e-mail address is dkildee@mail.house.gov, and Congressperson John Conyers' e-mail address is John.Conyers@mail.house.gov. Both addresses share the same domain name: mail.house.gov.

When you are ready to send a message, you press the Send button. The mail program formats the message and sends it to the mail server using **simple mail transfer protocol (SMTP)**—a set of rules for structuring and sending e-mail. The mail server sends a request to a domain name server to obtain the IP address of the computer that hosts the domain name to which the mail is addressed, and then it forwards the mail to that IP address. The mail server at the destination IP address stores the message until the user to whom it is addressed accesses it.

The intended recipient of the e-mail can receive the message in a variety of ways. The e-mail can be sent directly to a **personal digital assistant (PDA)**—a handheld computer such as a Blackberry—or an advanced cell phone, as shown in Figure 4.3.

BlackBerry
Friday October 3
Messages
SMS
Contacts
Calendar
Media
Clock
Camera

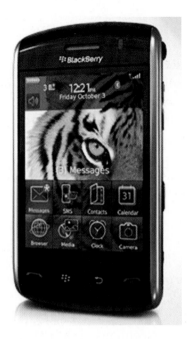

FIGURE 4.3
Phones and PDAs can receive e-mail.

The e-mail message can be accessed using client software on a computer. If the client software is on your personal computer, you can download the e-mail from the domain's mail server to your computer using ***post office protocol (POP3)***—a set of rules for delivering e-mail. The drawback to downloading e-mail is that the message is no longer available from the server and cannot be easily viewed from a different computer. An alternative to POP3 is the ***Internet message access protocol (IMAP)***. IMAP gives you a choice of downloading the message or leaving it on the server, where it can be read, stored, and retrieved from any computer that has Internet access.

When you view the e-mail message, the client displays an electronic postmark with the name and address of the sender and the date of delivery, as shown in Figure 4.4.

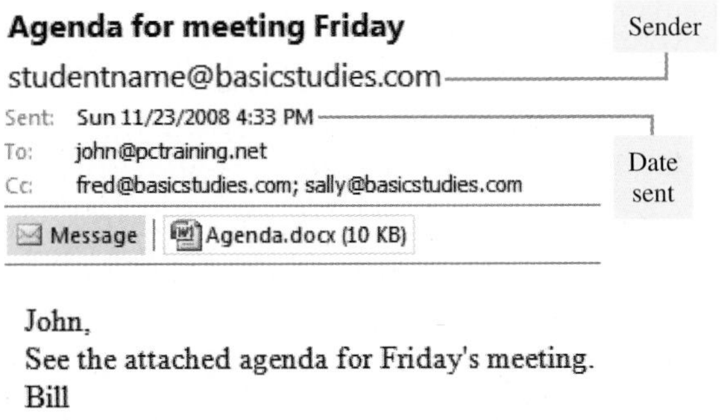

Agenda for meeting Friday
studentname@basicstudies.com
Sent: Sun 11/23/2008 4:33 PM
To: john@pctraining.net
Cc: fred@basicstudies.com; sally@basicstudies.com
Message
Agenda.docx (10 KB)
John,
See the attached agenda for Friday's meeting.
Bill
Sender
Date sent

FIGURE 4.4
Retrieved message.

Components of an E-Mail

Figure 4.2 shows the components of the Outlook Compose window. The **header area** consists of several boxes above the body of the message, which include the recipient addresses and subject line.

The following components are available in most e-mail programs.

- **From:** Your e-mail address from which you are sending the message.

- **To:** The e-mail address(es) of the primary recipient(s) of the message.

- **Cc:** The e-mail address(es) of other recipient(s) who will receive a duplicate of the message—a **carbon copy**, also known as a *courtesy copy*. The primary recipients will see the addresses of anyone copied using this line.

- **Bcc:** The e-mail address(es) of the other recipient(s) who will receive a **blind carbon copy** of the message. The primary recipients will not see the addresses of anyone copied using this line. This option may not be available with all free e-mail services or it might be necessary to change the display options to see it. It can be used when you do not want the recipients to see each other's e-mail addresses.

- **Subject:** A brief synopsis of the contents of the message. A descriptive subject is very important if you want the recipient to open the message.

- **Attachments:** Enables you to attach one or more files, such as Word documents, Excel spreadsheets, or zipped files. There is often a maximum attachment file-size limit.

- **Body:** The place where you type your message.

- **Send button:** Click this button to send a copy to each of the addresses entered in the To:, Cc:, and Bcc: boxes.

- **Signature option:** A shortcut for adding a stored signature, which could include your name, address, phone number, e-mail address, a quotation, or anything else you want to have at the end of messages on a regular basis.

- **Address book:** Storage area for e-mail addresses you use frequently. You can also click on To:, Cc:, and Bcc: to open the list of stored addresses.

Using E-Mail

E-mail can be accessed many different ways. Recall that some e-mail clients, such as Microsoft Outlook, run from your computer. E-mail messages are stored on your e-mail provider's mail server until they are copied to your computer.

Web mail systems use your browser as the mail client on your computer to communicate with the mail server. Messages are stored on the Web server so that e-mail can be accessed from anywhere in the world, as long as the computer has an Internet connection.

Reading E-Mail

When you start the e-mail program, it will display the messages that have arrived in the mail server since the last time you logged in. If you are using an e-mail client on your computer, the program must send a request to the mail server for the mail to be downloaded. Most e-mail programs display a list of messages that show the names of the senders and the subjects. To read one of the messages, you click or double-click it. When you are finished, you can leave the message on the server, delete it, or save the message to a folder using the options on the toolbar, as shown in Figure 4.5.

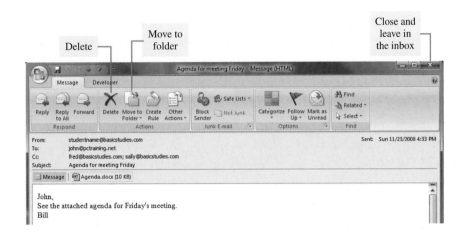

FIGURE 4.5
E-mail delete and save options.

Composing and Sending E-Mail

To compose a new message, you click a button on the toolbar to create a new message. The button is labeled *New* in Outlook, but in other mail programs it might be labeled *Compose*. A form displays in which you fill in the destination address, the subject, and the body of the message. When you are finished, you click the Send button.

Replying to and Forwarding E-Mail

When you receive an e-mail message, you have several options. You can delete the message without reading it, or read it and then delete it. You can read the message and then leave it in the inbox, or move it to a folder. For important messages, there are other options available. These include two ways to reply to the message and a forwarding option. You can also copy messages to one or more recipients in addition to the primary recipient.

There are two ways to reply to an e-mail message. You can *reply*—compose a new message automatically addressed to the original sender—or you can reply to the author and everyone who was copied on the e-mail. Figure 4.6 shows the message window that displays when the **Reply All** button is clicked. The e-mail will be sent to three recipients. Type the new message for the reply above the original message. Notice that the message will be sent to the author of the original message and also to the recipients to whom it was copied—excluding blind copies.

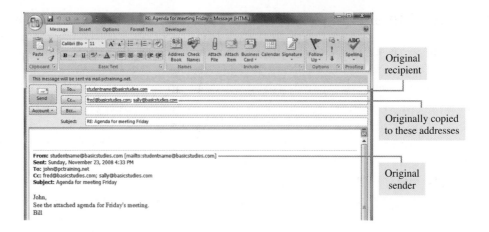

FIGURE 4.6

Reply options.

Often, you will receive an e-mail that you would like to pass on to another person. It might be an important message or a humorous story that you feel someone else would enjoy (be prudent, as many people do not like receiving this type of message). Figure 4.7 shows an Outlook message window after the **_Forward_** button has been clicked. A new message window is opened so that you can add a message to the original message you are forwarding. You are not required to add a message; clicking the Send Now button will forward the message to the address shown in the Send To: box. You can forward a message to multiple recipients by adding a comma between addresses. Some programs use a semicolon rather than a comma to separate addresses.

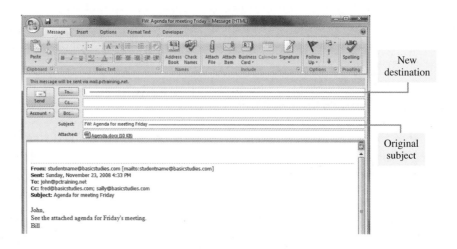

FIGURE 4.7

Forward options.

Managing Attachments

An advantage of using e-mail is that files can be attached to the messages. The file and an e-mail that explains what to do with it arrive at the same time. These files can be documents, spreadsheets, databases, or presentations. You can use this method to send a copy to yourself, creating a backup of important work. To attach a file to an e-mail message, you select the attachment option—usually by clicking a button with a paperclip icon—and browse your computer to locate and select the file. If you receive a file with an attachment, you can click the name of the attached file and a dialog box displays with the options for saving the file or opening it, as shown in Figure 4.8. If you intend to edit the attached file, save it to a known folder first and then open it from that location so that you can find it again.

FIGURE 4.8
Attachment management.

Using an Address Book

Most e-mail clients have an *address book* feature that stores a list of names with e-mail addresses and other information. Some clients have an auto-complete feature that will fill in the remainder of the e-mail address after you begin typing it. The names in an address book can be organized into groups to facilitate sending the same message to everyone in a group. When you specify a group as the intended recipient, the program substitutes the individual addresses of the members of the group.

Formatting E-Mail Messages

Most people are accustomed to writing documents with dedicated word processing software programs like Microsoft Word, which has many sophisticated features such as active spelling and grammar checking and multiple fonts. E-mail programs that reside on the user's computer—like MS Outlook—can connect to dedicated word processing software like MS Word, which is also installed on that computer, and use its advanced features to compose messages.

Web-based e-mail software is generally less sophisticated. Earlier versions of e-mail software were restricted to sending simple text messages, but modern e-mail programs offer the user the option of using hypertext markup language (HTML) to add the ability to use several different fonts, format text, and insert working hyperlinks. When you use a Web client for e-mail, features like spell checking usually take an extra step, and your choice of fonts is limited, as shown in Figure 4.9.

FIGURE 4.9

Gmail with font and spell-check options.

Advantages of Using E-Mail

E-mail has many advantages over the traditional postal service, including speed, remote accessibility, message management, and cost. These benefits are advantages, however, only if the people you want to reach have access to e-mail. Most employees in major organizations—and in many smaller organizations—have access to e-mail. Students in most universities, community colleges, and junior colleges are given e-mail accounts when they register, and many K–12 students also have accounts provided by their school districts.

E-mail systems can reduce the turnaround time of messages from weeks to minutes for purposes of including updates or elaborations of unclear points. Because of the rapid speed of transfer, e-mail messages are often sent during telephone conversations and with diagrams, pictures, URLs, or attached spreadsheets or databases to clarify points of discussion.

Traditional mail is sent to a specific address. If you are not at that address, you cannot access the mail. With e-mail, you can access your messages in a variety of ways and from an almost unlimited number of locations. You can access your school e-mail account, and often your work e-mail account as well, using a computer at a local library, at a friend's house, at home, or in a *cybercafé*—a place where you can eat or drink and connect to the Internet. If you do not know the e-mail address of the person to whom you want to send the message, there are ways of finding e-mail addresses (using Yahoo! People Search, for example) in much the same way as you would look for telephone numbers online. The only requirement is an Internet connection.

It is much cheaper to send messages using e-mail than traditional mail. With e-mail, you do not need paper, envelopes, or stamps. Several services such as Yahoo!, MSN, and Google provide free Web e-mail as an inducement to visit their sites.

Dealing with E-Mail Technical Problems

While the advantages of using e-mail outweigh the disadvantages, there are certainly problems associated with e-mail. These problems involve technical issues, content issues, and unwanted messages. While the vast majority of e-mail messages are sent and received flawlessly, there are occasionally technical issues that cause problems.

Delivery Failure

After you click the Send button to send an e-mail message, a dialog box indicates when the message has been sent. Sometimes, however, because of problems with the mail server, the message is never delivered. Even if the message is delivered, the recipient's mail server may not pass the message on properly. These things do not happen often, but they do happen, and usually for no apparent reason. Delivery failure can also be caused by the e-mail program itself. If a mail server has a filter that blocks certain categories of mail, it might mistakenly remove a legitimate message. The most common cause of delivery failure is an incorrect address, as shown in Figure 4.10. If you get a notice of failure to deliver, examine the notice and check the address to be sure it was correct. Save the notification. An advantage of e-mails is that it provides a paper trail to verify communications. Some massages might appear garbled because the message was composed using HTML but the recipient mail client only reads plain text.

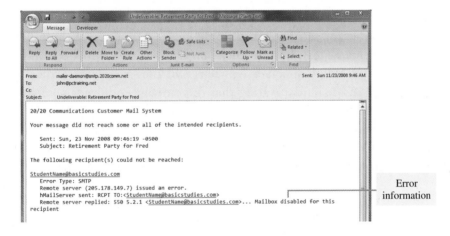

FIGURE 4.10
Mail delivery failure message.

Unreadable Attachments

Recall that e-mail messages are sent in small packets, which are reassembled once they reach their destination. Sometimes one or more packets become corrupted and the attachment does not display, will not download properly, or will download but not open. This often requires that the sender resend the message and attachment. You also might receive an attachment that has been created with a program that is not installed on your computer. When you attempt to open the attachment, the screen displays either gibberish or an error message. Look at the name of the attached file; specifically check the *file extension*—usually a three-letter code at the end of the file name following a period, which designates the type of file. For example, *.pdf* is a type of file that uses a special viewer from Adobe, and *.docx* is a Word 2007 file that might require a compatibility program to be read by an earlier version of Word. A program that makes Office 2007 files usable in earlier versions of Office is available from Microsoft, as shown in Figure 4.11.

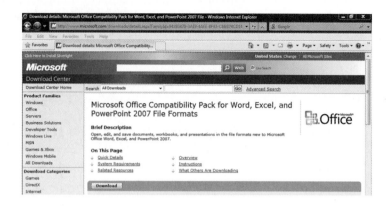

FIGURE 4.11

Conversion program for viewing Office 2007 files.

Inbox is Full

In addition to messages that are incorrectly blocked or sent to the trash, there is another reason people miss e-mail messages. The network administrator in charge of the mail server for an organization is responsible for setting e-mail guidelines. These often include the maximum number of messages recipients can have in their mail folders or a limit to storage space. If a user exceeds either quota, the mail server will reject all messages sent to that mailbox and respond with a message to the sender stating that the message could not be delivered. A user may be unaware that anything is wrong and will miss important messages. To avoid this problem, keep the number of messages stored in your e-mail program below the maximum allowed. You can do this by deleting unwanted messages or by removing them from active use and placing them in storage on a computer's memory, which is called ***archiving***.

Dealing with E-Mail Content Problems

It is very easy to send a message that has contents that elicit emotional responses or are misinterpreted because of poor wording or ill-advised attempts at humor or sarcasm.

Hasty Responses

Everyone has said something that they immediately wish they could take back. The speed with which e-mail is received and sent makes this situation a real possibility with electronic messages as well. If you receive an e-mail message that makes you angry or causes some other emotional response, your immediate reaction is to send a quick reply. Writing the reply is all right, but there are a few ideas you may want to consider in this situation to avoid sending a message you may later regret.

- Write your response without putting an address in the To: line. That way, you can't accidentally send a message before you want to.

- If you are particularly angry or upset, have a colleague or friend read and discuss your response.
- Save the message as a draft for an hour—or better yet, overnight—and then reevaluate your response.

These steps will help you avoid awkward and embarrassing e-mail responses.

Misinterpretation

Unless the recipient of your e-mail knows you well, there are things you should avoid in your messages to prevent misinterpretation or to prevent the recipient from taking offense at your response.

- Avoid extensive use of humor. The recipient's sense of humor may not be the same as yours.
- Avoid sarcasm. Some people don't understand sarcasm, and others are offended by it.
- Avoid slang. Phrases that are in everyday use by a 25-year-old may be alien to a 50-year-old. Also, in both work and school environments, there will be people for whom English is a second language, and they may misinterpret common slang expressions.

Dealing with Unsolicited E-Mail

Within hours of setting up a new e-mail account, your inbox may begin to fill up with unwanted messages. These messages could contain unsolicited electronic bulk mail, or unwanted responses to other people's messages.

Spam

One of the most annoying problems associated with e-mail is **spam**—unsolicited bulk messages that are offensive or waste your time. Spam is not just annoying; it is expensive. According to Commtouch, global spam averages 80% of all e-mail and reached a peak of 96% in October 2007. Most e-mail clients have software that attempts to filter out the spam, but these filters might mistake desired messages for spam, particularly if the message was sent to several people using a mailing list. Many network administrators use spam filters to block these unwanted messages from entering the network.

Too Many Messages from Known Sources

Individual users can also send too many messages by clicking the wrong button. If you get an e-mail from someone and the message has been copied to a dozen other people, clicking the Reply button sends the reply only to the sender. However, if you click Reply All, the message is sent to everyone who received the original message except for those who received blind copies. When an e-mail is sent to a department or a large block of people, clicking Reply All can result in dozens or hundreds of unnecessary messages.

Another source of unwanted e-mail is well-meaning friends, relatives, and coworkers. Some people receive e-mail messages that they think are funny, cute, or meaningful and forward the message to everyone in their address book. A few people appreciate these messages; many may not.

Ask people if they would like to be included in the group to whom you forward messages. In extreme cases, you can use the filtering software in the mail client or firewall software to block all messages from a particular domain or person. Refer to Lesson 5 for information regarding malicious use of e-mail.

▶▶▶ *lesson*
tWO | Asynchronous Communications

When there is an unspecified delay between the actions of two computers or people, they are not synchronized. The term for communication or activity that is not synchronized is *asynchronous*. E-mail is an example of asynchronous communications. One person can send an e-mail message and the other person might not read it or respond for days. In this lesson, you will study other types of asynchronous communication on the Internet.

E-Mail Lists

Most e-mail clients have an address book feature that will allow you to create groups to whom you can send the same message by simply using the group's name in the To: box of the message form. Organizations can communicate with their members by using similar lists of e-mail addresses. If an organization has thousands of names on its list, adding new addresses or changing existing ones can become a significant task. A large *electronic mailing list (e-list)* is similar to the type of mailing list you would create with an address book in an e-mail program. Mailing lists are available for sale from sites like Mailing Lists Direct, as shown in Figure 4.12.

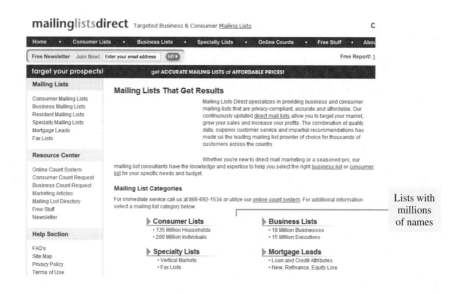

FIGURE 4.12

E-mail lists for sale.

Electronic mailing lists can be used to contact members of an organization who agree to be on the list. Special software is available to manage the e-list. The program has its own e-mail address—a *reflector*—to which an authorized person can send a message that will be distributed to all the addresses on the list.

Members of an e-list are called *subscribers*. Specialized e-list software can automatically handle requests to add a new subscriber or delete an existing one. Messages from e-list programs that have this feature usually include a notice to subscribers on how new members can subscribe or existing members can remove their names. For example, the message might instruct the reader to reply to a particular address with a message containing the word *unsubscribe* in the subject, and the program will remove the name and address automatically.

There are different types of e-lists.

- Announcement list: organizations send electronic newsletters to subscribers

- Direct marketing: a type of announcement list used by commercial groups to send announcements of sales or new products (more on this topic in Chapter 5)

- Discussion list: members are authorized to send messages to the reflector that are distributed to the other members to create a large asynchronous discussion

Most discussion lists have rules of behavior that are enforced by a *moderator*—a person who has administrative rights to delete postings or members. E-list programs can store—archive—messages and provide the ability to search the archive. Archives can be collected by other groups like Gmane that provide the ability to search thousands of archives and millions of postings.

to explore an e-list

1 **Start a Web browser. In the browser's address box, near the top of the Web browser screen, type** `https://lists.wikimedia.org/mailman/listinfo` **and then press** ⏎Enter.

2 **On the Wikimedia Mailing Lists page, scroll down and click on the link to a list of your choice.**

3 **Scroll down to the *Subscribing to* section. In the *Your email address* box, type your e-mail address. In the *Your name (optional)* box, type your name.**

4 **With your name displayed in the box, start the Snipping Tool. In the Snipping Tool dialog box, click the New Snip button arrow** ✂ **, and then click Window Snip. Point anywhere in the WikiEn-I Mailing List window, and then click one time.**

5 **Near the top of the Snipping Tool dialog box, click the Save Snip button** 💾 **. In the Save As dialog box, navigate to the folder where you store your files. In the File name box type** `U3Ch04ListStudentName` **substituting your name as indicated, and then click Save.** Alternatively, users of Windows XP can press the Print Screen (PrtScn) button on the keyboard and paste the captured screen into a word processing document. Users of Macintosh computers can press Command + Control + Shift + 3 to capture a screen image to the clipboard and paste the captured screen into a word processing document.

6 Close the browser without completing the subscription process. In the upper right corner of each open dialog box or window, click the Close button ![Close button].

7 Submit your snip as directed by your instructor.

Message Boards

Discussions can be posted on Web pages where postings and related responses are displayed next to each other. This is a Web-based version of a discussion list called an ***Internet forum*** or ***message board***. Nonmembers can visit and view the postings, but only members can post messages.

Postings are displayed by topic. To start a discussion on a topic, a member makes an ***opening post (OP)*** that declares the title of the topic with a brief description. Other members post their thoughts on the topic. Postings are displayed below the OP. They can be listed in reverse order, with the most recent postings at the top of the list, or in chronological order, with the oldest message at the top. The postings and the topic statement make up a ***thread***. Some boards post the messages in chronological order, with the oldest at the top of the list; others allow postings that respond to other postings within the thread and are indented below a posting to visually identify the relationship, as shown in Figure 4.13.

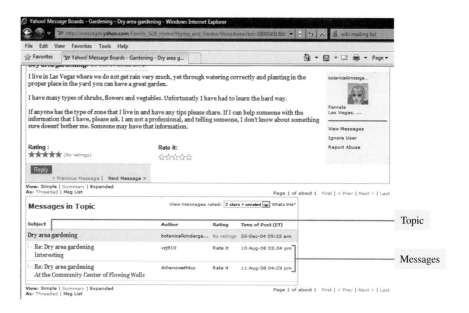

FIGURE 4.13
Thread with indented postings.

The software that manages the threads counts the frequency with which each thread is viewed and the frequency of new postings added to each thread. Threads that are most active can be identified as ***hot threads***.

Joining a message board is similar to joining an e-list, with some additional requirements. Users are often asked to confirm that they are over twelve years old so that the forum organizers do not have to meet the requirements of the ***Children's Online Privacy Protection Act***

(COPPA)—a law that protects information provided by children under thirteen. To assure that postings are from legitimate members and are not generated by a computer program in an effort to artificially increase the frequency rating of a thread, members might be asked to translate a visually distorted word—a *CAPTCHA*—that is hard for computers to translate, such as the examples shown in Figure 4.14.

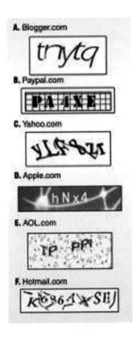

FIGURE 4.14
CAPTCHA Examples.

to explore a message board

1. **Start a Web browser. In the browser's address box, near the top of the Web browser screen, type** messages.yahoo.com **and then press** ⏎Enter. The Yahoo! Message Boards page displays. Notice the terms of service at the left of the page that describe proper behavior.

2. **On the Yahoo! Message Board page, under Browse, click the Cultures & Community link.** Notice that this category is made up of several subcategories.

3. **Under Browse Categories, click Names. Under Browse Categories, click Baby Names.** Notice that this category is divided into additional categories and the number of threads is listed under Topics, as shown in Figure 4.15. The names of the categories, topics, and dates will be different than those shown in the figure.

4. **Click the Girls' Names category to display a list of topics. Notice the number of replies and the date of the latest posting. Choose a topic with at least ten replies, in which the latest posting is less than a month old, and click its link. Scroll the screen, if necessary, to display the topic description and the postings at the top**

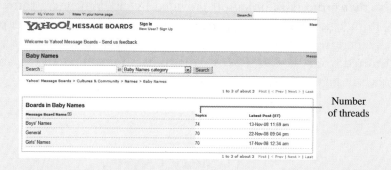

Number of threads

FIGURE 4.15
Message boards.

of the list. Notice the organization of the postings in chronological order, with postings that are responses to other postings indented below the earlier posting to which they refer.

5 With name topic and several postings displayed, use the skills you practiced previously to start the Snipping Tool program and do a Window Snip of the window. Save a copy of this Web page to the folder where you store your files. Name the file `U3Ch04MessageStudentName` substituting your name as indicated.

6 Close the browser, and then submit your snip as directed by your instructor.

Weblogs

A *weblog* is usually maintained by an individual who makes regular entries of a personal nature such as opinions, commentaries, descriptions of events from their point of view, personal picture or videos, and links to other sites that they find interesting. The term is usually shortened to *blog*. Many people use blogs as online diaries, but others use them as an alternative to mainstream media for learning about events. Search engines like Google have options for searching blogs. According to Technorati—a blog search engine—there are more than 112 million blogs, and over 175,000 new blogs are added each day. This collection of blogs is known as the *blogosphere*.

Most blogs are mainly text, but others specialize and are identified by terms that are combinations of the category and the word *blog*. Wikipedia lists broad categories of blogs.

- Personal blogs: ongoing diaries and personal opinions
- Corporate blogs: used to enhance internal communications or for external marketing, branding, or public relations
- Question blogging: also known as a *qlog*, this type responds to questions

Blogs can also be categorized by media.

- Video: made up of video postings known as *vlogs*
- Links: a *linklog* is made up of links to other sites or blogs
- Sketches: a *sketchlog* consists of a portfolio of drawings

- Photos: a *photoblog* contains photos
- Mixed media: a mix of media is a *tumbleblog*

Blogs can be organized by genre.

- Politics
- Travel
- Fashion
- Education
- Music

Blogs can also be categorized by the type of device used to access them, as in the case of a *moblog*, which is designed for use on handheld computers or advanced cell phones.

Video Sharing

According to the Organisation for Economic Co-Operation and Development (OECD), there are more than 220 million subscribers to broadband Internet services worldwide, and in the U.S., there are more than 66 million subscribers. Faster connections to the Internet and the availability of affordable digital video cameras make it practical for many people to create their own videos and share them over the Internet. A leader in providing video-sharing services is YouTube, which provides a wide variety of videos from which to choose. YouTube was founded in February 2005; in less than three years, YouTube activity increased to more than 79 million users, making more than 3 billion views per month. The convergence of technologies that made this phenomenal growth possible is discussed further in Chapter 6.

Video files are typically much larger—more megabytes of data—than text files or individual picture files and take longer to transmit over the Internet. A video file consists of many individual pictures that are taken in sequence. The human visual processing system retains each image for a short time, and if the next image is displayed before the last one fades out, the action seems to be continuous. Televisions display 24 to 30 images per second to achieve the appearance of motion. Consequently, even a few minutes of video can require thousands of individual pictures. The size of a video file depends upon the level of detail of each picture— the *resolution*—and the number of pictures taken or displayed per second. Video files usually include an audio component to provide sound. To make the video files small enough to transmit over the Internet in an acceptable amount of time, each of these components is usually compromised by using fewer low-resolution images and lower-quality sound.

Even these compromises are not enough to make video transmission over the Internet practical. To further reduce the size of video files, computers are used to analyze the pictures and reduce file size. One common method is to use a computer to analyze each picture to determine what parts of it changed from the previous picture. After the first picture is sent, only changes are transmitted. For example, if the background of a video does not change, there is no reason to take up transmission time to transmit the same background in each picture. Reducing the file size by applying this type of logic is called *compression*.

The process of changing a video into a sequence of codes in order to compress it and then decode it to reconstruct the video for viewing is done by a program or hardware device called a *codec*, where the acronym stands for *coding and decoding*. There are several different video codecs in use. To view a video, your computer must have the codec that was used to compress the video. Codecs are classified as *lossy* or *lossless*. A lossless codec can compress and then decompress an image repeatedly without losing any of the original detail. A lossy codec uses a method that does not recover all of the original data but usually achieves much smaller file sizes.

The type of codec used to compress an individual image or a video is usually indicated by the file extension—a short code following the file name. Refer to Table 1.2 for a list of commonly used video codecs and their file extensions.

CODEC NAME	FILE EXTENSION
Apple's version of the MPEG4 codec	avc1
Sorenson Spark	flv1
H.263	h263
MPEG-4 Video	mp4v
Apple animation	rle
Real Video 8	rv30
Sorenson Video 3	svq3
Adobe Shockwave	swf
Open Source MPEG-4	xvid
Windows Media Audio/Video	wmv

TABLE 4.2

The codecs are often bundled together in a single media player program to reduce confusion for the user.

to determine what program is associated with video files on your computer

Instructions are provided for Windows Vista. Alternative instructions are provided for Windows XP and Apple OSX.

1 **Click the Start button. On the menu, click Documents.** Alternatively, in Windows XP, click the Start button, and then click My Documents. In OSX, go to the Finder, and then click Movies.

2 **Click the My Videos folder.** Sample media files are provided with the Vista operating system.

3 **Right-click one of the files.** Alternatively, in Windows XP, open the Sample Files folder or search your hard drive for *.avi* files and right-click one of those files. In OSX, press the Ctrl key and click My Great Movie.

4 **On the menu, click Properties.** The type of file and the program that opens it is displayed, as shown in Figure 4.16. Alternatively, in OSX, point to *Open with*.

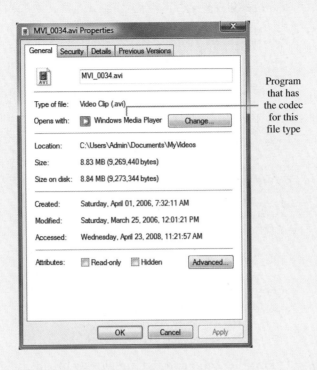

FIGURE 4.16
File type related to display program.

5 **Use the skills you practiced previously to start the Snipping Tool program and do a Window Snip of the window. Save a copy of this Web page to the folder where you store your files. Name the file** U3Ch04OpenWithStudentName **substituting your name as indicated.**

6 **In the upper right corner of each open dialog box or window, click the Close button** ❎ .

7 **Submit your snip as directed by your instructor.**

Streaming

Many users are only interested in viewing the video one time, or the copyright holder of the file does not want to provide the file in a reproducible form. In that situation, the recipient does not need to wait for the entire file to download before viewing it. The video or audio file can be transmitted in segments; as soon as the first segment is decoded, it can be played. If the download and decoding process is faster than playing the audio or video, the processed data is stored in a temporary memory location called a *buffer*. Media players often store a few minutes of processed data in the buffer before beginning to play so that interruptions in transmission will not stop play. Many radio stations provide their programming on the Internet as a live stream, as shown in Figure 4.17.

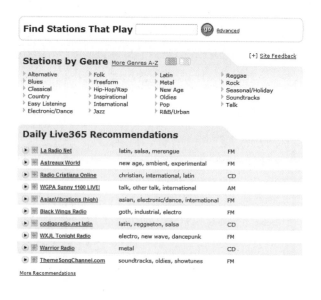

FIGURE 4.17
Streaming stations.

Because the audio and video files can be stored, previously broadcast episodes can be made available *on demand*—whenever the user requests it.

Using RSS Feeds

Instead of sending in a request for media, users can request that new content be sent to them automatically. For example, you can subscribe to a news service that automatically updates a pop-up window on your desktop with the latest news or sports scores. The challenge is to distribute the audio and video data, which uses a variety of codecs, for display on a variety of computers. This challenge is similar to the one that faced Tim Berners-Lee when he used the hypertext markup language (HTML) to define standard methods for displaying Web pages. Instead of choosing a standard codec and method for handling files, a very flexible standard is used: *extensible markup language (XML)*. Although the name implies that this is a specific language, it is actually a framework for writing a language, which is why the word *extensible* is part of the name. When a programmer creates an XML file, he or she defines the variables and the relationships between them and saves the definition in a *namespace*. The namespace can be stored on a server on the Internet with its own Web address. If anyone wants to use a file that was created with this set of definitions, the namespace can be found and downloaded from the server. This method provides the flexibility of using a variety of media types and coding programs.

XML is used to publish frequently updated information such as blogs, news headlines, and sports scores. Several sources use the acronym *RSS—really simple syndication*—to describe these files and their delivery method. RSS files are displayed using an RSS reader or *feed aggregator*. You can download a reader, or it might be built into your browser, such as Internet Explorer (IE). For example, if you wanted to keep track of stock market news as soon as it happens, you could subscribe to an RSS feed from Microsoft Money using IE. At the bottom of the Microsoft Money site, there is a link labeled RSS. When you click this link, a page of RSS feeds displays, as shown in Figure 4.18.

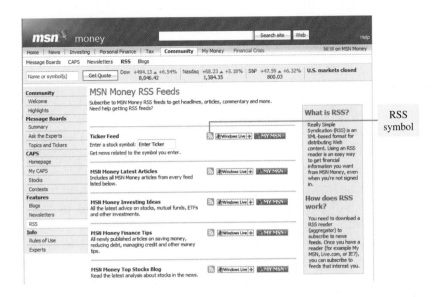

FIGURE 4.18

RSS links next to feeds.

If you are using IE8, you can click the RSS logo next to the feed you want. In this example, the RSS logo next to *MSN Money Investing Ideas* is clicked, which leads to a page displaying the titles of the latest articles and an option to subscribe. If you click the *subscribe to this feed* link, the feed will be added to your favorites under the Feeds tab, as shown in Figure 4.19.

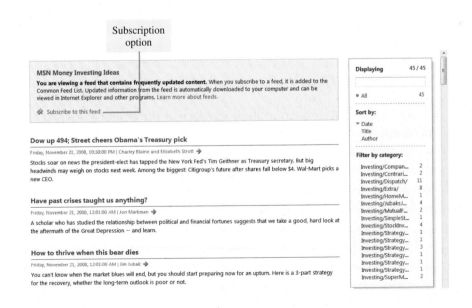

FIGURE 4.19

RSS link on Microsoft Money page.

A *podcast* is a file that is distributed through Web feeds that is specifically designed to play on portable media players like Apple's iPod. Most podcasts are audio files. Although the practice began with broadcasting media files to Apple iPods, other devices have been developed that can receive and play the files. Among other things, podcasts are used to distribute segments of radio shows and college lectures.

File Sharing

Unlike the client-server model, file-sharing systems do not store files on a server. Instead, they store files on individual computers in a peer-to-peer relationship where each computer can act like a server to provide files.

Early versions of file-sharing software, such as the original Napster software, stored an index on a server that kept track of where the files were stored. Because file sharing is often used to share music files without paying royalties to the copyright holders, this type of system could be shut down by suing the provider of the central index. Recent versions of file-sharing software such as GNUnet emphasize anonymous file sharing. Links are created between friends in a *friend-to-friend (F2F)* arrangement where files can be traded between friends without revealing an IP address. The content of the exchange, including the files, is encrypted so that it is difficult to determine if the files being transferred are copyrighted material. The stated goals of GNUnet include the anonymity of users in censorship-resistant file sharing.

▶▶▶ *lesson*
three | Synchronous Communications

A typical telephone conversation is an example of *synchronous* communication, where the parties to the conversation are present at the same time. In this lesson, you will study ways the Internet is used to support communications between people who are taking part in the exchange at the same time.

Internet Telephone Calls

One of the advantages of an established technology, such as the circuit-switched telephone system, is that the companies have had time to work out the problems with the system and add backup equipment that takes over when primary equipment fails. For example, most telephone systems have their own backup electric generators so that when the electric power to an area fails, the telephone system still works. Internet connections are becoming more reliable, and many people are switching from traditional telephone companies to Internet-based providers.

Recall that the Internet uses TCP/IP protocols for transferring data packets. A telephone call is a type of audio file, and the compression technologies that are effective at reducing the file size of music and video files can also be applied to telephone conversations. The process of coding telephone conversations into packets of compressed data, transmitting the packets over the Internet, and then decoding them fast enough to make synchronous conversation possible is called *Voice-over-the-Internet Protocol (VoIP)*. Because of the efficient use of broadband

Internet connections, the cost of VoIP is usually less than traditional telephone service—particularly for long distance calls, as shown in Figure 4.20.

FIGURE 4.20
VoIP options.

The ability to make telephone calls over the Internet from computer to computer has been available for many years. The early systems were not integrated with the existing telephone system, so usage was low. As the telephone switching system became computerized, it became increasingly practical to communicate between the two systems. Cable television networks like Comcast took advantage of this technology to offer telephone service along with television and Internet connections. Companies such as Vonage provide VoIP over broadband Internet connections from other providers.

The advantages of VoIP for home use include:

- The ability to use the same connection for more than one call at the same time.
- Computer-based extra features like conference calling, caller ID, automatic redial, and call forwarding are usually provided at no extra charge.
- Integration with video calling.
- Lower cost.
- Location independent—you can take and place calls from any computer that is connected to the Internet.
- Low-cost international calls.

The disadvantages of VoIP for home use include:

- Lack of mobility—wide-area Internet access is much less available than cell phone coverage.
- Quality of the calls is affected by the speed and quality of the Internet connection.
- Compatibility problems with devices designed for use over traditional telephone systems such as fax machines and home security systems.
- Needs electric power backup system such as an ***uninterruptible power supply (UPS)***—a unit with a battery that provides electric power for a short time—or an electric generator.
- Many people have cell phones that provide similar features plus mobility.
- Calls to traditional telephone numbers might have additional fees.

Advances in video compression and faster personal Internet connections make it possible to make video conference calls. One of the companies that offers this service is Skype. Users can download the Skype software and make free voice or video calls to other Skype users over the Internet. Both parties need a microphone, a camera that connects to a computer—*webcam*—a computer with adequate computing speed, and a fast broadband Internet connection, as shown in Figure 4.21.

FIGURE 4.21

Video calling.

Personal Conferencing

Conferencing refers to exchanges that take place while the parties are present to interact with each other. Businesses have used conference calls to facilitate meetings for many years, but they were expensive, especially if several long distance calls were required. The Internet can be used to facilitate conferencing at very low cost. A basic form of conferencing over the Internet is a live message center where text-based exchanges take place between users who are active at the same time. This type of exchange is called a *chat*. In a chat, users post comments and other members of the chat post responses. An advantage of a chat over a conference call is that it is self-documenting—there is a record of everything that was posted during the conference. Chats are available that you can join at sites like MSN and Yahoo!, as shown in Figure 4.22.

FIGURE 4.22

Chat box.

Voice-over-IP technology can be used to create a conference that is similar to a telephone conference call, except that users can exchange data files while talking. Video can be added to create a video conference in which users can see each other. This feature is useful in personal conferencing for communicating with family and friends. Business uses of Internet conferencing are discussed in Chapter 5.

Instant Messaging

Most conferences are limited in time and scope, and the participants agree to meet for a limited time and discuss a particular topic. If the participants want to stay in touch over a longer period of time and exchange short text messages on a variety of topics as the need arises, they can use *instant messaging (IM)*. Instant messaging is primarily a text-based service, where a person can post a message that appears immediately on another person's computer screen if that person is logged on and connected to the Internet. The recipient can quickly respond to the posting and return to what they were doing. Friends and family members can exchange information on an informal basis to keep each other informed of events and concerns.

IM messages tend to be informal and short. Abbreviations are commonly used to speed up typed responses and to indicate emotions. For example, *LOL* stands for *laugh outloud*. Early efforts to indicate emotions in text messages used combinations of characters such as :-) which resembles a sideways smiley face. Images called *emoticons* are available that can be pasted into messages, as shown in Figure 4.23.

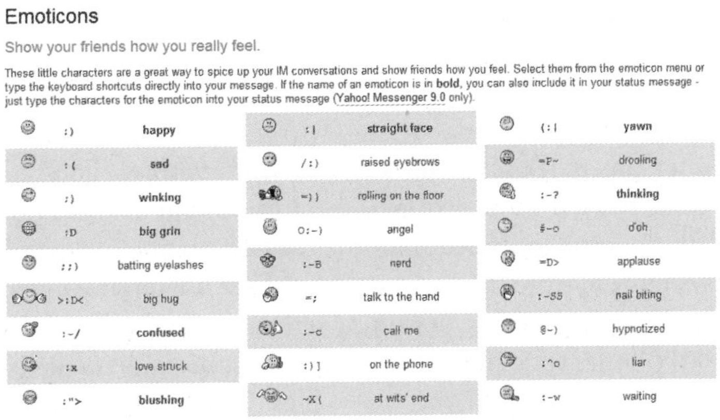

Emoticons

Show your friends how you really feel.

These little characters are a great way to spice up your IM conversations and show friends how you feel. Select them from the emoticon menu or type the keyboard shortcuts directly into your message. If the name of an emoticon is in **bold**, you can also include it in your status message - just type the characters for the emoticon into your status message (Yahoo! Messenger 9.0 only).

	:)	happy		:|	straight face		(:|	yawn
	:(	sad		/:)	raised eyebrows		=P~	drooling
	;)	winking		~))	rolling on the floor		:-?	**thinking**
	:D	big grin		O:-)	angel		#-o	d'oh
	;;)	batting eyelashes		:-B	nerd		=D>	applause
	>:D<	big hug		=;	talk to the hand		:-SS	nail biting
	:-/	confused		:-c	call me		8-)	hypnotized
	:x	love struck		:)]	on the phone		:^o	liar
	:">	blushing		~X(	at wits' end		:-w	waiting

FIGURE 4.23
Emoticons.

Each user determines a list of people from whom they will accept instant messages. Instant messaging might be offered as a service by an Internet service provider (ISP) like America Online (AOL) or content providers like MSN, Yahoo!, and Google. It is relatively easy to set up an IM with users of the same service, but it is more problematic if they use a different service.

Text and Multimedia Messaging

A mobile version of instant messaging is text messaging: *texting*. Texting software that is designed to use the *short message service (SMS)*—wireless service for sending short messages—works on mobile phones and personal digital assistants (PDAs) that have small screens, as shown previously in Figure 4.3. SMS limits each message to 160 characters, including spaces. For other alphabets such as Chinese, the SMS size is 70 characters.

The cell phone system is controlled by computers that are in frequent communication with each cell phone that is turned on. A cell phone periodically sends out a signal that is picked up by antennas on nearby towers. Computers connected to the towers compare the strength of the signal to determine which tower is closest to the phone and which antenna to use if a call comes in for that phone, as shown in Figure 4.24.

FIGURE 4.24
Cell phone tower.

The signal used for this purpose is called the ***control channel***. The short message service uses the control channel to send short text messages to a cell phone. Messages are kept short to avoid interfering with the primary function of the control channel. If the phone is not turned on, the cell phone system will store the message and deliver it later. If you have a digital phone, you can send a text message to another person by sending it to their mobile phone number.

Because many cell phones are equipped with digital cameras that take pictures and videos, the SMS was modified to send audio and video files. The service is called the ***multimedia messaging service (MMS)***. To use MMS to send media files between phones or PDAs, both devices must have Internet access using ***wireless application protocol (WAP)***, a standard for wireless access to the Internet. The MMS sends the text portion of the message using the control channel. If the message includes a multimedia file, the file is encoded, assigned a Web address, and uploaded to a server on the Internet using WAP. The text portion of the message that is delivered to the receiving cell phone contains the Web address where the media file is stored. If the receiving cell phone is also equipped to access the Internet, it uses its data connection to download the media file from the Internet.

▶▶▶ *lesson*

four | Uses of Online Communications

The wide variety of communications options that are available online have been put to use to supplement earlier forms of communication and have spawned new forms. In this lesson, you study some of the ways in which people are using synchronous and asynchronous communications.

Interest Groups

In Chapter 3, you studied the effects of worldwide communications on business-to-consumer commerce and observed that unusual products that do not sell enough in a local market can find a large enough market online to prosper. Similarly, people with special interests may not know enough people locally to form an interest group, but with access to millions of people online, anyone can find a group of people who share a common interest. With the synchronous and asynchronous communications available, interest groups can form and communicate online from anywhere in the world. The following are a few examples.

Medical

People who have a particular disease or who are close to those who do are often looking for information and support. Medical information websites such as WebMD have links to message boards and blogs of individuals and health experts.

to view a medical support group message board

1   **Start a Web browser. In the Address box, near the top of the Web browser screen, type** http://www.webmd.com/community **and then press** ⏎Enter. The WebMD Community page displays. Notice the types of communities listed at the left.

2   **In the left pane, under Community, click Message Boards.** A list of message boards displays on a variety of medical topics.

3   **Scroll down the list of message boards.** Notice that most areas of interest include a link to a support group.

4   **Choose any one of the general areas and click the link to the support group for that area of interest.** A list of discussion titles displays. The discussions with more than one posting have a plus sign next to them.

5   **Choose a discussion title that has more than three postings, and then click the plus sign to expand the list to display the individual postings.** Notice the user names of people posting messages and the time since the last message was posted.

6 Use the skills you practiced previously to start the Snipping Tool and create a Window Snip of the window that displays a list of postings on a particular topic in a support group. Save a copy of this window to the folder where you store your files. Name the file U3Ch04SupportStudentName substituting your name as indicated.

7 In the browser window, point to the Close button ![X] in the upper right corner, and then click the left mouse button. The browser window closes.

Politics

Political forums are a place for individuals and groups to state their opinions on issues and public figures. Most political blogs are openly biased toward a party or philosophy. Many people consider such openness to be more honest than sites that present themselves to be unbiased but which—according to their detractors—are not. Blogs on most political topics can be found at directories such as eTalkingHead.

Blogs are generally uncensored and unverified. People who make untrue statements are subject to the same laws that punish *libel*—publication of false and malicious information for the purpose of defaming a living person—but few people are prosecuted. It is common in political blogs for biased or untrue statements to be widely circulated. It is up to the reader to assess the accuracy of any statements they read in a blog, message board, or e-mail. Fortunately, there are sites like Factcheck.org that research statements made in blogs, message boards, and websites. If you post a political opinion or comment about someone, be aware that postings in blogs or social networking sites are public and can be saved permanently. A harsh statement made in the heat of the moment can be embarrassing years later.

to check a political statement

1 Start a Web browser. In the Address box, near the top of the Web browser screen, type http://www.factcheck.org and then press [↵Enter]. The FactCheck page displays. Notice the communication options at the left of the page, including an RSS feed, as shown in Figure 4.25. This is an example of where an RSS feed would provide information from FactCheck to your desktop regarding a breaking story.

FIGURE 4.25
FactCheck.

2 **Under Recent Postings, choose a topic that interests you and click the title of the topic, which is a link.** The topic is discussed and, at the bottom, sources are cited. Elements of the topic that can be confirmed are identified, and elements that are false or misrepresentations are also identified.

3 **Use the skills you practiced previously to start the Snipping Tool and create a Window Snip of the window that displays your choice of article. Save a copy of this window to the folder where you store your files. Name the file** U3Ch04FactsStudentName **substituting your name as indicated.**

4 **In the browser window, point to the Close button** ▢ **in the upper right corner, and then click the left mouse button.** The browser window closes.

Hobbies

People enjoy collecting, restoring, and studying unusual things. A person might collect rare glass bottles, restore a particular model automobile, or be interested in rare butterflies. Websites that are devoted to a particular hobby often provide discussion forums. For example, MustangForums has thousands of threads.

Playing Games

There are many games that can be played on a computer, and many of them are available for downloading. Instead of playing against a computer program, people can play against real people using synchronous and asynchronous communications. Before the age of electronic communications, people would play chess by correspondence, where each move had to wait for a letter to arrive via the postal system. With Internet connections, people can play against each other using synchronous communications. Numerous games are available, as shown in Figure 4.26.

FIGURE 4.26

Playok.

Social Networking

A person who is a member of one group is often a member of other groups. There is a concept known as *six degrees of separation* that asserts that anyone on the planet can be connected to anyone else through an average of only six personal contacts. This theory was tested on the Internet in 2001 by Duncan Watts at Columbia University. People were asked to send an e-mail to a complete stranger—the target, about whom they only knew the name, occupation, and general location—by having a friend with whom they were on a first-name basis forward the message to someone they knew. Watts found that 48,000 people sending messages to 19 targets succeeded in delivering the message by forwarding it through an average of only six intermediate friends.

The Internet simultaneously provides a way for special interest groups to form and for people to connect to anyone on earth through a friend-of-a-friend connection. In this lesson, you study how the Internet is used to form social groups that are interconnected to form a *social network* of personal contacts with other individuals. Business applications of social networking are discussed in Chapter 5.

Facebook, MySpace

Social networking pages like Facebook and MySpace provide a place where individuals can post information about themselves, including biographical information, photos, and videos.

Users can search for people they know who might already be members and invite them to view their pages. Users can interact using asynchronous tools like e-mail or synchronous tools such as instant messaging. Social networking pages are very popular. According to Alexa.com—an Internet activity-ranking service—Facebook and MySpace have approximately the same number of page views per day as Google's search engine. A social networking site that is intended to be shared with anyone who wants to join is called an *external social network (ESN)*. Specialized social networks that are intended for use by limited groups of people, in which membership is by invitation, are called *internal social networks (ISN)*. Examples are doctors who specialize in a particular disease, professional groups, or a network of your invited friends.

To get started in a social network, you sign up and create a profile. The profile can be a mix of text, videos, pictures, links to other sites, or whatever you choose to disclose about yourself. The next step is connecting to other people. Most sites have a search option that helps you find people you know who are already members. You can send invitations by e-mail to view your page through the program that coordinates the site. The person who receives the message must agree by responding to the invitation. The response goes to the program's server, which establishes the link and adds the person to your list of friends. Similarly, other people can invite you to view their page and join their list of friends.

Online Dating Services

The Internet can be used to arrange meetings between individuals who are interested in establishing a romantic or sexual relationship. Some service providers like eHarmony have members fill out questionnaires that help identify a person's views and values. The answers are analyzed by a computer program, and the result of the analysis is used to match the member with other members who might be compatible. An introductory page is made available for potential matches, but contact information is not available until a membership fee is paid.

Free sites, such as Datehookup, provide an e-mail forwarding service where the member's user name and e-mail address are stored on a server. E-mail sent to the person's user name is forwarded anonymously to the e-mail address. In general, you should avoid posting your e-mail address in a public site.

Dating service sites are designed to protect the identity of users while they provide enough details about a person to determine if the person is attractive and meets specified criteria. Computerized communications are used to provide videos, live video chats, or discussion threads to allow people to interact until such point as they agree to identify themselves and arrange direct contact.

to use a dating service

1. **Start a Web browser. In the Address box, near the top of the Web browser screen, type** `http://personals.yahoo.com` **and then press** `⏎Enter`**. The Yahoo! Personals page displays.**

2. **In the *Find someone special near you* box, click the arrow on the *I am a* box and choose a relationship. Fill in the two ages to specify an age range, and then enter a zip code or city and state. Click the Search Now button.** A list of postings by individuals displays.

3. **Scroll the screen to display at least four postings.**

4. **Use the skills you practiced previously to start the Snipping Tool and create a Window Snip of the window that displays the individuals you located. Save a copy of this window to the folder where you store your files. Name the file** `U3Ch04DatingStudentName` **substituting your name as indicated.**

5. **In the browser window, point to the Close button** [X] **in the upper right corner, and then click the left mouse button.** The browser window closes.

Education Online

Educators have used communication technology to teach students who were not physically in the classroom since the development of the postal system, when it was known as ***distance education***. As the name indicates, the assumption was that students did not attend class in person because they were too far from the classroom to attend regular meetings. Students can be prevented from attending regular class meetings in person for other reasons. Many of today's students are working adults whose travel or work conflicts with traditional class schedules. Even full-time students who live on campus find that it is much easier to schedule a full load of classes if one or two of the classes are taken online using asynchronous communications so that they do not conflict with other class meeting times.

Course Support Suites

An online course utilizes several communication technologies. Most courses use websites or course delivery systems that have a grade book where students can view their own grades but not those of other students. The site contains links to other pages that describe assignments and required reading. The website has an e-mail feature that has a mailing list of student e-mail addresses and a live-chat area. There is usually a document management system that allows students to send attachments to the instructor that are not seen by other students. Presentations are available in slides, text, or video formats. One of the commercial providers of software to support online education is Blackboard, and Moodle is an example of an open-source support software. Schools that have sufficient computer and support resources can host the Blackboard software on their own servers. Otherwise, the company will provide a hosting service for additional fees.

Higher Education

Learning that utilizes a computer for delivering instruction is known as ***e-learning***. Many classes supplement on-campus courses with an online component such as a grade book or list of class assignments. Other classes take place entirely online, where instructors use synchronous and asynchronous technologies to communicate with students. According to an article from Inside Higher Ed magazine, more than three million students are taking at least one online course each year, and approximately 60% of chief academic officers maintain that the quality is as good as or better than on-campus courses and that e-learning is critical to their institutions.

Use of e-learning in higher education varies from schools that offer no classes that are entirely online to schools that offer entire degrees online where a student is not required to physically attend a single class. Before the Internet, universities served a particular geographic area and students who lived in other areas had to move to campus to take classes. With the availability of Internet connections, this pattern is changing. An institution that represents this change is the University of Phoenix. It is based in Phoenix, Arizona, but it offers degrees online that can be taken anywhere, as shown in Figure 4.27. Inexpensive training and learning opportunities are available on the Internet to people of all income levels. Some institutions such as the Massachusetts Institute of Technology make lectures available online at no cost.

FIGURE 4.27

University of Phoenix.

K-12 Schools

Younger students typically need more structured learning environments than college students, but e-learning plays a role in the kindergarten through senior high school environment. According to a study funded by the Sloan Foundation, over half of the school districts surveyed had at least one student who was taking a class fully online. In many cases, these are senior high school students who are taking college courses online, but in some cases school districts offer their own courses. The State of Michigan requires that all high school graduates have an online learning experience.

Home Schooling

Many states allow parents to teach their children at home. Online resources provide access to a rich environment of support materials, as shown in Figure 4.28.

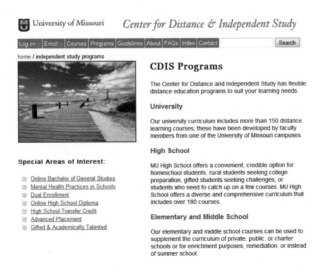

FIGURE 4.28

Home-schooling support online.

Group Projects

Online communities can direct their efforts toward common goals where thousands of volunteers can produce outcomes that are often free of charge to other online participants.

Open-Source Software

Many people share the belief that computer software should be available at no charge, and they are willing to develop software applications that can be used without paying royalties or licensing fees. According to the Open Source Initiative, the software is *open source* if it meets ten criteria.

1. Free redistribution: The software can be sold or given away with other software.

2. Source Code: The *source code*—program code written in text form before it is translated into machine code—is available.

3. Derived works: must allow modifications that are distributed under the same terms as the original software

4. Integrity of author's source code: may restrict redistribution of source code only if distribution of patch files is allowed

5. No discrimination against persons or groups

6. No discrimination against fields of endeavor

7. Distribution of license: Rights attached to the program must apply to any redistribution.

8. License must not be specific to a product: Rights must not depend on being part of a particular distribution.

9. License must not restrict other software: cannot require that other programs distributed with it are open source

10. License must be technology-neutral: cannot assume a particular technology or style of interface

Two examples of open-source software are the Linux operating system and OpenOffice—a suite of software applications shown in Figure 4.29 that is similar to Microsoft Office.

FIGURE 4.29

OpenOffice.org home page.

Wikis

A *wiki* is a server program that allows users to collaborate to create the content of a website. The term *wiki* is a Hawaiian word that means *fast*. The most famous wiki is *Wikipedia*, which is a free online encyclopedia. Wikipedia has more than 2.5 million articles in English and hundreds of thousands of articles in more than twenty other languages, as shown in Figure 4.30.

FIGURE 4.30

Wikipedia home page.

Wikis are designed to make it easy to correct mistakes, not prevent them. Recent changes are typically displayed prominently. Many wikis provide a log of changes—called a *revision history*—and a *diff* feature that highlights the changes made in an article to make it easier for users to spot changes that are not correct.

If a more recent viewer disagrees with a change, he or she can view the revision history and choose to reset it to an earlier version. If a person is willing to maintain a page, they can receive notifications whenever the page is changed. Sites like Wikipedia use automated programs— *bots*—that automatically identify and undo vandalism. To reduce vandalism, some sites require users to register and then enforce a waiting period before granting editing privileges. Wikis are used to share information about a variety of topics such as travel destinations, law, and shopping.

Wikipedia is a collection of articles that do not have a single author but consist of information that can be edited or changed by anyone. In Wikipedia, readers can become editors by clicking the *edit this page* tab. The underlying code of the page displays, as shown in Figure 4.31.

FIGURE 4.31

Wikipedia editing screen.

Citing a Wikipedia article in a research paper is not acceptable in most situations, because the article that a person might retrieve at a later date based on the reference might not be the same as when it was cited. Wikipedia requires that authors of articles provide citations for any facts or references to other sources. If an article lacks citations for its facts, it can be tagged to indicate that lack and ultimately removed if the appropriate citations are not added within a certain time period. The citations at the bottom of a Wikipedia article can provide a good starting place for finding sources that are acceptable references, as shown in Figure 4.32.

FIGURE 4.32

Wikipedia citations.

Many libraries contain academic journals, databases, and books that are not available to the general public in electronic format or on the Internet. The content of these libraries can be searched online by authorized users. Some journals are available in electronic format and others may be reserved for use in person.

to enter the editing mode of a Wikipedia article

1 **Start a Web browser. In the Address box, near the top of the Web browser screen, type** `wikipedia.org` **and then press** `↵Enter`. The Wikipedia page displays.

2 **Under the Wikipedia title, click the link to the English version.**

3 **At the left of the window, in the** *search* **box, type** `Scio Township` **and then press** `↵Enter`. A page displays with information, including a map, about this small township in Michigan, as shown in Figure 4.33.

FIGURE 4.33

4 **Scroll down to the History section and read the first paragraph.** According to this site, the history of the name is not known, but possible explanations are provided.

5 **Scroll back up to the top of the page. At the top of the page, click the** *edit this page* **tab.** An editing pane that has its own scroll bar displays the content of the posting.

6 **Use the scroll bar in the editing pane to scroll down to the history section.** If someone wanted to add another explanation for the unusual name, they could edit this paragraph. Do not make changes—just observe.

7 **Use the window scroll bar to scroll downward to display the options below the editing pane. Adjust the two scroll bars to display the history section in the editing pane and the option buttons below the editing pane.** Notice the buttons that provide an option to preview or save the changes, as shown in Figure 4.34.

Editable
text

Save or
preview

FIGURE 4.34

Editing a Wikipedi posting.

8 Use the skills you practiced previously to start the Snipping Tool and create a
Window Snip of the window that displays the editing pane and option buttons
shown in Figure 4.34. Save a copy of this window to the folder where you store
your files. Name the file U3Ch04WikiStudentName substituting your name as
indicated.

9 In the browser window, point to the Close button [X] in the upper right
corner, and then click the left mouse button. The browser window closes.

Choosing Appropriate Communication Technologies

To choose the appropriate communication technology, attempt to match the characteristics of
the medium to your needs. Begin by evaluating your choices by considering the following
questions.

- What do you want to accomplish?

- Is the communication one-way or two-way?

- Do the parties need to interact at the same time (synchronously) or not (asynchronously)?

- What mode of communication do the parties use most?

- Is group membership open or closed?

- How fast is the slowest Internet connection in the group?

When you have considered these questions, apply what you know about e-mail, other
forms of asynchronous and synchronous communications, and social networking tools, and
then choose the method or combination of methods that have those characteristics.

▶▶▶ *lesson*
five | Security, Privacy, and Ethics

A small percentage of people behave unethically and attempt to take advantage of others, waste their time, or do harm. A problem that accompanies living online is that you will come into contact with some of these people, and you must know how to protect yourself. In this lesson, you study their methods and how to counteract them so that you can use the Internet as safely, privately, and securely as possible.

Malware

Software programs that are designed with malicious intent are called ***malware***. They fall into several categories.

Computer Viruses

Like a biological virus, a computer ***virus*** is a program that is capable of tricking its host into using its resources to make copies of itself and distribute them to other hosts without their consent. Similarly, if a computer's security has been compromised by malware, it is ***infected***. Computer virus programs can be hidden within other programs or attached to files or e-mail messages that are exchanged between computers. A virus can also contain additional code that is intended to operate on the host computer—called a ***payload***. The virus uses computer resources to duplicate and distribute itself, which can slow down the computer and the network. The payload can perform any function, from simply placing a notice on the computer screen to deleting key files.

Worms

A ***worm*** is a program that can duplicate itself and spreads by sending copies of itself to other computers on a network. It does not need to attach itself to another program, file, or e-mail message. Unlike a virus, the target of a worm is the network itself rather than individual computers. A worm can contain a malicious payload, or it can simply overload the network with traffic as the number of worm programs multiply and use network resources to transfer copies between nodes.

Some worms generate e-mail messages with the worm program attached. They locate your e-mail contact list and then send messages to all the people on your list. To disguise the origin of the message, they replace your name in the From: part of the message with other names from your contact list. This practice is called ***spoofing*** and it makes it difficult to locate the infected computer. If a recipient receives an infected e-mail message and then uses the Reply feature to warn the person who sent the file that their computer is infected, the reply goes to the wrong person. The term spoofing is also used to describe Web pages that hide their true purpose.

Trojan Horse

A *Trojan* is a program that spreads by tricking users into granting permission to install it by pretending to be something else. For example, you might see a notice for a free screen saver that you download and then agree to install. The screen saver might work as described, but there could be another program hidden within it that you do not know about.

Rootkit

A *rootkit* is a program that gives an outsider access to the computer's operating system at the administrator level. The program makes changes to the operating system to hide its activities from normal operating system security measures so that the intruder can take control of the computer as an administrator without the real system administrator's knowledge. The rootkit may include a program called a *backdoor* that allows the intruder to bypass normal system security to communicate with the system and take control.

Denial of Service

If malware succeeds in getting past your computer's defenses, it can install programs that give outsiders control. Instead of attacking your computer, your computer can be used to mount attacks on servers by flooding them with service requests from thousands of controlled computers at the same time. The server becomes overloaded and cannot provide timely service to its normal users. This is called a *denial of service (DoS)* attack.

Spyware

Programs that are designed to monitor a user's behavior and then report it without the user's consent is called *spyware*. Spyware can go beyond monitoring and redirect browsers to Web pages or divert click-through advertising revenue to different sites.

Crimeware

A type of program that is designed to steal information about a user for the purpose of impersonating them and stealing money from financial institutions is called *crimeware*. Legitimate programs can be used as crimeware. For example, a program that records every keystroke—a *keylogger*—can be used as crimeware to capture the keystrokes used to enter a password, social security number, or an answer to a challenge question. Crimeware can redirect a browser to a fake website when the user types in the bank's Web address or steal passwords that are stored on a user's computer. Sending out messages to many people on the chance that a few of them will respond or by misrepresenting a Web page as a trustworthy site so that something of value can be stolen is called *phishing*.

To understand the difference that the Internet makes to criminals, think about a petty criminal who walks through a neighborhood looking for houses where no one is home, and then walks up to each of those houses and tries the door to see if it is unlocked. Because it takes time and effort to identify and check each house, the success rate must be frequent enough to justify the effort. Because the effort and cost required to send e-mail messages over the Internet to millions of people is so little, even extremely low success rates can be profitable.

Fraud and Hoaxes

Some malicious or criminal activities do not involve sophisticated computer programs. Instead, they use lies. A lie that is intended to convince its audience that something is real when it is not is a *hoax*. A malicious hoax might involve a warning about a nonexistent virus that infects computers with a particular file. The user is instructed how to find this file in the system's hidden operating files and delete it. The file is actually a necessary part of the operating system, and the computer fails to start the next time it is turned on.

A hoax that is intended to trick someone out of their money is *fraud*. According to the FBI's 2007 Internet Crime Report, the total dollar loss from Internet fraud that year was $239 million. The median dollar loss per complaint was $680. The most common categories of fraud are auction and nondelivery, as shown in Figure 4.35.

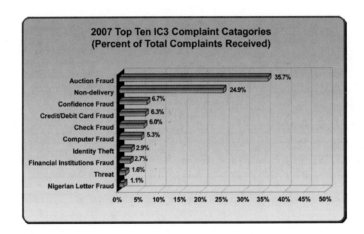

FIGURE 4.35
2007 Internet Crime Report.

Directory Harvest Attacks

Lists of valid e-mail addresses are valuable because they can be sold to companies who want to send unsolicited advertising to valid e-mail addresses. A ***directory harvest attack (DHA)*** attempts to determine what e-mail addresses at a domain are valid. It utilizes a long list of possible user names and sends e-mail messages to everyone by that name at a particular domain. A DHA program could send e-mail messages to all the likely combinations of last names and first names along with the domain name, such as ajohnson@basicstudies.com, bjohnson@basicstudies.com, cjohnson@basicstudies.com, and so on. The mail server would send back a notice that it could not deliver messages for each address that does not exist. The program would assume the others must exist and create a mailing list of existing addresses for that domain name. A variation on this method is to simply send the unsolicited e-mail to all likely user names at a domain and rely on a certain percentage of them being delivered.

Instant messaging systems are also subject to DHA if they keep a directory of users. Unwanted messages sent to instant messaging users are called ***SPIM*** to indicate that they are similar to e-mail spam.

Defenses Against Malware, Hoaxes, and Other Attacks

A good defense has several layers that work together. They include awareness by end users, well-informed system administrators, and computer programs that block malicious programs at network and individual user levels.

What System Administrators Can Do

The computer system administrator must provide an environment that is accessible enough to allow users to do their jobs but restricted enough to protect those users from malicious intruders or unwanted distractions. This is an ongoing battle, and the administrator needs to have allies. The government provides assistance in the form of advice, warnings, and prosecution of cybercriminals. For example, administrators can go to the ***Computer Security Resource Center (CSRC)***—a government site for security information—at *csrc.nist.gov/itsec* for technical advice about installing and managing Windows operating systems, as shown in Figure 4.36.

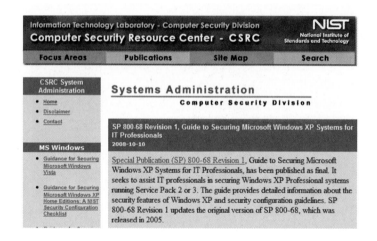

FIGURE 4.36
NIST home page.

Network administrators must be informed about legal issues, and they must be able to work together if a worm is spreading from network to network. An example of this type of collaboration is the ***Internet Storm Center (ISC)***—an emergency response site maintained by the SANS Institute—where administrators exchange information and coordinate during attacks on their systems, as shown in Figure 4.37.

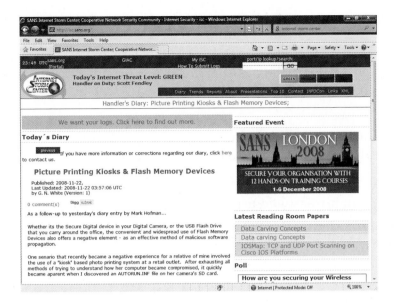

FIGURE 4.37

ISC home page.

Administrators have a variety of tools they can use to help provide a secure environment, including:

- firewall sofware and hardware to scan incoming and outgoing packets for known problems and for general categories of undesirable communications

- establishing user groups that have different levels of access to system resources or communications outside the network

- updating security software regularly on servers and individual computers

- checking computers on the network for unlicensed software

- backing up vital data files in a secure location

- monitoring network resource usage for unauthorized activity

- warning users of hoaxes and other security threats

- providing user training on security practices

- encrypting wireless network communications

- providing secure virtual private network (VPN) connections for workers outside the network

What Individuals Can Do

Individuals must be aware of the battle that is being fought to protect them and must cooperate with their network administrator. Awareness and the practice of basic security procedures will help greatly. They include:

- Protecting your passwords
  - Use passwords that are strong—a mix of uppercase and lowercase letters, numbers, and special characters that are not dates or common words.
  - Do not write them down near the computer or give them to someone else.
  - Do not use your personal information, like your birth date, in your password.
  - Change the password at least every three months.
  - Do not use the same password on all of your accounts.
- Backing up important files regularly
- Protecting your personal information
  - Do not respond using a link in a message that warns of a problem.
  - Do not provide financial information unless the connection is secure. Look for the lock symbol in the browser and *https* in the website address.
  - Read website privacy policies.
  - Look for the *eTrust* logo on sites that subscribe to this privacy certification service.
- Confirming the identity of the site and researching its reputation before doing business
  - If they provide a contact number, call it to confirm that it works.
  - Use a search engine to search for the name of the site or its sponsor to see if there are negative comments.
- Avoiding illegal activity
  - Do not download or install unlicensed software.
  - Do not download, view, or play copyrighted text, audio, or video files. Dealing with criminals exposes you to other criminal activity.
- Being skeptical of hoaxes
  - Double check any message that claims to be a warning that asks you for your password or login information. Your service provider should never ask you for your password.
- Not using the company network for unauthorized Web browsing, especially adult entertainment sites

If you do not have a network administrator, you have to take on some of those responsibilities yourself that include:

- Using security software
  - Install antivirus software and turn on the automatic update feature.
  - Set the antivirus software to scan at regular intervals when the computer might be turned on but unused, such as during meal breaks.
  - Use antivirus software to scan e-mail attachments.

- Install or activate antispyware software.

- Install or activate firewall software so that you can identify trusted sites or block unwanted traffic from particular sites.

- Updating operating system software automatically—when a vulnerability is discovered, the operating system provider distributes a *patch*, a program that automatically modifies the operating system program to repair the flaw

- Stopping use of your computer for financial purposes if you suspect that your computer security is compromised

  - Use security software to scan the computer to look for malware. If that does not work, seek professional help from a computer service company.

If you think you might have shared information that could be used to impersonate you, go to the Federal Trade Commission site for advice.

to deal with identity theft

1   **Start a Web browser. In the Address box, near the top of the Web browser screen, type** `http://www.ftc.gov/bcp/edu/microsites/idtheft/` **and then press** **Enter**. The Fighting Back Against Identity Theft page displays.

2   **To the right of *Learn more about identity theft*, click the More button.** A list of links to sections on the *About Identity Theft* page displays.

3   **Under *About Identity Theft*, click *How can you find out if your identity was stolen?* This section contains a link labeled *Detect Identity Theft*, as shown in Figure 4.38.**

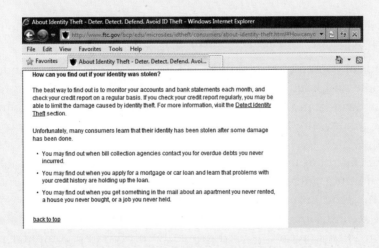

FIGURE 4.38
FTC page.

4 At the end of the first paragraph, click the *Detect Identity Theft* link. Another page of tips on detecting identity theft displays.

5 Use the skills you practiced previously to start the Snipping Tool and create a Window Snip of the window that displays the links on the Detect Identity Theft page. Save a copy of this window to the folder where you store your files. Name the file U3Ch04IDStudentName substituting your name as indicated.

6 In the browser window, point to the Close button in the upper right corner, and then click the left mouse button. The browser window closes.

Behaving Appropriately

You behave differently in a group of strangers than you do with your friends or at work. The rules that describe appropriate behavior in social groups are called *etiquette*. Similarly, the rules that describe appropriate behavior on the Internet are called **netiquette**. General rules for online communications and group participation are:

- Avoid hostile comments or insults—called *flames*—that lead to hostile exchanges called *flame wars*.
- Do not use all capital letters; this practice is similar to shouting at someone.
- Do not assume online exchanges are private; servers keep copies of messages.
- Limit use of copying and forwarding messages and reply-to-all features.
- Do not bully or intimidate people in discussions.
- Do not use communication tools for unethical or illegal behavior such as cheating or fraud.
- Refer to the guidelines for each group to determine the specific expectations and rules governing participation, and abide by them.

Many methods of communicating online can be done annonymously under an assumed name. Many people find it enjoyable to join a discussion where no one can form a preconcieved idea about them from their age, sex, race, or physical appearance. Some people take advantage of this annonymity to behave badly because they do not fear the consequences of their actions.

To have some control of member behavior, some groups require a verifiable identity as a condition for joining and participating. The identity requirements and verification methods vary. In some groups, it is sufficient to provide a working e-mail address. However, e-mail accounts are given out freely at many sites to anyone who takes the time to fill out a form, so this method is used primarily to prevent a computer program from joining a group and adding many false members. If a person must pay to be a member, the group needs a real identity for billing purposes. Members can choose user names, but their real identity is on file with the service. Similarly, texting requires a cell phone number that is associated with a billing name and address. Wikipedia will allow anyone to submit a modification to an article without identifying themselves. Some groups are restricted to people who are known to at least one current member, who must send a code or e-mail that the person can use to join.

When you register with a group, check the terms of service. If you falsify the information on the registration form and such an act violates the terms of service, then you are technically guilty of unauthorized access, which is a felony under the Computer Fraud and Abuse Act of 1986. This law was cited in the prosecution of a woman in 2008 who posed as a teenage boy on MySpace and whose online arguments with a girl allegedly contributed to the girl's suicide.

SUMMARY

In this chapter, you learned about synchronous and asynchronous methods of communication online and how they are used. You also studied how to protect yourself and your computer from malicious attacks.

You can extend your learning by reviewing concepts and terms, and by practicing variations of skills presented in the lessons.

KEY TERMS

address book

archiving

asynchronous

backdoor

blind carbon copy (Bcc)

blog

blogosphere

body

bots

buffer

CAPTCHA

carbon copy (Cc)

chat

Children's Online
Privacy Protection Act
(COPPA)

codec

compression

Computer Security
Resource Center (CRSC)

control channel

crimeware

cybercafé

denial of service (DOS)

diff

directory harvest att
(DHA)

distance educatio

e-learning

electronic mail
(e-list)

emoticons

eTrust

extensil
langua

exter
(ES

fe

fraud

friend-to-friend (F2F)

header area

ad

d

instant messaging (IM)

internal social network
(N)

internet forum

Internet message access
protocol (IMAP)

Internet Storm Center
(ISC)

keylogger

libel

linklog

lossless

lossy

malware

message board

moblog	reflector	synchronous
moderator	reply	texting
multimedia messaging service (MMS)	reply to all	thread
	resolution	Trojan
namespace	revision history	tumbleblog
netiquette	rootkit	uninterruptible power supply (UPS)
on demand	short message service (SMS)	
open source		virus
opening post (OP)	simple mail transfer protocol (SMTP)	vlog
patch		Voice-over-the-Internet Protocol (VoIP)
payload	sketchlog	
personal digital assistant (PDA)	social network	webcam
	source code	weblog
photoblog	spam	wiki
podcast	spim	Wikipedia
post office protocol (POP)	spoofing	wireless application protocol (WAP)
qlog	spyware	
really simple syndication (RSS)	subscriber	worm

CHECKING CONCEPTS AND TERMS

MULTIPLE CHOICE

Circle the letter of the correct answer for each of the following.

1. The difference between POP mail protocol and IMAP mail protocol is that _____. [L1]

   a. POP is used to send mail and IMAP is used to download mail from the server

   b. IMAP can leave the mail on the server, whereas POP downloads it

   c. IMAP is used to send mail and POP is used to retrieve it

   d. they are both used to send mail, but IMAP is newer

2. What percentage of e-mail messages are unsolicited bulk mailings that are also known as *spam*? [L1]

   a. less than 10%

   b. between 10 and 40%

   c. between 40% and 70%

   d. more than 70%

3. What is a lossy codec? [L2]

   a. a compression and decompression process that loses some of the original content

b. a compression and decompression process that can reproduce the original content without loss

c. a very bad codec

d. a disposable camera

4. When watching a streaming video, what is the role of the buffer? [L2]

a. to clean up distortions or transmission errors so the result looks more polished

b. to decompress the signal

c. to store the incoming data so it can be displayed at a constant rate in spite of inconsistent or slow transmission

d. to play the audio portion of the content

5. Why are VoIP telephone services generally cheaper than traditionally wired telephone services? [L3]

a. The phone service is bundled with television service.

b. Wireless transmission systems do not have to pay for extensive wiring networks.

c. The combination of audio compression and packet transmission makes much more efficient use of communication links.

d. Few people use it, so the price is artificially low to attract customers.

6. Why are text messages restricted to 160 characters? [L3]

a. They are 20 bytes long.

b. They must avoid interfering with the control functions of the cell phone system on the control circuit.

c. They are 20 bits long.

d. The buffer on most cell phones can handle 1280 bits.

7. What is libel? [L4]

a. an untrue verbal statement that is intended to defame a living person

b. unauthorized use of a trademark

c. any untrue statement

d. a false and malicious publication printed for the purpose of defaming a living person

8. Software that may be redistributed without paying royalty or license fees and which makes its source code available is called _____. [L4]

a. copyrighted

b. patented

c. fair use

d. open source

9. The defining characteristic of a wiki is _____. [L4]

a. the ability of users to collaborate to create the content of a website

b. its speed

c. its Hawaiian origin

d. its acceptance as an authoritative source for research papers

10. How are infected computers used in a denial-of-service attack? [L5]

a. They all suddenly refuse to reply to e-mail or other requests.

b. They all ask the same server for service at the same time and overload it with requests so that it denies requests from legitimate users.

c. They send infected e-mail to the same server until one of them gets through, and then the payload destroys the server's ability to respond to service requests.

d. They destroy the infected computers at the same time on a given date.

MATCHING

Match each term in the second column with its correct definition in the first column by writing the letter of the term on the blank line in front of the definition.

_I_ 1. Spam directed at instant messaging systems

_C_ 2. Exchange of hostile or insulting messages

_A_ 3. Distorted word that is recognizable by humans

_E_ 4. Very active Web discussion

_J_ 5. Rules for connecting mobile devices to the Internet

_B_ 6. Software or device that compresses and decompresses files

_D_ 7. Method of delivering content to subscribers that uses XML

_H_ 8. Program that gives outsiders access to a computer and administrator rights

_G_ 9. E-mail address to which a message is sent that will be distributed to the e-list

_F_ 10. Program that duplicates itself on a network

A. CAPTCHA

B. Codec

C. Flame war

D. RSS

E. Hot thread

F. Worm

G. Reflector

H. Rootkit

I. SPIM

J. WAP

SKILL DRILL

Skill Drill exercises reinforce chapter skills. Each skill reinforced is the same, or nearly the same, as a skill presented in the chapter. Detailed instructions are provided in a step-by-step format.

Each exercise is independent of the others, so you can do the exercises in any order.

1. Searching Message Boards

The major search engines have options for searching message boards.

To find a message board on a topic that interests you, follow these steps:

1. Start a Web browser.

2. In the **Address** box, type `groups.google.com` and then press `↵Enter`.

3. In the **Search for a group** box, type `travel` and then press `↵Enter`. A list of current threads displays.

4. Choose a thread from the list and click its link.

5. Scroll down to display the thread. Choose one that includes postings from several individuals.

6. Click the **Start** button, click **All Programs,** click the **Accessories** folder, and then in the list of programs, click the **Snipping Tool.**

7. In the **Snipping Tool** dialog box, click the **New Snip** button arrow, and then click **Window Snip.** Point anywhere in the **message board** window, and then click one time.

8. Near the top of the **Snipping Tool** dialog box, click the **Save Snip** button. In the **Save As** dialog box, navigate to the folder where you store your files. In the **File name** box, substituting your name as indicated, type `U3Ch04TravelStudentName` and then click **Save.**

9. In the upper right corner of each open dialog box or window, click the **Close** button.

10. Submit your snip as directed by your instructor.

2. Searching for Blog Postings

Search engines like Google can help you find a blog on a topic.

To use Google to find a blog, follow these steps:

1. Start a Web browser.

2. In the **Address** box, type `google.com` and then press ⏎Enter.

3. Along the toolbar, near the top of the screen, click the **More** arrow. On the menu, click **Blogs.**

4. Near the top of the page, in the box, type `computer security` and then click the **Search Blogs** button.

5. Examine two or three blogs, and then return to the one you find most interesting.

6. Use the skills you practiced previously to start the **Snipping Tool** program and do a Window Snip of the window. **Save** a copy of this Web page to the folder where you store your files. Name the file `U3Ch04SecurityStudentName` substituting your name as indicated.

7. In the upper right corner of each open dialog box or window, click the **Close** button.

8. Submit your snip as directed by your instructor.

3. Contact your Representative

You can communicate asynchronously with your elected representatives. Some of them have public e-mail addresses, and others use online forms that automatically tabulate and summarize the contacts. Many have websites that stream video or audio messages.

To locate the contact information for your elected officials, follow these steps:

1. Start a Web browser.

2. In the **Address** box, type `http://www.usa.gov/Contact/Elected.shtml` and then press ⏎Enter. The Contact Elected Officials page displays with links to directories for federal and state elected officials.

3. On the Contact Elected Officials page, click the **U.S. Senators** link.

4. Scroll down the list of senators and click one of the names.

5. Scroll down the page to find an example of an asynchronous communications technology.

6. Click the **Start** button, click **All Programs,** click the **Accessories** folder, and then in the list of programs, click **Snipping Tool.**

7. Use the skills you practiced previously to start the Snipping Tool program and do a Window Snip of the window. Save a copy of this Web page to the folder where you store your files. Name the file U3Ch04SenatorStudentName

8. In the upper right corner of each open dialog box or window, click the **Close** button.

9. Submit your snip as directed by your instructor.

EXPLORE AND SHARE

Explore and Share questions are intended for discussion in class or online. Look for information that is related to the learning outcomes for this chapter as directed. Submit your answers as directed by your instructor.

1. The popularity of Facebook and MySpace has grown greatly. To compare the popularity of the two, use a browser to go to **Alexa.com.** This is a site that analyzes the use of popular websites. You can compare three domain names to see how many Internet users visit each site. Under the title Website Traffic Comparisons, in the first box, type **facebook.com** and in the second box, type **myspace.com** and in the third box, type **hi5.com.** Above the existing chart, confirm that the **Reach** and **3m** tabs are chosen. Click the **Compare Sites** button. Use the **Snipping Tool** to copy the window and save it as U3Ch04AlexaStudentName If other factors were about the same, would the relative popularity of the site influence your choice of which one to use? Explain your decision. Prepare to share what you learned about Alexa and the three social networking sites. Submit your answer and the file as directed by your instructor. [L4]

2. *Truste* is an organization that verifies that member sites respect the privacy of their users. Learn more about this site and who its sponsors are. Start a Web browser. Go to **truste.com.** Near the top of the page, click the **For Consumers** tab. Explore the content of this page and follow some of the links. Use the browser's **Back** button to return to this page, if necessary. Under **Privacy** Resources, click **Online Privacy-A Tutorial for Parents and Teachers** to display this brochure in PDF format. Alternatively, go to http://www.truste.org/pdf/parent_teacher_tutorial.pdf. In your browser, reduce the zoom magnification to **100%.** Scroll to the table of contents page. Use the **Snipping Tool** to copy the window and save it as U3Ch04TrusteStudentName Prepare to share what you learned about this site. Submit your answer and the file as directed by your instructor. [L5]

3. Many colleges offer individual classes and entire degree programs online. Begin your exploration of this topic by using a browser to go to elearners.com/online-degrees/index.asp In the **Search Online College Degrees** box, type information systems Confirm that the **Online Degree Programs** option button is selected, and then click the **Go** button. Review the list of online degrees available. Next, go to your school's website or to a college in which you are interested. Search their site for online degrees and courses. Choose a screen that displays online course

offerings at any one of the colleges you explored. Use the **Snipping Tool** to copy a window that shows the online courses or degrees, and then save it as U3Ch04DegreeStudentName Prepare to share what you learned about online courses and degrees. Submit your answer and the file as directed by your instructor. [L4]

4. Music is available to download or as streaming audio. The combination of music and computer analysis is used in the **Music Genome Project.** Begin your exploration by starting a browser and going to **Wikipedia.org.** Choose the English version, and then search for the **Music Genome Project.** Read the first few paragraphs about this approach to analyzing music. Next, use the browser to go to **Pandora.com.** Create your own "radio station" and let the program suggest similar music using the Music Genome Project method. You might have to register to continue using the site beyond a few songs, and the site might not be available outside the U.S. Use the **Snipping Tool** to copy a window that shows the songs you select, and then save it as U3Ch04MusicStudentName Prepare to share what you learned about this site and its method of suggesting music options. Submit your answer and the file as directed by your instructor. [L2]

IN YOUR LIFE

In Your Life questions are intended for discussion in class or online where you can share your personal experience. Restrict your answers to the topics described in each exercise. Submit your answers as directed by your instructor.

1. If you are working in a lab or on someone else's computer and you forget to bring any portable memory device, you can still get your file back home by sending an e-mail message to yourself from that computer if you have an Internet-based e-mail program. Most colleges or schools provide an e-mail account that can be accessed from the Internet. If you do not have an e-mail account that you can reach using a browser, start a browser and go to Google mail at **mail.google.com** and create a free account. Once you have an account, compose a new message and use your own e-mail address in the To: box. Attach your file using the Attach button and send the message. Move to another computer at home or in the lab and log into the mail program. Open the message and click the attachment. Use the dialog box to save the file on the second computer. Describe what you learned from this exercise. Is there another method you would use instead of this one if you had to move a file between computers but did not have portable media available? [L1]

2. People often forget to write their names on e-mail messages, and it might not be apparent from their user name who they are. You can add your name automatically, plus your favorite closing or saying to each e-mail message you compose, using the **Signature** feature that is available on most e-mail programs. For example, in Google's Gmail program, you click the Settings link at the top of the window. Under the **General** tab, click the **Signature** option, and then in the adjacent box, type whatever you want to appear at the bottom of the body of each e-mail message. Describe which e-mail program you use and the steps necessary to add an automatic signature line to each new e-mail message. [L1]

3. Many people use the Internet to meet others for romantic purposes. Learn more about one of these sites, focusing on the asynchronous and synchronous technologies they use to help strangers communicate. You can begin by starting a browser and going to **datehookup.com**, which is a free site. At the bottom of the screen, click the **Help** link. Explore several of the links on the Help page to get tips on how to communicate effectively online. These tips apply to many other situations besides dating. Return to the home page. At the bottom, click the **Terms** link and review the rules for participating in this group. New users can do a few searches before they are required to register. Explore this site, and then describe what you learned about communicating in this type of online community. [L4]

RELATED SKILLS

Related Skills exercises expand on or are related to skills presented in the lessons. The exercise provides a brief narrative introduction, followed by instructions in a numbered-step format that are not as detailed as those in the Skill Drill section.

1. Compress a JPEG Picture in Word 2007

One of the most common picture formats is JPEG, which is a format that allows lossy file compression. Most digital cameras save files in this format, and individual pictures can be several megabytes in size. The detail in these multi-megabyte pictures is more than most computer monitors and many printers can display, so it is a waste of storage space and transmission capacity to use them in Web pages and low-quality flyers. Compression of JPEG pictures is built into several programs that manage or use pictures, including Microsoft Office 2003 and 2007. A new feature of Office 2007 is that it uses a lossless compression on all of its files called ZIP, but you can compress the pictures even further using the lossy JPEG compression method. The following instructions are written for Word 2007, with tips for compressing pictures in Office 2003.

To compress pictures in a Word 2007 document to reduce file size, follow these steps:

1. Start Microsoft Word 2007. If a blank document does not open by default, in the upper left corner, click the round **Office** button, and then click **New.**

2. In the first line of the document, type **your name,** and then press ⏎Enter. On the **Insert** tab, in the **Illustrations** group, click **Picture.**

3. Navigate to the folder where the student files for this chapter are stored and locate **U3Ch04Magnolia.** In the **Insert Picture** dialog box, on the toolbar, click the **Views** button arrow, and then click **Details.** Notice that the size of this picture is 941 KB.

4. Click **U3Ch04Magnolia,** and then click the **Insert** button. The picture is placed in the document. Alternatively, insert a digital picture of your choice that has the file extension *jpg* or *jpeg* and is more than 1 megabyte in size.

5. At the bottom of the window, on the right side, drag the zoom slider to its highest magnification. Scroll to different parts of the picture and notice the detail that is visible at this magnification. Drag the zoom back to **100%.**

6. Click the **Office** button, and then click **Save as.** Navigate to the folder where you save files for this chapter. Save the document as U3Ch04Pic1StudentName Click the **Office** button, and then click **Close.**

7. In Word 2007, at the upper left of the window, click the **Office Home** button. On the menu, click **Open.** Navigate to the folder where you stored the file, if necessary. In the **Open** dialog box, on the toolbar, click the **Views** button arrow, if necessary, to display the details of the file size. Notice that the file size is reduced to 224 KB by the Office 2007 compression method. Using Word 2003, the file is slightly larger than the picture file by itself.

8. Click the file name, and then click the **Open** button. Drag the zoom to its maximum and examine the details of the picture. No detail has been lost, which is an example of a lossless compression method—the original is restored completely.

9. Click the picture to select it. On the **Picture Tools Format** tab, in the **Adjust** group, click **Compress Pictures.** In Word 2003, right-click the picture, and then on the shortcut menu, click **Compress.**

10. In the **Compress Picture** dialog box, click the **Options** button. In the **Compression Settings** dialog box, in the **Target Output** area, click the **E-mail** option. Click **OK** twice to close both dialog boxes.

11. Drag the zoom setting to its maximum, and scroll across the picture to examine the amount of detail that is lost at high magnification. Drag the zoom back to **100%.** Notice that the quality of the image on the screen is acceptable for many purposes.

12. Save the file as U3Ch04Pic2StudentName and then close it.

13. Click the **Office Home** button. On the menu, click **Open.** Navigate to the folder where you stored the file, if necessary. Compare the sizes of the two files you have just saved. Recall that the original picture file was 941 KB.

14. **Close** all open windows without saving any changes. Submit the files as directed by your instructor.

2. Archive Old E-Mail in Outlook 2007

If you allow old e-mail messages to accumulate in the inbox, it can slow down your search for messages. You can move old files out of the active folders using the Archive feature.

To begin the process of archiving old messages using Outlook 2007, follow these steps:

1. Start Microsoft Outlook 2007 or another e-mail client. If it is the first time the program has been used, you will have to go through some initial steps to set it up.

2. On the menu bar, click **File,** and then on the menu, click **Archive.**

3. In the **Archive** dialog box, confirm that the **Inbox** folder is selected. On the **Archive items older than** box, click the arrow. On the calendar, choose a date that is three months prior to the current date.

4. Use the **Snipping Tool** to copy the **Archive** dialog box and save the file as U3Ch04ArchiveStudentName

5. Click the **Cancel** button. Do not complete the archive process. Submit the file as directed by your instructor.

DISCOVER

Discover exercises give students general directions for exploring and discovering more advanced skills and information. Each exercise is independent of the others, so you may complete the exercises in any order.

1. Try Open Office

One of the major online collaborative projects is *open software*. Begin your discovery of the genre by using a browser to go to **OpenOffice.org.** On the OpenOffice.org home page, click the **I want to participate in OpenOffice.org.** Explore the links on this page to appreciate the many ways in which volunteers contribute to this project. Return to the home page, click **I want to learn more about OpenOffice,** and read some of the articles. If you have a fast Internet connection, return to the home page, click **I want to download OpenOffice.org,** and follow the directions to download the program file, which is about 146 MB. If you do not have a fast connection, go to a computer that does and download the file, and then save it to portable memory on a flash drive or burn it to a CD. After you download the file, use Windows Explorer to locate the file and double-click it to run the installation program. Experiment with the Writer and Spreadsheet programs. You will find that the interface is very similar to that of Microsoft Office 2003. See if you can find a feature of Microsoft Office that you like that is not available. Use OpenOffice Help to assist your search for those features. Use OpenOffice Writer to record a description of what you learned about OpenOffice. Save the file as U3Ch04OpenStudentName and choose the .doc file format that is compatible with Microsoft Word. Submit the file in the format designated by your instructor.

2. Learn to Edit a Wikipedia Article Using the Sandbox

Making a change to an encyclopedia that is viewed worldwide is a daunting task for many people. To learn how to edit or create articles using Wiki tools, you can use the **sandbox** which, as the name implies, allows you to play around with the tools. Open a browser and go to **en.wikipedia.org** to open the English-language version. In the **Search** box, type wiki sandbox and then press ⏎Enter. On the **Wikipedia: Sandbox** page, explore the tutorials and options for editing a Wikipedia article that will not be saved permanently. Use the tools to place your name at the bottom of one of the sandbox articles. Use the **Snipping Tool** to capture the screen that shows your name in the article, and save it as U3Ch04SandboxStudentName Edit the article again to delete your name. Submit the file as directed by your instructor.

ASSESS YOUR PROGRESS

At this point, you should have a set of skills and concepts that are valuable to an employer and to you. You may not realize how much you've learned unless you take a few minutes to assess your progress.

1. From the student files, open U3Ch04Assess. Save it as U3Ch04AssessStudentName

2. Read each question in column A.

3. In column B, answer Yes or No.

4. If you identify a skill or design concept that you don't know, refer to the learning objective code next to the question and the table at the beginning of the chapter to find the skill and review it.

5. Print the worksheet if your instructor requires it. The file name is already in the header, so it will display your name as part of the file name.

6. All of these skills and concepts have been identified as important by surveying hundreds of individuals working at over 200 companies worldwide. If you cannot answer all of the questions affirmatively even after reviewing the relevant lesson, seek additional help from your instructor.

chapter **five**

Working Online

Lesson	Learning Outcomes	Code	Related IC3 Objectives
1	Identify the services provided by a network mail server	5.1	2.2.9
1	Identify options for filtering junk e-mail	5.2	2.3.6
1	Identify options for creating a signature block	5.3	2.2.9
1	Identify methods of applying rules in Outlook to presort e-mail	5.4	2.2.7
1	Identify methods of creating an out-of-office notice	5.5	2.2.9
1	Identify methods of categorizing and searching e-mail messages	5.6	2.2.7
1	Identify methods of using references instead of attachments	5.7	2.2.5
1	Identify methods of deleting and archiving e-mail	5.8	2.2.7
1	Create a professional e-mail	5.9	2.3.7
1	Identify use of e-mail to document telephone conversations	5.10	2.3.1
1	Identify procedures to make effective use of e-mail	5.11	2.3.7
2	Identify uses of e-mail for direct marketing	5.12	2.3.3
2	Identify business uses of message boards and weblogs	5.13	2.3.1
2	Identify applications of video streaming and video on demand	5.14	2.3.1
2	Identify uses of RSS and texting in business	5.15	2.3.1
2	Identify examples of online social networking in business	5.16	2.3.1
3	Identify business uses of VoIP and audio conferencing	5.17	2.3.1
3	Identify methods of integrating voice and data communications	5.18	2.1.1
3	Identify special requirements of audio and video conferencing	5.19	2.1.2
3	Identify uses of IM and Chat for business purposes	5.20	2.1.3
4	Identify advantages and disadvantages of virtual teams	5.21	4.1.1
4	Identify advantages and disadvantages of telework	5.22	4.1.3
4	Identify advantages and disadvantages of outsourcing	5.23	4.1.1
4	Identify advantages and disadvantages of insourcing	5.24	4.1.1
5	Identify the risks to data	5.25	4.2.3
5	Identify the reasons for monitoring employee communications	5.26	4.2.6
5	Identify methods of finding rules and policies	5.27	4.2.9
5	Identify computer-related safety practices	5.28	4.2.1
5	Identify healthy practices related to computers	5.29	4.2.2

?Why Would I Do This?

The Internet has revolutionized the way people communicate with each other to do their jobs and earn a living. In this chapter, you learn skills and information pertaining to living online that you can use in the work environment.

visual summary | In these lessons, you will study how the communications technologies that you studied in Chapter 4 are used at work and how they can be used to change the way you work.

FIGURE 5.1

List of Student and Solution Files

In most cases, you will create files using text or pictures found on Web pages. You will add your name to the file names and save them on your computer or portable memory device. Table 5.1 lists the files you start with and the names you give them when you save the files.

ASSIGNMENT	STUDENT SOURCE FILE:	SAVE AS:
Lessons 1–5	none	U3Ch05OutlookStudentName
		U3Ch05SPAMStudentName
		U3Ch05VideoStudentName
		U3Ch05TeleworkStudentName
		U3Ch05OutsourcingStudentName
		U3Ch05PolicyStudentName
		U3Ch05ErgonomicsStudentName
Skill Drill	none	U3Ch05VotingStudentName
		U3Ch05ChainStudentName
		U3Ch05ElistStudentName
Explore and Share	none	U3Ch05CalendarStudentName
		U3Ch05DocsStudentName
		U3Ch05SchoolStudentName
In Your Life	none	none
Related Skills	none	U3Ch05RuleStudentName
		U3Ch05MeetingStudentName
Discover	none	U3Ch05ArchiveStudentName
		U3Ch05RecoverStudentName
Assess Your Progress	U3Ch05Assess	U3Ch05AssessStudentName

TABLE 5.1

▶▶▶ lesson
one | Using Electronic Mail at Work

Electronic mail is being replaced by texting and instant messaging for personal communications outside of the workplace, but it is still a very important method of communication at work. Compared to paper-based communications, electronic mail is faster and cheaper. It is more flexible because it can be accessed by portable devices, including cell phones, and it can be forwarded, duplicated, and distributed to lists of addresses easily. Electronic mail can be used to share documents and media files. It also creates a record of communication to track the history of a communication.

E-Mail Servers

A workplace has much more control over e-mail than an individual does. This is because all of the employees have the same mail client and server that operate behind a firewall, separate from the rest of the Internet.

If all of the employees have the same e-mail client and use the same e-mail server, more features are available. For example, if you send someone an e-mail message, the server can let you know if the other person retrieved or read the message, even if they do not reply. There is usually a suite of related software where the e-mail, meeting management, and calendar programs interact. You can send out an e-mail message to several people in a work group in which you announce a meeting. The mail client can distribute the notice to everyone in the group, and the meeting can automatically be placed on each person's personal calendar. The person who schedules meeting rooms can let everyone know where the meeting will take place, and then if someone does not come to the meeting, there is evidence that they were notified.

An example of commercial software that provides this type of service is Microsoft's Exchange Server, designed to work with Microsoft Outlook. Outlook is a program that has several functions such as e-mail, calendar, task list, and contact management, which are designed to work together. The server software from Microsoft that works with the Outlook client can manage voice messages and communications with workers who are in remote or mobile locations, as shown in Figure 5.2.

FIGURE 5.2
Exchange Server provides additional functions.

Another example of this type of software is IBM's Lotus Domino, which was originally named Lotus Notes. Lotus Notes was one of the first widely used messaging systems in business. It was purchased by International Business Machines (IBM). Its market share has declined from its once dominant position. A third example is Novell GroupWise, which runs on several operating systems, including Linux and Windows.

Managing Large Amounts of E-Mail

It is not uncommon for someone to receive more e-mail messages each day at work than they have time to read. Fortunately, there are tools that make this task manageable.

Filtering Junk E-Mail

Workers who are using e-mail within an organization have fewer problems with unsolicited advertising—spam—because the network administrator can use firewall software to block most of it. People who are working outside the protection of an organization's firewall have to rely on their own filtering software. Microsoft Outlook 2007 has several options for dealing with unsolicited and unwanted e-mail—*junk e-mail*—as shown in Figure 5.3

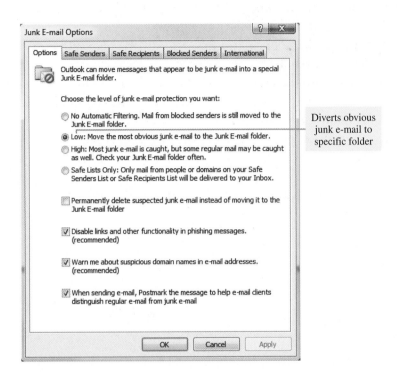

FIGURE 5.3
Options for managing junk e-mail in Outlook 2007.

Presorting E-Mail

Notice in Figure 5.3 that the program can divert messages that it classifies as junk e-mail into a special folder by that name. It recognizes junk e-mail by referring to a set of rules that identify characteristics typical of unsolicited advertising or messages that have been forwarded many times. You can define your own rules for presorting incoming mail and placing messages in folders that you choose. A folder can be added to the existing mail folders by right clicking a folder and choosing the New Folder option from the shortcut menu. Messages can be moved between folders using drag-and-drop.

For example, suppose that you send out an invitation for a coworker's retirement party to a list of dozens of people. You ask them to reply only if they plan to attend and to reply by a certain date so that you have an estimate of how much food to order. You do not need to read each reply. To make this task more manageable, you can divert the replies into a folder and then simply count them after the reply deadline has passed. If you used the term *retirement* in the subject, it will be in the subject of the replies, and then you can set up a rule in Outlook to place those replies in a special folder, as shown in Figure 5.4.

FIGURE 5.4
Rule for sorting.

You can set up rules to filter out some messages or flag others as important. An option that is useful is to separate incoming mail based on whether the message was sent to you as the primary addressee or just as a copy or blind copy.

Out-of-Office Notice

If you are on vacation or away from work for another reason and do not expect to reply to e-mail messages, you can set up an automatic reply to let people know that they should not expect a timely response. If you are using Outlook as your client and Microsoft's Exchange Server, you can use the *Out of Office Assistant*, as shown in Figure 5.5.

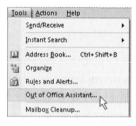

FIGURE 5.5
Optional feature with Exchange Server.

If you are using Outlook without the Exchange Server, you can download and modify a template from Microsoft's website. Then create a rule to automatically reply with the modified template, which contains your message regarding the length of your absence and who to contact while you are gone. Similarly, if you use a mail server, you can request notification when a message is delivered or read. If you are not using the same mail server, the recipient is notified of your request for verification but they do not have to comply.

Categorizing E-Mail Messages

Sorting incoming mail into separate folders usually requires that you check messages often. Another option is to keep messages in the inbox but categorize them by color or flag them by importance and type of response as they come in. You can set up rules to determine the categories to which messages belong, and the messages that meet those criteria are shaded with a particular color, as shown in Figure 5.6.

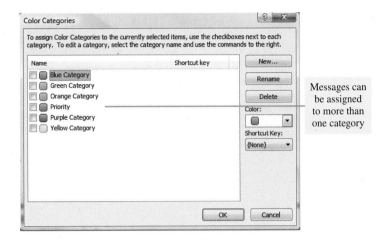

FIGURE 5.6
Categorize by color.

Using Fields

Outlook has more than two dozen items of information called *fields* that can be displayed when it lists the e-mail messages. You may choose which fields to display and the order from left to right, as shown in Figure 5.7. The Priority field is commonly used to identify high or low priority messages.

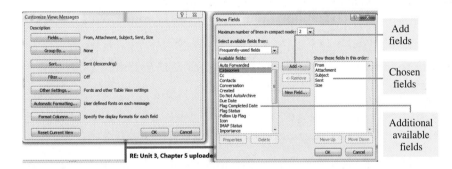

FIGURE 5.7
Choice of fields to display.

Sorting E-Mail Messages

The list of e-mail messages can be sorted in ascending or descending order in any one of the fields by clicking the field heading at the top of the column. To change the sort order, you click the heading again. Messages that have not been viewed are listed in boldface font and those that have been viewed at least once are in normal font.

Searching for E-Mail Messages

To find a message that contains a particular word or date, you can enter the content you want to match in the Search box, and then press ⏎Enter as shown in Figure 5.8.

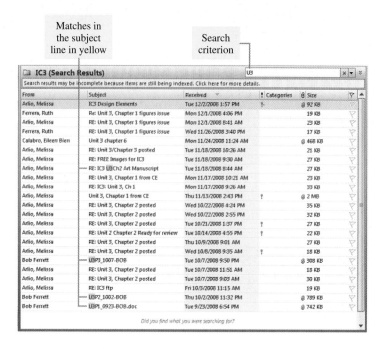

FIGURE 5.8
Searching.

to explore Microsoft Outlook

Outlook is designed to function in a business environment using Microsoft's Exchange Server. You can view a demonstration of Outlook's features online. This exercise requires speakers or headphones.

1 **Start Microsoft Internet Explorer.** Microsoft's websites often work better if you use their browser.

2 **In the Address box, type** `Microsoft.com/Outlook` **and then press** ⏎Enter. The Microsoft Outlook page displays.

3 **At the left side of the page, under Product Information, click** *See It in Action.* The Microsoft Outlook demo page displays. If this page has changed, look for a link to a demonstration of Outlook.

4 **Click the Play Demo button. A window opens and the presentation begins.**

5 **Near the bottom of the demonstration window, point at the Pause button, as shown in Figure 5.9.**

6 **Click the pause button to stop the presentation.** The button changes into a Play button.

Pause
button

FIGURE 5.9
Outlook demonstration video.

7 **Click the Play button to resume the demonstration.** Notice that the two buttons to the right are the Back and Forward buttons used to navigate the demonstrations.

8 **Watch the demonstration. Stop the demonstration at a screen that shows a sample screen illustrating one of Outlook's features.**

9 **Start the Snipping Tool. In the Snipping Tool dialog box, click the New Snip button arrow** ✂, **and then click Window Snip. Point anywhere in the demonstration window, and then click one time.** Alternatively, users of Windows XP can press the Print Screen (PrtScn) button on the keyboard and paste the captured screen into a word processing document. Users of Macintosh computers can press Command + Control + Shift + 3 to capture a screen image to the clipboard and paste the captured screen into a word processing document.

10 **Near the top of the Snipping Tool dialog box, click the Save Snip button** 💾. **In the Save As dialog box, navigate to the folder where you store your files. In the File name box, substituting your name as indicated, type** U3Ch05OutlookStudentName **and then click Save.**

11 **In the upper right corner of each open dialog box or window, click the Close button** ❌.

12 **Submit your snip as directed by your instructor.**

Managing E-Mail Resources

E-mail servers store messages and their attachments. Old messages can fill up available storage on hard disks and slow down indexing and retrieval functions. There are several practices that workers can use that will allow network administrators to manage mail server resources more effectively.

Use References Instead of Attachments or Embedded Media

Many companies provide storage space on a network server that is accessible to groups of people within their organizations. If you have a file that you wish to share with several people, you can place the file on the server instead of attaching it to an e-mail. In an e-mail, you provide the location where the file is stored. By using this technique, only one copy of the file exists on the server rather than a copy attached to many e-mail messages. Mail clients that can display messages using HTML can also display graphics or other media within the e-mail message. Inserting images and video clips can greatly increase the storage requirements and decrease the transfer speed of the e-mail message. If the image or video is also available on a Web server, provide the URL of its source or its location on a stored file server.

Passing on Chain E-Mail

Before the Internet, letters were circulated that contained a message urging each recipient to write ten duplicate letters to their friends. The message usually contained a dire warning that bad luck would trouble anyone who failed to keep the process going. These letters were called *chain letters*. The process has transferred to the Internet as **chain e-mail** but is magnified by the ease with which people can forward messages to friends. The dire warning is seldom used with chain e-mail, because it takes so little effort to pass on the message. Instead, most people think they are doing their friends a favor by passing along the opportunity for a good deal, an unsubstantiated warning about a new virus, a funny story, or a good recipe. The messages multiply rapidly and become part of the load of unsolicited e-mail. E-mail filters are less successful blocking these messages than other junk e-mail because they might be from trusted sources. The messages consume company resources without supporting the objectives of the company. You should not pass along chain e-mail or encourage people who send these messages to you at work.

Deleting E-Mail

Some e-mail messages should not be on the organization's computers in the first place. Personal videos or pictures that are downloaded from the Internet that are not related to work should be deleted. To delete an e-mail message, select it, and then right-click it and choose Delete from the menu, click the Delete button on the mail client's toolbar as shown in Figure 5.10, or press Delete on the keyboard.

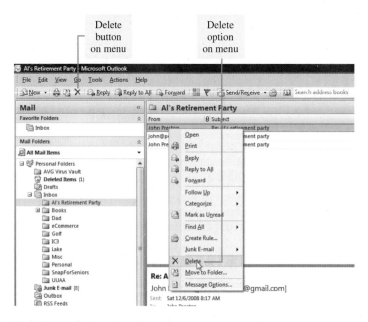

FIGURE 5.10
Delete options.

The message is not deleted yet. Instead, it is moved to the Deleted Items folder from which it can still be recovered. To complete the process, the message must be deleted again by emptying the Deleted Items folder. Outlook and some other mail programs can be set to do this automatically when you exit the mail program. Others accumulate deleted messages until you specifically choose to empty the folder. To empty the Deleted Items folder in Outlook, you can right-click on the Deleted Items folder and choose the *Empty "Deleted Items" Folder* option from the menu, as shown in Figure 5.11.

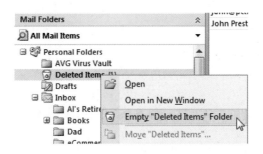

FIGURE 5.11
Empty Deleted Items.

Archiving E-Mail

Instead of deleting work-related e-mail messages, you can move them out of the active folders in the inbox to inactive **archive** folders. Mail in the archive folders can be stored on the same computer or placed on removable storage media that can be placed in low-cost, long-term storage.

Archiving requires judgment. Most archiving decisions are based on the date of the message. Messages that have not been used for months can usually be archived. To archive messages in Outlook, you can select a folder, and then on the menu bar, click File, Archive. The Archive dialog box displays, as shown in Figure 5.12.

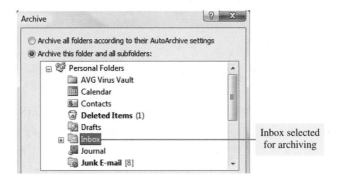

FIGURE 5.12
Archiving files.

You can choose the folder for storage, the date of archiving, and the location where the archive file is stored. Outlook stores the files in a proprietary format, and the archive files have the .pst file extension. The archive file can be copied and duplicated on removable storage media for secure off-site storage. The archive file should not be copied or moved while the Outlook program is open.

You can set Outlook to archive files automatically using ***AutoArchive***. To turn on this feature in Outlook, choose Tools, Options on the menu. In the Options dialog box, click the Other tab, and then, under AutoArchive, click the AutoArchive button. The AutoArchive dialog box displays. Here you can choose how often to check the folder and move files to the archive folder that have not been active for a specified number of months, as shown in Figure 5.13.

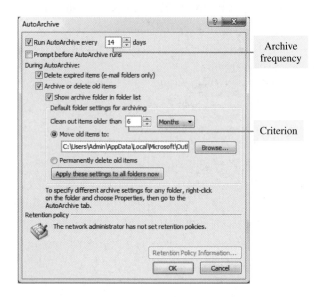

FIGURE 5.13
Outlook AutoArchive options.

Synchronizing E-mail

Electronic mail can be accessed from portable devices including personal digital assistants and cell phones. If the mail remains on the mail server all the client devices see the same mail. If the mail is downloaded to a user's computer, mail activities by other devices must be coordinated or ***synchronized.*** The mail client in the portable device must be able to communicate with the mail client on the user's computer.

Professional and Effective Use of E-Mail

Communicating in a work environment has different priorities than communicating personally. The main purpose is to exchange information efficiently and effectively.

Subject Lines

When you write an e-mail at work, be aware that the person to whom you are sending the message has to deal with hundreds of messages. In the subject line, write a very brief description of the content or purpose of the message. Be aware that the recipient might use filtering to categorize messages, so include key words that would assist in that process, such as the name of the project.

Salutation

A ***salutation*** is a courteous recognition with which you begin a message. Rules for writing business e-mail messages are similar to those for writing business memos. An e-mail message does not have to begin with a salutation if it is an impersonal announcement or if it distributed to several people. If the message is sent to an individual, it is appropriate to begin with a salutation. It is important to use the right degree of formality in the greeting. An informal salutation such as *Dear Doug,* or *Doug,* is appropriate for greeting peers. Notice that the salutation is followed by a comma.

If you are writing to someone you do not know or with whom you have a more formal relationship, use the person's title and follow the salutation with a colon. For example, *Dear Mr. Jones:*

It is usually better to be more formal than necessary rather than less so. People who have worked most of their professional lives to achieve their current status might be offended if you do not use their titles. For example, use *Dear Dr. Smith:* instead of *Dear Mr. Smith:* if the person has a doctorate degree. Similarly, people who are older might expect a certain amount of respect due to their age.

Body

The body of the e-mail message should have the following characteristics:

- as short as possible
- short, single spaced paragraphs with an empty line between paragraphs
- focus on one topic, as stated in the subject
- If you have more than one topic, use headings or labels to separate them.
- If you are responding to a series of questions, number or label the responses.
- Include text of previous message to provide content for your response—most e-mail programs do this by default when you reply.

Avoid certain types of content:

- hasty responses that are written in anger or with poor grammar
- critical comments about others that could be forwarded or circulated
- criticisms of people who report to you, which should be delivered in person
- assessments of worker performance that should be private

Texting systems often allow users of PDAs and cell phones to compose or reply to e-mail messages. Users who are accustomed to texting on these devices might use the same abbreviations and style for writing e-mail messages. This is only appropriate for informal messages to people with whom you would also exchange text messages. Otherwise, use standard grammar, capitalization, and spelling.

Be aware of the audience of the message. Many companies have international operations that involve people for whom English is a second language or who are not familiar with local slang or recent events.

Closing

The closing should match the salutation. If the message did not require a salutation, no closing is required. If the salutation was informal and included a phrase like *Good morning, Bill,* the closing can consist of a phrase such as *Best regards,* If the salutation was formal, close with *Sincerely,* Notice that both closings are followed by commas.

Signature Block

The recipient must be able to identify the sender and how to contact them. The sender's name and optional contact information should follow the closing. If your e-mail address completely identifies your name in the From: part of the message and the message is informal, you may use only your first name. If your salutation is formal, use your own title and full name, followed by alternative contact information such as telephone numbers. The name and contact information constitute a *signature block*. Figure 5.14 is an example of an informal e-mail message.

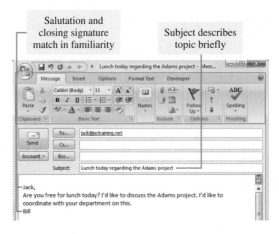

FIGURE 5.14
Informal e-mail message.

Figure 5.15 is an example of a formal e-mail message. Both of these examples can be used in a work environment, depending on which level of formality is appropriate.

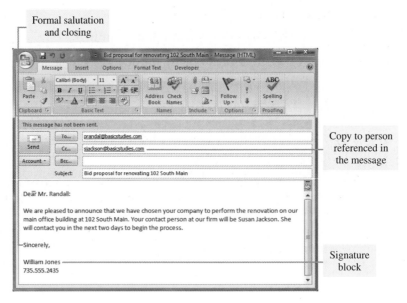

FIGURE 5.15
Formal e-mail message.

Documenting Meetings and Telephone Conversations

When people meet and discuss issues face-to-face, they often remember the meeting differently afterwards. To avoid confusion that could result in problems later, you can take notes during a meeting and then circulate an e-mail message afterwards in which you summarize the main points of the discussion. This allows others to correct any misunderstandings you may have, and the message can be used as a reference by all parties.

The Importance of Writing Skills

Online communication still relies heavily on written documents, and this is particularly true in the working world where electronic mail is widely used. In many cases, the first impression you make on a potential employer, a potential customer, or fellow worker is formed by what you write in an e-mail. Unlike many first meetings, you have more control over the impression you make in an e-mail, because you can take time to correct errors and make improvements. When you are preparing to send an e-mail to people who have no other way of knowing you, be sure to demonstrate to them that you value their opinion of you by taking time to do the following:

- Check the address to be sure it is correct so that the message arrives when it is expected.
- Show consideration for busy people by limiting the use of copies.
- Show consideration for busy people by making the subject short and descriptive.
- Choose the appropriate level of formality in the salutation and the closing. If you are not sure of how to handle a situation, refer to a style guide for business writing.
- Use the spell-check feature to find any misspelled or mistyped words that the program recognizes as errors.
- Look for words that spell-checking programs do not catch, such as words that are spelled correctly but used incorrectly. Examples are *there, their, or they're* which are used in the wrong place.
- Check grammar and capitalization. Many e-mail clients have spell-check programs but fewer have grammar checking. If you are weak in this area, write your message in an advanced word processing program that has grammar checking, like Microsoft Word. Revise the text to comply with basic grammar rules and then paste the text into the body of the e-mail.
- Show consideration for busy people by avoiding long paragraphs of text. Use bulleted or numbered lists to make concise points.
- Consider your audience. Avoid using slang, abbreviations, or cultural references that might not be understood.
- If a message is very important, or if you are acting as a representative of the organization to outsiders, ask someone else to look it over. A fresh perspective will find errors or identify weaknesses. Be prepared to return the favor.

Following these rules demonstrates to the recipient that you care about their opinion—the first step in making a good impression.

▶▶▶ *lesson*
two | Asynchronous Communications at Work

Recall that the parties are not present at the same time during asynchronous communications. This is a common occurrence in organizations that span many time zones and have busy people who are often occupied with meetings or travel. The asynchronous communication technologies that are used for personal communication can also be used at work.

Address Book

The address book in Outlook is a valuable resource of business and personal contact information. You can add new addresses to the address book by right-clicking the address on an incoming message and choosing *Add to Outlook Contacts* on the shortcut menu. To modify or delete an existing address, open the Contacts group and scroll through the alphabetized list to locate the individual address. Right-click the contact and use the Shortcut menu to open it for modification or to delete it. You can group several addresses together under one name to make it easier to send a message to members of a group. To create a distribution list, on the File menu, you would click New, and then click Distribution list. In this dialog box, you can select members from your contacts list as shown in Figure 5.16 and assign a name to the group.

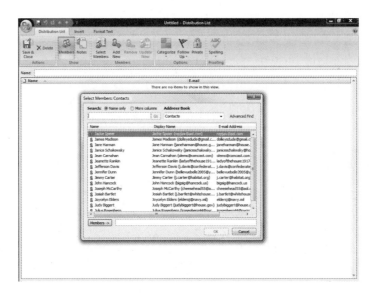

FIGURE 5.16
Distribution list from contacts.

E-Mail Lists

Selling products by sending unsolicited messages is an electronic version of a practice that has been used with the postal system. Many companies advertise their products using the postal service to send out advertising circulars, catalogs, CDs, and credit card applications—***direct mail***. The companies pay the postal service to deliver these materials, and they pay for design and printing of the materials. This type of advertising is called ***direct marketing***. The percentage of recipients who actually buy a product is low, but these methods often generate enough business to pay for materials and delivery and still create a profit for the company. The companies are rarely charged for the cost of disposal of the materials in local landfills or the time consumed by the recipients for handling the waste of unused materials—which is why it is often called *junk mail*. People who do not want to receive this type of mail can ***opt out***—choose not to participate—by asking their local post office not to deliver this type of mail. Alternatively, they can indicate the type of direct mail they want or do not want at websites like DMAchoice.org.

Direct marketing companies use electronic mail to advertise their products in a similar manner but with some important differences. It still costs money to design an attractive advertisement to include in an e-mail, but the cost of delivery is far lower. The advertising companies do not pay for the storage and handling of their e-mail messages. The low cost of distributing millions of e-mail messages means that extremely small success rates can be profitable. The U.S. government enacted the CAN-SPAM Act of 2003 to provide some protection for consumers. The law requires that e-mail advertising not use deceptive addresses or subject lines and must include the sender's valid physical postal address. It also requires the company to include an opt-out procedure. If your company or organization decides to use e-mail to promote its product or to solicit donations, you should know what the law requires.

to explore the CAN-SPAM law

If your browser does not display PDF files and you need a PDF viewer, go to Adobe.com, download Adobe Reader, locate the Adobe Reader installation file on your computer, and then double-click the file name to install the PDF viewer.

1 **Start a Web browser. In the browser's address box, near the top of the Web browser screen, type** `www.ftc.gov` **and then press** `↵Enter`. The home page of the Federal Trade Commission displays.

2 **Near the top of the Web page, move the pointer onto the Consumer Protection tab.** Notice that the second row of tabs changes to display an additional level of options.

3 **Under the Consumer Protection tab, click Business Information. At the left of the Business Information page, click E-commerce. On the E-commerce Web page, under Facts for Business, click *The CAN-SPAM Act: Requirements for Commercial Emailers*.** A Web page that describes the act displays, as shown in Figure 5.17. Alternatively, go directly to http://www.ftc.gov/bcp/edu/pubs/business/ecommerce/bus61.shtm or use a search engine to look for *FTC CAN-SPAM*.

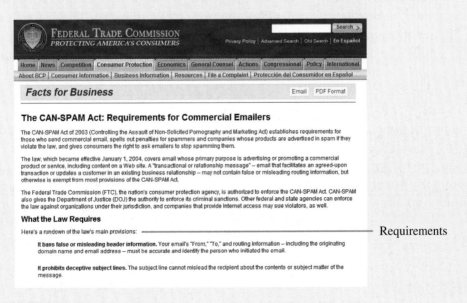

FIGURE 5.17
Restrictions placed on senders.

4   Read the section titled *What the Law Requires*. Scroll down and display the Penalties section.

··

if you have **problems**

PAGE WILL NOT SCROLL

In some cases, this window will not display properly in Internet Explorer 8.0. If you are using IE8 and cannot scroll this page to display the Penalties section, open the page using a different browser or an earlier version of Internet Explorer.

··

5   Start the Snipping Tool. In the Snipping Tool dialog box, click the New Snip button arrow 📷, and then click **Window Snip**. Point anywhere in the FTC window, and then click one time.

6   Near the top of the Snipping Tool dialog box, click the Save Snip button 💾. In the Save As dialog box, navigate to the folder where you store your files. In the File name box, substituting your name as indicated, type U3Ch05SPAMStudentName and then click **Save**.

7   In the upper right corner of each open dialog box or window, click the Close button ❌.

8   Submit your snip as directed by your instructor.

Message Boards and Weblogs

Message boards can be used by businesses and organizations to allow employees or members to contribute their knowledge and experience toward solving problems. They also allow employees to ask questions in a forum where the questions and answers can be viewed by other people with similar questions. This type of message board is usually hosted on the company server and is not open to outsiders. Some managers use private blogs to record their daily thoughts during a project so that they can review them after the project is finished and critique their decision-making process once the outcome is known.

Searches of public message boards and blogs can reveal how a segment of the public views a company's product or how an event has affected an organization's reputation. For example, if rumors are circulating about a product's safety, a company can determine the type of information campaign it needs to respond to those rumors. According to a survey of more than 300 companies—sponsored by the American Management Association and ePolicy Institute in 2007—only 10% of organizations monitored social networking sites like MySpace or Facebook to see what the public was saying about the organizations or their products.

Video Streaming and Video on Demand

Organizations can communicate with their members, employees, or customers with videos that are better than text at displaying products or evoking emotion. The videos can be displayed over broadcast television networks, but the cost can be more than $500,000 for thirty seconds during prime viewing time. The same videos can be played repeatedly over the Internet using streaming video—***webcasting***—whenever the viewer wants to watch and at practically no cost. If an organization wants to add streaming video to its website, it can obtain open-source software or purchase commercial software packages that integrate the process of creating video, storing it, and then managing delivery over the Internet, as shown in Figure 5.18.

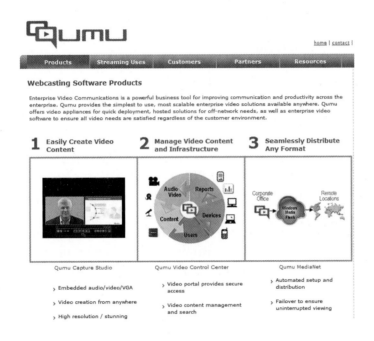

FIGURE 5.18
Commercial webcasting.

Low resolution segments of popular television shows can be distributed using streaming technology, but high definition video that is intended for large-screen television sets requires faster data transmission rates than are currently available. An alternative to streaming is to download large video files over the Internet to a home ***digital video recorder (DVR)***. The DVR can record the video on a hard disk and then replay it at a later time after the entire file has arrived. This service is called ***video on demand (VOD)***. The customer connects the DVR to a high-speed Internet connection and then chooses from a list of previously broadcast episodes. The DVR contacts the company's file server and manages the file download in the background. When the file download is complete, the show appears on the list of recorded shows. Downloads can be timed to occur at night during low-usage periods when transmission rates are fastest. The same feature can be used to sell movies that can be watched at any time until the rental expires, as shown in Figure 5.19. See Chapter 6 for a discussion of 1080p video.

FIGURE 5.19
VOD options.

Using RSS and Texting

Companies often have to keep their employees informed about the latest developments that affect their markets. Recall that *really simple syndication (RSS)* feeds download information automatically to your computer, phone, or PDA. Companies can use this technology to keep their workers informed. Typical uses are providing stock market prices, international currency values, and weather predictions.

Many workers who travel or work outside the office use personal digital assistants to keep in touch with fellow workers and with customers. Text messaging is used to alert them of appointments or important e-mail messages. Airlines like American Airlines use texting to alert travelers of changes in departure times and gate assignments, as shown in Figure 5.20.

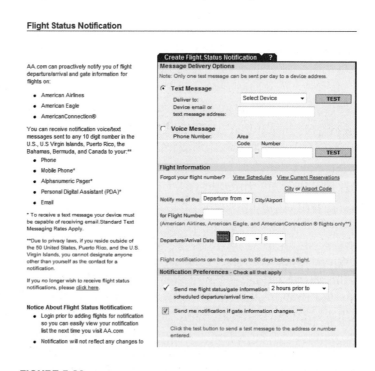

FIGURE 5.20
Flight status notification.

Business Networking

Informal networking has always been a part of business. Traditionally, networking took place in conventional meetings of professional , service, or social groups in which people shared expertise and information about employment opportunities. Business people can network online using the same networking services they use for social purposes—like MySpace and Facebook—or use a networking service such as LinkedIn that is intended for professional networking, as shown in Figure 5.21.

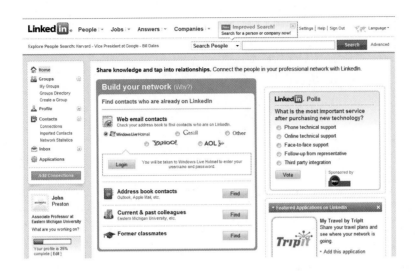

FIGURE 5.21
Professional networking.

▶▶▶ *lesson*
three | Synchronous Communications

Recall that synchronous communications take place when the parties are present at the same time. Businesses depend on synchronous communications to exchange information as rapidly and as effectively as possible. Synchronous communications allow participants to develop new ideas rapidly and to correct mistakes or misunderstandings immediately.

Internet Telephone Calls

Companies and organizations have an internal telephone system where calls are routed between phones within the organization by a central device called a *private branch exchange (PBX)*. The PBX is connected to the *public switched telephone network (PSTN)* that uses the older circuit-switching system to connect callers to outside numbers. When callers from inside the company dial 9 to get an outside line, they are asking the PBX to connect them to the PSTN.

Recall from Chapter 1 that companies have a parallel system for computer data that uses a local area network (LAN) to connect computers, and the LANs are often connected to each other using encrypted connections over the Internet. Voice over IP (VoIP) systems use the

Internet connection to send voice over the Internet at much lower cost, especially for international calls. Systems are available that combine the strengths of both systems—widespread connection to existing phone systems and low-cost long distance calling. A **voice gateway router** is used to connect the LAN and PBX to the telephone company's network to use the low-cost Internet connection. The PBX can still connect to the PSTN for local calls, and the telephone company can route voice to the PSTN using a **hop-off gateway** to reach the PSTN at the destination if the call recipient does not have a voice gateway router. See Figure 5.22 from an AT&T brochure.

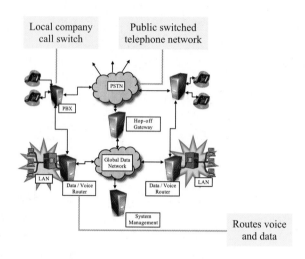

FIGURE 5.22
Hybrid data and voice telephone network.

The telephone company can use this system to provide organizations with local telephone numbers in their markets so that customers do not have to pay long-distance charges to call the organizations. It also makes it appear as if the businesses have local offices.

Audio Conferencing

Conference calls can be expensive if each caller is using a traditional telephone connection, but VoIP systems can offer conference calling between several people for less than the cost of a single long-distance call. A PBX is not needed for online conference calls through service providers like ConferenceCalls.com, where a telephone conference call can cost as little as 2.7 cents a minute per caller. A conference call can be augmented—for an additional fee—with a Web connection to make it possible for participants to connect their computers to share files, simultaneously edit documents and spreadsheets, and poll members on issues, as shown in Figure 5.23.

Managing the audio in a conference is not difficult if all of the participants use handsets or personal headphone/microphone devices. However, some conferences involve a group of people who are sitting around a table sharing a connection.

This type of arrangement requires special equipment. There are two problems to overcome in this type of arrangement. First, any source of noise that is closer to the microphone than the participant's mouth will sound much louder to the other conference participants than it will to the people in the room. For example, shuffling papers or tapping a pencil on the table near the microphone will be very distracting.

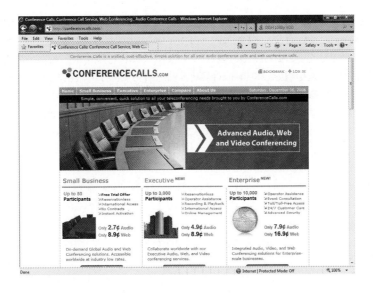

FIGURE 5.23
Conferencing options.

The other problem is suppressing the echo. When the audio speaker produces the voices of the other participants, those voices can be picked up by the microphone and transmitted back. To prevent this problem, conference telephone units combine the speaker with several directional microphones. Special software records the sounds just emitted from the speaker and blocks them when they are picked up by the microphone. Audio conferencing units are available that combine a telephone, speaker, and microphones, as shown in Figure 5.24.

Many business phone systems play music or a radio station when someone is put on hold. If you are a member of a conference call but decide to leave the call for a few minutes and use the hold feature on your phone, you could return to the call to find that the other people have had to listen to your system's music while you were gone. If you have to leave a call, let the other people know, and either hang up and reconnect later or leave the line open.

FIGURE 5.24
Conferencing phone with directional microphones and speaker.

Video Conferencing

People communicate with gestures of their hands and faces and with movements of their bodies—called **body language**. These visual cues are missing in audio conferencing. The success of many business meetings depends on evaluating the emotions of the participants. For instance, if they are skeptical, disinterested, nervous, or angry and you cannot see them well enough to recognize the emotions from the visual cues, this could affect the outcome of the meeting. Consequently, video conferencing for business purposes must be high quality to enable interpretation of body language.

Recall that video consists of a series of still images that simulate smooth motion when many pictures are shown in sequence each second. The transmission rates necessary to transmit high-quality digital video is usually greater than typical Internet connection speeds can handle, so compromises are required. Compression codecs are effective at compressing video conferences, especially when most of the image does not change from one picture to the next and where the background is one color—which is typical of someone speaking into a camera in a conference room. Video compression codecs have evolved from the early **H.261** standard to **H.264/MPEG-4 Part 10**. The standards used for transmitting video conferences depend upon the type of transmission system used. The **International Telecommunications Union (ITU)**—a group that manages international radio and telecommunications standards—has three general standards for video conferencing.

- **H.320**: used with standard public switched telephone networks (PSTN), digital networks, T1, and satellite networks
- **H.323**: used with LANs
- **H.324**: used with traditional telephone systems and **third generation (3G)** mobile phones that provide high-speed Internet access and video calls

Video conferencing systems must be able to interface with older systems and with a mix of transmission standards to interoperate with conferencing systems at other organizations.

Video conferencing in business can take place between individuals who use personal computers and inexpensive webcams, or with more expensive systems that have higher-quality cameras with remote control and wide-screen displays, as shown in Figure 5.25.

FIGURE 5.25
Video conferencing system.

to explore business videoconferencing

Companies that have offices in many countries coordinate their efforts using dedicated video conferencing facilities.

1 **Start a Web browser. In the Address box, type** `Polycom.com` **and then press** `↵Enter`. **Choose your region, and then click the Go button.** The Polycom home page displays. Alternatively, type `http://www.polycom.com/usa/en/home/index.html`

2 **Near the top of the page, point at Products, and then on the menu, click Telepresence and Video. On the Telepresence and Video page, under the introduction screen, click Videos.**

3 **Under Watch More, click *Telepresence Complete Portfolio Video*.** The video starts. If the website has changed and this video is not available, choose another option that shows video conferencing equipment.

4 **Near the bottom of the demonstration window, point at the Pause button, as shown in Figure 5.26.**

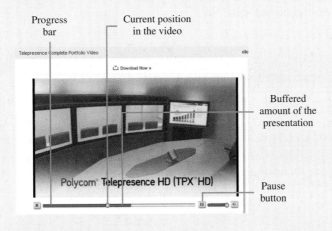

FIGURE 5.26
Video on teleconferencing.

5 **Click the Pause button to stop the presentation.** The button changes into a Play button.

6 **Click the Play button to resume the demonstration.** You can drag the circle on the progress bar to move backward or forward in the video.

7 **Watch the demonstration. Stop the demonstration at a screen that shows a sample screen illustrating one of Polycom's features.**

8 **Start the Snipping Tool. In the Snipping Tool dialog box, click the New Snip button arrow** ✂, **and then click Window Snip. Point anywhere in the video window, and then click one time.**

9 Near the top of the Snipping Tool dialog box, click the Save Snip button 🖫 . In the Save As dialog box, navigate to the folder where you store your files. In the File name box, substituting your name as indicated, type U3Ch05VideoStudentName and then click Save.

10 In the upper right corner of each open dialog box or window, click the Close button ❌ .

11 Submit your snip as directed by your instructor.

Using Chat and IM for Customer Support

Many businesses use online chat to provide customer support instead of using telephones. An online chat has two significant advantages over telephone support. If the support person needs to hand off the contact to a specialist or a supervisor, that person can scroll through the chat and quickly get up to speed on the situation instead of asking the customer to repeat everything. Support personnel can manage more than one chat at a time to maximize the value of specialists. The chat software integrates with the company website to offer more personalized service than static text and at lower cost than telephone support. Free trials are available, as shown in Figure 5.27.

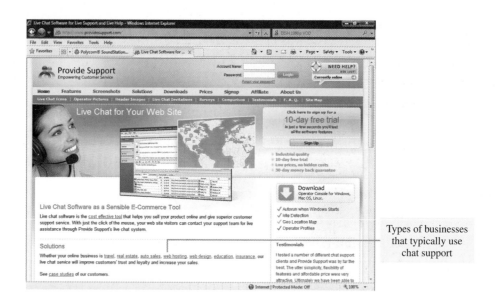

Types of businesses that typically use chat support

FIGURE 5.27
Chat for e-commerce.

Information workers who share expertise can band together in small groups using instant messaging. If one person in the group needs a quick answer to a question, he or she can IM someone in their group of trusted friends to interrupt their work and ask a question. Each person in the group must be willing to be interrupted to provide this help. Using IM, customer support people can get answers to customer questions quickly.

four | Using Computers Online at Work

Some jobs can be done at an isolated computer that is not networked to other computers, but such jobs are becoming rare. Most computers are connected to other computers on a network, and many jobs require access to the Internet. Synchronous and asynchronous communication technologies have become part of most jobs and have changed the way some organizations conduct business and manage their employees.

Virtual Teams

In traditional organizations, employees are organized by the type of work they do into departments like engineering, marketing, human resources, finance, operations, and management. In this type of organization, each employee reports to a manager who allocates tasks and evaluates that person's performance. When a new product or process is in the design stage, some organizations create teams made up of representatives from each department to provide input so that the final product functions well with each of the organization's processes. The teams are assembled for a particular project and for a limited time.

Improved communications technologies have made it possible to assemble teams that are separated by distance and time—known as ***virtual teams***. There are several advantages to virtual teams compared to traditional teams:

- The best person for a particular task might work at a different location.
- Team members can meet without spending time traveling.
- Members can be selected from other countries and cultures to provide diverse views.
- Part-time or contract employees can be included as needed for each project to reduce the number of full-time employees.
- Team members can participate from any location that has adequate connectivity.
- Work can be done on the project twenty-four hours a day by teams dispersed over different time zones.

Some disadvantages of using virtual teams are:

- Team members might feel isolated from coworkers.
- Communication technologies are not adequate for all of the tasks.
- It is difficult to find common meeting times for synchronous communication.
- Online projects might not be considered as important for personal advancement.

Telework

Managing a virtual team requires the manager to consider new ways of evaluating a worker's performance. Because the manager is not in the same location as many of the team members, issues related to a worker's presence are less important. Instead of focusing on the time at which workers arrive in the morning and leave at night or how many breaks they take, the manager must set objectives for each worker—including a timeline—and then leave the specific schedule up to the employee and the team members. Some tasks are easier than others to manage by objective. For example, if a salesperson gets paid a percentage of the product they sell, the manager can evaluate the salesperson by how much they sell, not how much time it took them to sell it.

Many tasks performed by workers involve work on computers using commonly available software and communications with fellow workers and customers using online communications. In many cases, workers have the necessary computer equipment, software, and Internet connections at home to do those tasks. Instead of spending time in a car or train to commute from home to work and back each day, some workers *telecommute*—work from home.

There are several advantages of telecommuting:

- Reduces time wasted traveling to and from a place of employment.
- Reduces environmental impact of burning fossil fuels for transportation.
- Reduces traffic congestion.
- Reduces dependence on foreign oil.
- Reduces company overhead for parking and office space.
- Provides flexibility for parents and caregivers to deal with the needs of children and dependents.
- A physically distributed workforce is less of a target for terrorist attacks.

Some government agencies are encouraging telecommuting, which they call *telework*. For example, the Government Services Administration (GSA) administrator, Lurita Doan, stated in 2007 that she wanted half of GSA employees to be able to telework by 2010.

to explore telework

The Government Service Administration (GSA) is encouraging people to work from home.

1 **Start a Web browser. In the Address box, type** www.telework.gov **and then press** ⏎Enter**. The telework.gov home page displays.

2 **Under *i am an employee,* click *Become a teleworker.***

3 **Under *Basics for Employees,* click *Step 4: Conduct a self assessment.* A bulleted list displays, as shown in Figure 5.28. If the website has changed and these steps do not match the website, choose another option that shows information about becoming a teleworker.**

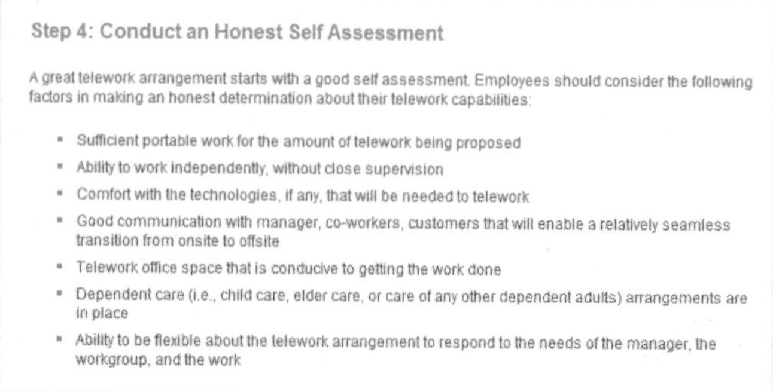

Step 4: Conduct an Honest Self Assessment

A great telework arrangement starts with a good self assessment. Employees should consider the following factors in making an honest determination about their telework capabilities:

- Sufficient portable work for the amount of telework being proposed
- Ability to work independently, without close supervision
- Comfort with the technologies, if any, that will be needed to telework
- Good communication with manager, co-workers, customers that will enable a relatively seamless transition from onsite to offsite
- Telework office space that is conducive to getting the work done
- Dependent care (i.e., child care, elder care, or care of any other dependent adults) arrangements are in place
- Ability to be flexible about the telework arrangement to respond to the needs of the manager, the workgroup, and the work

FIGURE 5.28
GSA telework guidelines.

4 Start the Snipping Tool. In the Snipping Tool dialog box, click the New Snip button arrow ✂, and then click Window Snip. Point anywhere in the window that shows Step 4, and then click one time.

5 Near the top of the Snipping Tool dialog box, click the Save Snip button 💾. In the Save As dialog box, navigate to the folder where you store your files. In the File name box, substituting your name as indicated, type U3Ch05TeleworkStudentName and then click Save.

6 In the upper right corner of each open dialog box or window, click the Close button ✖.

7 Submit your snip as directed by your instructor.

Telework is not appropriate for many situations or for all types of employees, and it can have several disadvantages.

- Supervisors might send extra work home with the worker, assuming willingness to work additional hours at night and on weekends to get a project done on time.
- Fellow employees might view such an arrangement with envy or resentment.
- There can be less sense of belonging to an organization, accompanied by a sense of isolation.
- Lack of security when data is transferred to a home computer.
- Some home work environments have too many distractions.
- Some workers are not self-disciplined enough to work effectively without a structured environment.
- Friends and relatives do not respect the worker's need for dedicated work time.
- Many managers judge effort by observing workers visually instead of monitoring online work.

Telework must be carefully structured to be sure that the work and worker match the environment and that the worker has the appropriate access to company data.

Online Business Practices

In his best-selling book *The World is Flat*, Thomas Friedman identifies ten factors that have changed the world and made it more competitive. His metaphor refers to a level playing field on which developed and emerging countries now compete equally. Several of these factors involve online communications, and some of them—such as the rise of the Internet and the use of standards like TCP/IP, SMTP, and XML—have been mentioned in previous chapters. Some of these factors specifically affect the way organizations do business online. If you understand how companies use computers and communications technologies to compete in the new *flat* world, you will be able to make better decisions about how your online skills can fit into a company.

Outsourcing

The communications technologies that enable people to work from home can be used to enable someone to work on a project from another country—called *outsourcing*. The global network of fiber optic cable makes it just as easy to join a project from India as from Indiana. Some companies have entire departments in other countries, while others outsource particular functions or hire contract workers for particular projects.

to explore outsourcing

Companies like Accenture provide connections between local and foreign companies that provide services.

1 **Start a Web browser. In the Address box, type** `accenture.com/Global/Outsourcing/MoreServices.htm` **and then press** `↵Enter`**.** The Accenture Global Delivery Network page displays, as shown in Figure 5.29.

FIGURE 5.29
Accenture website.

2 **At the right of the page, under Related Links, click the map of the world to enlarge it.**

3 **Start the Snipping Tool. In the Snipping Tool dialog box, click the New Snip button arrow** 🔗 **, and then click Window Snip. Point anywhere in the map, and then click one time.**

4 **Near the top of the Snipping Tool dialog box, click the Save Snip button** 💾 **. In the Save As dialog box, navigate to the folder where you store your files. In the File name box, substituting your name as indicated, type** `U3Ch05OutsourcingStudentName` **and then click Save.**

5 **In the upper right corner of each open dialog box or window, click the Close button** ⊠ **.**

6 **Submit your snip as directed by your instructor.**

One of the functions that is commonly outsourced to India is the ***call center,*** where workers at a particular location talk to customers using synchronous audio communications to handle questions or requests for help, as shown in Figure 5.30.

FIGURE 5.30
Call center.

Hospitals in the United States outsource evaluation of X-rays, as shown in Figure 5.31. Because of the time difference, a radiologist in India can work a normal daylight shift, but as far as the hospital in the U.S. is concerned, they receive an evaluation overnight that is ready to use the next morning.

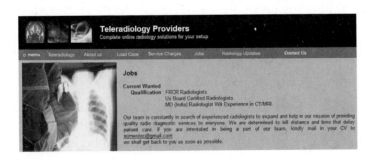

FIGURE 5.31
Analysis of X-ray images outsourced.

Insourcing

Because of fast Internet connections, call centers can be located anywhere in the world, but one of the challenges of outsourcing tasks that involves synchronous audio exchange between people is the need to understand regional accents and slang. To overcome this problem, some companies use call centers that are in the same country as the customers. Using a separate group for service that is located within the same country is called *insourcing*. For example, more than half of the McDonald's restaurants in Hawaii use a call center in Texas to handle the requests made in their drive-throughs. An order is taken by a worker in Texas using a synchronous audio connection, transcribed onto a computer, and then posted over the Internet to a screen inside the restaurant a few yards from the customer. Even though the calls are handled in another state in the same country, call center employees in Texas have to be trained to understand local slang and use Hawaiian words such as *aloha* and *mahalo*—the greeting and *thank you*. Because the workload at a restaurant peaks at mealtimes, the workers at a centralized call center can handle the calls as the peak demand period moves from one time zone to the next, reducing the need for workers at each site who would not be utilized between mealtimes.

Some foreign companies have discovered that they can get better service on equipment repairs inside the U.S. For example, Toshiba found that instead of shipping defective laptop computers all the way back to Japan for service, they could hire UPS—the shipping company—to repair the laptops at a repair center located next to UPS's central transfer airport in Louisville, Kentucky. UPS uses its computing services to track the laptops and return them to the customer in much less time than it would take Toshiba to repair them at their own repair center in Japan.

Supply Chains

Products that are manufactured start as raw materials that must be processed in several steps, shipped to distribution centers, and then transported to retail sales outlets. This sequence is called a *supply chain*. Companies use standardized communication systems to link their computers to control this process and thereby reduce waste, excess inventory, and response time.

▶▶▶ *lesson*
five | Security, Privacy, Safety, and Health

When you work for someone else, you are responsible for how your actions affect the organization, and the organization has responsibilities toward you and its other workers. In this lesson, you study rules of ethical behavior at work that affect security and privacy. You also study behaviors related to computers that affect safety and personal health.

Reducing Risks to Organizational and Personal Data

Data can be stolen, lost through equipment malfunctions, or copied, altered, or destroyed through malicious actions. Viruses that spread via e-mail, worms that replicate on the network, and Trojans that disguise themselves can affect stored data as discussed previously.

Data Theft

There are two ways to steal data: directly from the computer or (far more frequently) through an Internet connection. To steal data directly from a computer requires access to the computer. When an organization loses data directly, it is almost always stolen by an employee. When someone enters a computer from the outside, it is referred to as *hacking* the computer and is performed by a clever programmer called a **hacker**. Some hackers follow a special code of ethics and do not damage or steal data; they get into the computers to prove that they can and often claim to be performing a service by exposing security flaws. To protect data from unauthorized access, users must be identified. Traditional methods of identification utilize a combination of user name and password. Some sites require the user to provide a working e-mail address to which a pass code is sent, while others require a working telephone number that has a billing address.

Malicious Tampering

Another data problem—often even more damaging than data theft—is the malicious tampering of data. Tampering can occur internally by a disgruntled employee, through the use of viruses or other malicious programs, or by hackers. Data can be damaged, erased, or subtly altered so that the changes are not noticed for some time.

Data Storage Failure

Data storage failure can result in lost data. Electrical power surges can damage storage media and result in lost data. Power outages and low power conditions can cause computers to shut down prematurely, which can result in the loss of recently entered, unsaved data. Storage devices can also fail—or crash—making the data stored on them inaccessible. A surge suppressor is a simple device that is often built into a plug strip for a few extra dollars. Many people use them at home, but they are often neglected at work, even in workplaces with heavy motors that can cause low power when they start or surges when they stop.

Avoiding Data Loss

A preventive measure to avoid data loss is saving your work frequently. If the power goes out and you saved your work five minutes earlier, you have only lost a maximum of five minutes' worth of work. If you haven't saved your current document for two hours, you could lose a lot of work. The default setting in Microsoft Office 2007 is to save your work automatically every ten minutes, but other software programs might not have this feature.

Privacy on Company Computers

The attitudes toward worker privacy vary significantly between the European Union (EU) and the United States. In the EU, there is a presumed right of privacy for the worker. EU directive 95/46/EC requires that people be given notice when their data is being collected. In the United States, a simple statement in the company handbook is sufficient notice in most situations. A survey of 304 companies in 2007, which was sponsored by the American Management Association and the ePolicy Institute, provides a profile of how organizations in the United States manage issues related to worker privacy. Some of their findings related to the use of communications technologies and privacy are:

- 45% monitored time spent, content, or keystrokes.
- 84% of those that monitored workers informed them of company policy.
- Only 27% of the organizations that informed workers of monitoring did so during training sessions; most relied on Internet postings (32%), e-mail notices (40%), or employee handbooks (70%).
- 66% monitored and reviewed website visits.
- 45% monitored telephone use.
- 16% recorded telephone conversations, and 10% recorded and reviewed voice mail messages.
- 47% used video surveillance to counter theft, violence, or sabotage; 7% used video to monitor employee performance.
- 3% monitored or tracked the location of company cell phones.

Companies can dismiss employees for violating company policies. The same survey of these organizations found that:

- 28% have fired an employee for e-mail misuse.
- 30% have fired an employee for Internet misuse.
- Only 6% have fired an employee for misuse or private use of the telephone.

Personnel Policies on Computer Use

Organizations can be sued for failing to monitor employee behavior. To protect themselves from lawsuits, companies often monitor e-mail or other electronic communications to look for evidence of the following activities:

- sexual harassment
- profanity
- criminal activity
- pornography viewing or forwarding
- using company resources to generate personal income
- admissions of incompetence

Companies can go too far if they single out a particular person to monitor, and some forms of personal communications are protected from government monitoring by the Electronic Communications Privacy Act. In general, workers in the United States should not assume a right to privacy while using company resources for communications.

Companies and organizations have policies that govern employee behavior regarding use of computers. Violation of the company policy is often grounds for dismissal, so you should know what they are. To locate an organization's policies regarding computer use, begin by examining the company's website and using its internal search engine to look for key phrases such as *computer policy*. If that does not produce the desired results, contact the human resources department and ask for assistance.

Most policies regarding computer use by employees include the following topics:

- Illegal activity is banned, including violation of copyright or software licenses.
- Use of company resources is for company purposes.
- Protecting the security of the system from unauthorized access and how to respond to a virus attack.

to explore computer use policy

Organizations like the National Energy Research Scientific Computing Center (NERSC) require employees to sign a form that specifies acceptable and unacceptable behavior.

1 **Start a Web browser. In the Address box, type** `www.nersc.gov/nusers/accounts/usage.php` **and then press** `↵Enter`. The NERSC Computer Use Policies Form page displays, as shown in Figure 5.32.

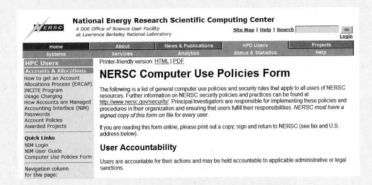

FIGURE 5.32
NERSC Policy.

2 **Scroll down the page and read the policies related to using computers. Stop scrolling at a point that displays the policy labeled *Monitoring and Privacy*.**

3 **Start the Snipping Tool. In the Snipping Tool dialog box, click the New Snip button arrow , and then click Window Snip. Point anywhere in the NERSC window, and then click one time.**

4 **Near the top of the Snipping Tool dialog box, click the Save Snip button . In the Save As dialog box, navigate to the folder where you store your files. In the File name box, substituting your name as indicated, type** `U3Ch05PolicyStudentName` **and then click Save.**

5 **In the upper right corner of each open dialog box or window, click the Close button .**

6 **Submit your snip as directed by your instructor.**

Company policies should include a statement that complies with relevant laws about records retention and how long copies of e-mail or other electronic records must be kept. Electronic records must not be erased if they could be used as evidence in an investigation. Laws, policies, and guidelines are usually available online. Search the organization's Web site and Web sites of related professional organizations for links to laws and policy statements. Stay informed about changes in policies and laws by reading newsletters from the organization and related professional organizations.

Safety in the Workplace

Your working environment needs to be safe, both for you and your equipment. You need to maintain a safe working environment for your equipment to help minimize the risks of data loss, electrical overload, fire, and employee accidents. Maintaining a healthy work environment for people involves proper equipment setup, unobtrusive room lighting, proper seating, and special techniques to avoid computer-related injuries.

Techniques to keep your work environment safe range from simple, commonsense safety measures to installation of special electrical backup equipment. Some solutions are inexpensive or free, while others can be quite costly.

Your computer equipment should be positioned for maximum safety. Electrical cords should be secured, preferably in an out-of-the-way place where no one will trip over them or snag clothes on them. If an electrical cord must cross the floor in an area that receives any foot traffic, it should be enclosed in a plastic runner created for that purpose to avoid a hazardous situation, as shown in Figure 5.33.

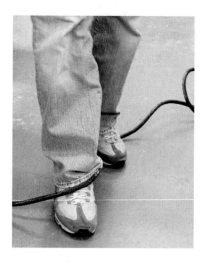

FIGURE 5.33
Cover or remove wires from walkways.

Electrical outlets should not be overloaded. Adding multiple adaptors to a single outlet will often overload the circuit and create either a fire hazard or the potential for lost data when a circuit breaker shuts off. As more equipment is added to an area, a power strip will often provide enough outlets; however, it may become necessary to hire an electrician to add another outlet or circuit to the area.

Finally, as more and more equipment is attached to your computer, you may run low on desk space. Always be sure that each piece of equipment is on a solid base and does not overhang the edge of the desk or table you are using. Equipment that is balanced precariously on the edge of a workspace often ends up on the floor.

Maintaining a Healthy Working Environment

Computers have become part of our lives, and many people spend hours each day sitting in front of a desktop computer. When you perform a repetitive movement from the same physical position, parts of your body become fatigued. Incorrect positions can accelerate the onset of fatigue and even result in painful chronic problems. It is especially easy to work in unhealthy positions when you use a laptop computer.

The following tips may be effective at reducing fatigue but are not right for everyone. Remember to stretch and change your position often and get up and move around on a regular basis. Seek professional medical advice if you have a health problem related to computer use.

Ergonomics is the applied science of equipment design to reduce operator fatigue and discomfort. Computers are often added to a workspace with little regard for operator comfort or fatigue factors. Whether you work on a computer or manage people who do, it is very important to understand the basics of ergonomic design. To maximize comfort and cause the least amount of stress to your body while working at a computer, you need to have proper vertical and horizontal alignment between yourself and the computer. You also need to have proper lighting to avoid eye fatigue.

Imagine holding a bowling ball above your head at the end of your outstretched, upright arm. If the center of the ball is directly in line with your arm, then holding the ball is not too difficult. Imagine bending your wrist slightly so that the weight of the ball is not directly above your forearm but is supported by your bent wrist. You can imagine how much more difficult this would be and how much more quickly your wrist would tire. Your head weighs about as much as a bowling ball, and it sits on top of your neck and spine. If you move your head forward so it is not directly above your spine, your neck muscles must work harder to support its weight, and the disks between the vertebrae in your spine will be compressed unevenly, which may result in disabling pain. The ***Occupational Safety & Health Administration (OSHA)***—an agency in the Department of Labor—provides a website that guides you through an analysis of your computer workstation to help you avoid computer-related injury.

to explore good working positions

The OSHA website has illustrations of positions and workstation components and a checklist to help you test your setup.

1 **Start a Web browser. In the Address box, type** www.osha.gov/SLTC/etools/computerworkstations **and then press** ⏎Enter**. The U.S. Department of Labor's Occupational Safety & Health Administration Web page displays, as shown in Figure 5.34.**

FIGURE 5.34
Ergonomics.

2 **At the left of the window, click *Good Working Positions*. Notice the instruction to keep the head in line with the torso.**

3 **At the left of the window, point at *Workstation Components*. On the menu, click Chairs.**

4 **Start the Snipping Tool. In the Snipping Tool dialog box, click the New Snip button arrow ✂, and then click Window Snip. Point anywhere in on the Chairs window, and then click one time.**

5 **Near the top of the Snipping Tool dialog box, click the Save Snip button 🖫. In the Save As dialog box, navigate to the folder where you store your files. In the File name box, substituting your name as indicated, type** U3Ch05ErgonomicsStudentName **and then click Save.**

6 **In the upper right corner of each open dialog box or window, click the Close button ✖.**

7 **Submit your snip as directed by your instructor.**

SUMMARY

In this chapter, you learned about using e-mail at work. You studied the uses of asynchronous and synchronous communications at work and how these technologies are used to facilitate work done by teams that include people who are working from home or from other countries. You also learned about privacy and security policies and about practices related to using computers safely and protecting the health of workers.

You can extend your learning by reviewing concepts and terms, and by practicing variations of skills presented in the lessons.

KEY TERMS

archive

AutoArchive

body language

call center

chain e-mail

digital video recorder (DVR)

direct mail

direct marketing

ergonomics

fields

H.261

H.264/MPEG-4 Part 10

H.320

H.323

H.324

hacker

hop-off gateway

insourcing

International Telecommunications Union (ITU)

junk e-mail

Occupational Safety & Health Administration (OSHA)

opt out

outsourcing

private branch exchange (PBX)

public switched telephone network (PSTN)

salutation

signature block

supply chain

telecommute

telework

third generation (3G)

video on demand (VOD)

virtual team

voice gateway router

webcasting

CHECKING CONCEPTS AND TERMS

MULTIPLE CHOICE
Circle the letter of the correct answer for each of the following.

1. Which of the following salutations is most appropriate for an e-mail message to a potential customer you have never met named Dr. William Cross? [L1]

   a. Dear Mr. Cross:

   b. Good morning, Bill,

   c. Dear Dr. Cross:

   d. Hey,

2. If you have to distribute a file to several people in your organization who use the same e-mail and network servers, what is the best option for using server resources wisely? [L1]

   a. Attach the file to an e-mail and send it to each person.

   b. Place the file on the network server in a folder that is available to all the intended recipients, and provide the address in an e-mail that you send to all of them.

c. Compress the file using a codec and attach it to an e-mail that you distribute to all of them.

d. Attach the file to an e-mail, send it to one person, and copy it to all the others.

3. Why is direct marketing by e-mail profitable even if very few people respond? [L2]

a. People still respond positively to the product because they have seen it often.

b. The direct marketers are paid a small fee for each message by the network infrastructure providers to keep traffic high on their systems so they can get government rebates.

c. The costs of distributing e-mail are extremely low for the direct mailers, so small success rates are still profitable.

d. Providers of junk mail filtering software pay them a percentage of their software sales.

4. What are examples of uses of RSS for business purposes? [L2]

 not on test

a. Providing inexpensive ways to exchange text messages with mobile employees

b. Enable desktop video conferencing

c. Enable audio conference calls

d. Keep employees informed of changing situations like weather conditions and stock prices

5. How can companies combine their telephone and data communications? [L3]

a. By training employees to use the one that is cheapest for the appropriate type of communication

b. By using a gateway router that combines voice and data

c. By using codecs to compress voice and then transmitting over dial-up connections

d. By using data communications during the daytime and restricting long-distance calls to off-peak hours

6. Why is special software needed to manage input signals from microphones during an audio conference call when participants are at a table sharing the same microphone and speaker unit? [L3]

a. The software blocks sounds picked up by the microphone and just emitted by the speaker to reduce echoes.

b. The sensitivity of the microphone to voices of different pitches is dynamically changed to match the participant's voice.

c. Cameras are pointed automatically at the participant who is speaking, based on pickups by directional microphones.

d. The software automatically distinguishes between noises on the table, like shuffling papers, and blocks them.

7. Which of the following is **not** an advantage of telework? [L4]

a. Managers are accustomed to managing by objective, and existing management techniques transfer easily to teleworkers.

b. It reduces pollution from transportation vehicles.

c. It provides flexibility for care providers.

d. It reduces time wasted commuting to and from work.

8. Which of the following is a **disadvantage** of working on a virtual team? [L4]

a. It can use the best people regardless of location.

b. Team members can be selected from other countries to provide a diverse viewpoint.

c. Work can be done around the clock in different time zones.

d. Synchronous communications are not convenient if workers are in different time zones.

9. The medium most commonly used by employers in the United States for informing employees about computer-related policies is _____. [L4]

a. the employee handbook

b. training classes

c. the company website

d. circulated e-mail

10. Which of the following is **not** a safe practice when using computers? [L5]

a. Installing additional electrical circuits if additional computer equipment needs more power than the rating of existing outlets

b. Assuring that the base of the monitor is entirely resting on the table or desk

c. Using an extension cord that lies across a walkway without a protective cover

d. Secure connecting wires so they will not catch on clothing and pull components off the desk

MATCHING

Match each term in the second column with its correct definition in the first column by writing the letter of the term on the blank line in front of the definition.

D___ 1. Inactive storage

A___ 2. Group of people at one location who use audio communications to provide service

F___ 3. Video recorder that uses a hard disk

H___ 4. Applied science of equipment design to reduce operator fatigue

C___ 5. An agency in the Department of Labor concerned with worker safety

I___ 6. Having work done in another country

B___ 7. Device for routing telephone calls within a company

E___ 8. Courteous recognition or greeting

G___ 9. Working from home

J___ 10. Group whose members are separated by distance or time

A. Call center

B. PBX

C. OSHA

D. Archive

E. Salutation

F. DVR

G. Telework

H. Ergonomics

I. Outsourcing

J. Virtual team

Skill Drill exercises reinforce chapter skills. Each skill reinforced is the same, or nearly the same, as a skill presented in the chapter. Detailed instructions are provided in a step-by-step format.

Each exercise is independent of the others, so you can do the exercises in any order.

1. View Video on Using Outlook for Voting

A feature that is available to users of Outlook and Exchange Server is voting.

To learn more about polling coworkers using Outlook and Exchange Server, follow these steps:

1. Start Internet Explorer. In the **Address** box, type `office.Microsoft.com/Outlook` and then press ⏎Enter.

2. At the left of the screen, under **Training**, click **Outlook 2007 Demos**.

3. Scroll down the list of demos, and then click **Demo: Voting made easy-Create and send polls in Outlook**. On the following page, click **Play Demo**.

4. Watch the demo all the way through, and then close the demo window. Start the demo again.

5. While the demo is playing, click the **Start** button, click **All Programs**, click the **Accessories** folder, and then in the list of programs, click the **Snipping Tool**.

6. In the **Snipping Tool** dialog box, click the **New Snip** button arrow, and then click **Window Snip**. Point anywhere in the **Demo** window, and then click one time to capture any one of the screens in the demo.

7. Near the top of the **Snipping Tool** dialog box, click the **Save Snip** button. In the **Save As** dialog box, navigate to the folder where you store your files. In the **File name** box, substituting your name as indicated, type `U3Ch05VotingStudentName` and then click **Save**.

8. In the upper right corner of each open dialog box or window, click the **Close** button.

9. Submit your snip as directed by your instructor.

2. Learn More About Chain E-Mail

Chain e-mail can be used for fraud or to spread hoaxes.

To learn more about chain e-mail that could affect your company's mail server by flooding it with unnecessary mail, follow these steps:

1. Start a Web browser program such as Internet Explorer, Firefox, or Safari.

2. In the **Address** box, type `breakthechain.org` and then press ⏎Enter.

3. Read samples from the home page.

4. On the left of the home page, click **Virus Warnings**.

5. Scroll down the list of chain e-mail about false warnings and click one of the links.

6. Click the **Start** button, click **All Programs**, click the **Accessories** folder, and then in the list of programs, click the **Snipping Tool**.

7. In the **Snipping Tool** dialog box, click the **New Snip** button arrow, and then click **Window Snip**. Point anywhere in the description you selected, and then click one time.

8. Near the top of the **Snipping Tool** dialog box, click the **Save Snip** button. In the **Save As** dialog box, navigate to the folder where you store your files. In the **File name** box, substituting your name as indicated, type `U3Ch05ChainStudentName` and then click **Save**.

9. In the upper right corner of each open dialog box or window, click the **Close** button.

10. Submit your snip as directed by your instructor.

3. Direct Mail Lists

Direct mailing is a legal form of advertising if you follow the rules. You can purchase the service for distributing your requests for donations or product advertising by bulk e-mail.

To learn about using direct e-mail advertising or solicitation, follow these steps:

1. Start a Web browser program such as Internet Explorer, Firefox, or Safari.

2. In the **Address** box, type `emailcustomers.com` and then press ⏎Enter. This site specializes in sending e-mail to customers who have elected to receive direct e-mail.

3. Near the top of the Web page, click **EMAIL LISTS FOR SALE**. In the **Opt-in Emailing Overview** box, read about opt-in e-mail and expected response rates.

4. Scroll down to the sections titled **List Buying** and **Some Definitions**. Adjust the scroll bar so that both boxes are on the screen.

5. Click the **Start** button, click **All Programs**, click the **Accessories** folder, and then in the list of programs, click the **Snipping Tool**. In the **Snipping Tool** dialog box, click the **New Snip** button arrow, and then click **Window Snip**. Point anywhere in the window that displays information about list buying and definitions, and then click one time.

6. Near the top of the **Snipping Tool** dialog box, click the **Save Snip** button. In the **Save As** dialog box, navigate to the folder where you store your files. In the **File name** box, substituting your name as indicated, type `U3Ch05ElistStudentName` and then click **Save**.

7. In the upper right corner of each open dialog box or window, click the **Close** button.

8. Submit your snip as directed by your instructor.

EXPLORE AND SHARE

Explore and Share questions are intended for discussion in class or online. Look for information that is related to the learning outcomes for this chapter as directed. Submit your answers as directed by your instructor.

1. Virtual teams can share a calendar to assist in coordinating their efforts. If the team members do not share a common server, they can use Web-based software such as Google Calendar. Use a browser and go to **calendar.google.com**. Use the online help and introductory screens to set up a free calendar. You will have to register with Google

to use this free service. Invite a friend or classmate to join you, and grant them the ability to make changes to the calendar as if they were a virtual team member. Schedule an event for some time in the next week. Use the **Snipping Tool** to copy the calendar window, and save it as U3Ch04CalendarStudentName Prepare to share what you learned about using a shared online calendar. Submit your answer and the file as directed by your instructor. [L2]

2. Virtual teams can create documents and spreadsheets online in a shared environment. If the team members do not share a common server, they can use Web-based software such as Google Apps. Use a browser and go to **docs.google.com**. Use the online help and introductory screens to sign up to use Google Docs, which is a free service. Create a word processing document, and then invite a friend or classmate to join you. Grant them the ability to make changes to the document as if they were a virtual team member. Write a short paragraph and ask your friend to make changes to it. Use the **Snipping Tool** to copy the document window, and save it as U3Ch04DocsStudentName Prepare to share what you learned about using a shared online document. Submit your answer and the file as directed by your instructor. [L2]

3. Find out more about the policies at a school regarding computer use. The school could be the one you are attending or the school of a child you know. Search the school's website for a link to the school's handbook. Look for the policy regarding use of school e-mail and Internet use. Use the **Snipping Tool** to copy a window that clearly identifies the school's name and part of the policy. Save it as U3Ch04SchoolStudentName Prepare to share what you learned about this site. Submit your answer and the file as directed by your instructor. [L5]

IN YOUR LIFE

In Your Life questions are intended for discussion in class or online where you can share your personal experience. Restrict your answers to the topics described in each exercise. Submit your answers as directed by your instructor.

1. Evaluate the workstation where you use a computer the most. Start a browser and go to **http://www.osha.gov/SLTC/etools/computerworkstations/** At the left of the window, click **Checklist**. Review the **Evaluation** checklist; it is the first 33 questions. Answer each of the 33 questions as Yes or No. Keep track of how many No answers you have. Describe how well your work environment checks out on this list, and describe what you learned from this exercise. [L5]

2. Many jobs are never advertised; instead, people learn about upcoming openings through a network of friends. To learn more about job searching through networking, start a browser and go to **jobsearch.about.com/cs/networking/a/networking.htm** Describe the tips found on this website that you think might work best for you.[L5]

3. Personal Outsourcing: Outsourcing is not just for large companies; small businesses and even individuals can outsource. Begin by reading more. Start a Web browser and go to **online.wsj.com/article/SB118073815238422013.html** Scroll down the page to **WSJ.com Podcast**. Click **Hear the podcast** and listen to it. Go to one or two of the sites mentioned in the article. Describe what you learned about personal outsourcing and the cost. [L5]

Related Skills exercises expand on or are related to skills presented in the lessons. The exercise provides a brief narrative introduction, followed by instructions in a numbered-step format that are not as detailed as those in the Skill Drill section.

1. Sort Incoming Mail in Outlook

In Outlook and several other mail clients, you can create rules to sort incoming mail. To presort incoming mail based on a word in the subject line, follow these steps:

1. Start Outlook 2007. Display the mail folders. Right-click the **Inbox** folder, and then on the menu, click **Create New Folder**.

2. In the **Create New Folder** dialog box, in the **Name** box, type `Retirement Party` and then click the **OK** button. The subfolder, Retirement Party, is added to the mail folders.

3. On the menu bar, click **Tools**, and then on the menu, click **Rules and Alerts**. On the **E-mail Rules** tab, click **New Rule**. The Rules and Alerts dialog box displays.

4. Under **Stay Organized**, click **Move messages with specific words in the subject to a folder**.

5. At the bottom of the window, on the right side, in the **Step 2** panel, click the **specified words** link. The Search Text dialog box displays.

6. In the Search Text dialog box, in the **Specify words or phrases to search for in the subject** box, type `Retirement` and then click the **Add** button. At the bottom of the dialog box, click **OK**. The Rules Wizard dialog box displays again. Notice that the link *specified words* is replaced by *Retirement*.

7. In the **Step 2** panel, click the **specified** link. The Rules and Alerts dialog box displays. Under **Choose a folder**, next to the **Inbox** folder, click the plus sign next to **display the subfolders**, and then click the **Retirement Party** folder. In the **Rules and Alerts** dialog box, click **OK**. The Rules Wizard dialog box displays again.

8. Use the Snipping Tool to save an image of the Rules Wizard dialog box as `U3Ch05RuleStudentName` and then close the Snipping Tool window.

9. In the Rules Wizard dialog box, at the bottom, click the **Finish** button. The Rules and Alerts box displays.

10. In the Rules and Alerts dialog box, confirm that a new rule named **Retirement** is listed, and then click **OK**.

11. Test the rule by composing an e-mail message that is addressed to you, and include the word **Retirement** in the subject line.

12. Check the **Retirement Party** folder to confirm that your message arrived and was automatically moved to that folder.

13. On the menu bar, click **Tools**, and then on the menu, click **Rules and Alerts**. On the **E-mail Rules** tab, click the **Retirement** rule to select it, and then just above the list of rules, click the **Delete** button to remove the rule. Close the dialog box.

14. In the Mail folders pane, right-click the **Retirement Party** folder. On the menu, click **Delete "Retirement Party"** and then confirm that you want to delete it.

15. **Close** all open windows without saving any changes. Submit the file as directed by your instructor.

2. Explore Windows Meeting Space

Windows Vista has a feature that allows Vista users to collaborate and share applications and files even if they just have wireless network cards in their laptops and are not near a wireless server. This is done by setting up a peer-to-peer wireless connection. The feature is called *Windows Meeting Place*. You do not have to have Vista to do this exercise.

To learn about Windows Meeting Place, follow these steps:

1. Start a Web browser and go to Microsoft.com/Windows.

2. In the **Search** box, type Meeting Space and then click the **Go** button.

3. On the list of search results, select **Explore the features: Windows Meeting Space**.

4. On the **Windows Meeting Space** page, notice that this feature is not included in Vista Home Basic version.

5. Review the features of Meeting Space. Scroll to the section titled **Ad-hoc collaboration**. Use the **Snipping Tool** to capture the screen, and then save the image as U3Ch05MeetingStudentName Submit the file as directed by your instructor.

DISCOVER

Discover exercises give students general directions for exploring and discovering more advanced skills and information. Each exercise is independent of the others, so you may complete the exercises in any order.

1. Create an Outlook Archive File

You need to have the Outlook program to do this exercise; it can be any recent version. Start Outlook. On the menu bar, click **File**, and then click **Archive**. In the Archive dialog box, choose the folder to archive. In the Archive dialog box, choose a date to use as a criterion for archiving the files. Click the **Browse** button and choose a location on your hard disk or removable storage device on which to place the archive file. Use the **Snipping Tool** to capture an image of the Archive dialog box, and save the image as U3Ch05ArchiveStudentName Click **OK**. Submit the file in the format designated by your instructor.

2. Change the Default Backup Setting in Word 2007

Start Microsoft Word 2007. In the upper left corner, click the **Office** button, and then click **the Word Options** button. In the Word Options dialog box, click **Save**. In the Save dialog box, confirm that the **Save AutoRecover information every** option is selected. In the box to the right, change the time to **5**. Use the **Snipping Tool** to capture the screen that shows the new setting for AutoRecover, and save it as U3Ch05RecoverStudentName At the bottom of the Save dialog box, click the **Cancel** button. Close Word and any other dialog boxes. Submit the file as directed by your instructor.

ASSESS YOUR PROGRESS

At this point, you should have a set of skills and concepts that are valuable to an employer and to you. You may not realize how much you've learned unless you take a few minutes to assess your progress.

1. From the student files, open **U3Ch05Assess**. Save it as U3Ch05AssessStudentName

2. Read each question in column A.

3. In column B, answer Yes or No.

4. If you identify a skill or design concept that you don't know, refer to the learning objective code next to the question and the table at the beginning of the chapter to find the skill and review it.

5. Print the worksheet if your instructor requires it. The file name is already in the header, so it will display your name as part of the file name.

6. All of these skills and concepts have been identified as important by surveying hundreds of individuals working at over 200 companies worldwide. If you cannot answer all of the questions affirmatively even after reviewing the relevant lesson, seek additional help from your instructor.

chapter six

The Future of Living Online

Lesson	Learning Outcomes	Code	Related IC3 Objectives
1	Identify analog relationships between voltages and sound waves	6.1	1.1.6
1	Identify the use of binary numbers to digitize analog signals	6.2	1.1.6
1	Identify the function of an A to D converter	6.3	1.1.6
1	Identify the process by which analog signals are converted to digital signals	6.4	1.1.6
1	Identify the advantages of using digital signals	6.5	1.1.6
1	Identify the advantages of digital radio	6.6	4.1.3
1	Identify the way digital images are recorded and reproduced	6.7	4.1.3
1	Identify the analog method used in a CRT to create an image	6.8	4.1.3
1	Identify the difference between interlaced and progressive scanning	6.9	4.1.3
1	Identify the meaning of HDTV ratings like 720p and 1080i	6.10	4.1.3
1	Identify the role of a DVR and a DVD player in a home entertainment center	6.11	4.1.3
2	Identify how GPS is used to increase capacity of a 2G mobile phone system	6.12	4.1.2
2	Identify how the same frequencies are used in a cellular phone system without interference	6.13	4.1.3
2	Identify how a first generation mobile phone identifies itself in a cell	6.14	4.1.3
2	Identify the security problems with first generation mobile phones	6.15	4.1.3
2	Identify how time division multiple access and code division multiple access increases the capacity of a 2G mobile phone system	6.16	4.1.2
2	Identify differences between the GSM system and other systems used in the U.S.	6.17	4.1.2
2	Identify the characteristics of a 3G phone system	6.18	4.1.2
3	Identify virtual input and output devices		4.1.4
3	Identify the characteristics of a human neuron	6.19	4.1.4
3	Identify two methods that use computers to assist hearing	6.20	4.1.4
3	Identify how a microprocessor aids the blind with artificial sight	6.21	4.1.4
4	Identify risks to data and appropriate steps to protect it.	6.22	4.2.3
4	Identify methods and tools to protect and supervise children online	6.23	4.2.5
4	Identify methods and tools to protect and supervise employees online	6.24	4.2.3
4	Identify methods to protect the integrity of the system	6.25	1.1.7, 4.2.4
4	Identify methods to protect privacy	6.26	4.2.8
4	Identify practices that conserve and recycle materials	6.27	4.2.11
4	Identify methods to stay informed about virus threats	6.28	4.2.10

Why Would I Do This?

The way we communicate and compute is becoming more digital and more mobile. Computers are merging with other devices like cell phones and the keyboards and monitors we use every day might soon be replaced by virtual images. Soon, we might be able to manipulate our environment by using computers to interpret our brain activity and then give commands to mechanical devices. These changes could clear desktops at work of bulky equipment and make it even more practical to work from home. If these changes happen in the next few years, you can be prepared for them if you keep informed about progress in these areas and consider how it might affect your workplace. You will conclude this book by reviewing some guidelines for behavior online that remain fundamentally the same, regardless of technological advances, and which provide stability in changing times.

visual summary | In these lessons, you will study how communication technologies that rely on computers are merging and interacting. You will learn how to reduce risks and behave responsibly.

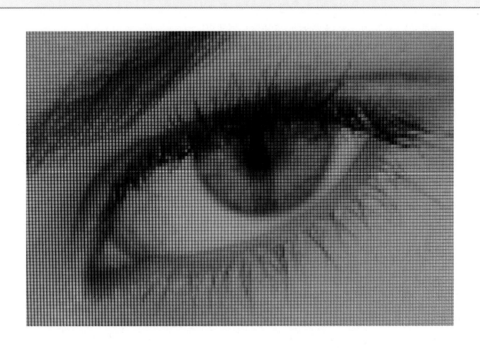

FIGURE 6.1A

FIGURE 6.1B

List of Student and Solution Files

In most cases, you will create files using text or pictures found on Web pages. You will add your name to the file names and save them on your computer or portable memory device. Table 6.1 lists the files you start with and the names you give them when you save the files.

ASSIGNMENT	STUDENT SOURCE FILE:	SAVE AS:
Lessons 1–5	none	U3Ch06SampleStudentName
		U3Ch06HDTVStudentName
		U3Ch06ZoneStudentName
		U3Ch06UnlockStudentName
		U3Ch06ServiceStudentName
		U3Ch06CochlearStudentName
		U3Ch06FBIStudentName
Skill Drill	none	U3Ch06RateStudentName
		U3Ch06StarStudentName
		U3Ch06EmergencyStudentName
Explore and Share	none	none
In Your Life	none	U3Ch06TrackStudentName
		U3Ch06UnlockStudentName
		U3Ch06DisabledStudentName
Related Skills	none	U3Ch06BrainStudentName
		U3Ch06IridiumStudentName
		U3Ch06OrbitStudentName
Discover	none	U3Ch06TopStudentName
		U3Ch06FourGStudentName
Assess Your Progress	U3Ch06Assess	U3Ch06AssessStudentName

TABLE 6.1

▶▶▶ *lesson*
One | Becoming More Digital

The world we experience with our senses usually varies continuously like the flow of a stream or the passing of time, but computers process information using individual numbers. To take advantage of the computer's ability to compress information and transmit it efficiently and accurately, we convert information about our environment into numbers. For comparison, this lesson begins with a description of previous methods of transmitting voices without computers, and then it describes how computers are used to do it more accurately and efficiently.

Analog Telephone

Traditional telephones rely on a system where the electrical voltage in a wire varies the same way that sound waves from a person's voice cause the air pressure to vary on a microphone. The microphone turns the variation in air pressure into a variation in electrical voltage. The variation in voltage changes continuously to match the variation in air pressure of a person's voice, as shown in Figure 6.2.

   If one system mimics another continuously so that you can use it to represent the original, it is an *analog* system. The variation in electrical voltage changes continuously, the same way the air pressure changes. It is carried over wires to a speaker that reproduces the voice, as shown in Figure 6.3, by converting the variations in voltage back into variations in air pressure.

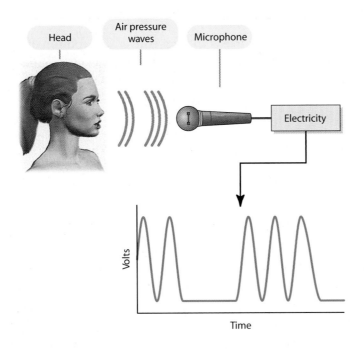

FIGURE 6.2
Microphone converts sounds into analog electrical voltages.

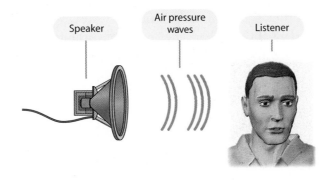

FIGURE 6.3
Speaker converts electrical voltages back into sound waves.

Digital Computers

Most computers use electrical voltage in a much simpler way. Instead of varying continuously, the voltage in a computer's central processing unit jumps back and forth between two voltages. Any system that has only two parts or states is a ***binary*** system. The two voltages used in a computer's processor are represented by the binary numbers 0 and 1. One of the advantages of using a binary system is that many physical devices can be used to represent or store information in binary form. Computers that use binary devices and numbering systems—the large majority of computers—are called ***digital*** computers. Computers were introduced into the telephone system to control the connection of the telephone circuits because that function is binary; i.e., circuits are either connected or not connected.

The central part of a computer is a collection of millions of tiny electrical switches, ***transistors***, that are made of solid crystals and do not have any moving parts. Millions of them can be connected in devices called *microprocessors*, where they perform logical operations. The input devices that are attached to a computer convert the motion of a mouse, the pressing of a key, audio signals from a microphone, or video signals from a camera into simple binary voltages that the microprocessor can use to switch other circuits on or off, based on recorded instructions. Output devices take the simple voltages produced by the microprocessor and convert them into a form that humans understand, such as the visual displays on the monitor or sound waves coming from a speaker. These microprocessors accomplish complicated tasks by doing billions of simple tasks each second.

Analog to Digital Converters

To convert analog voltages—for example, the voltages that vary with the sound of your voice—into binary digital voltages, a device called an *analog to digital (AD) converter* samples the analog voltage many times each second and assigns a binary number to the voltage at each point in time.

To understand this process, assume you are given the task of keeping a record of the outdoor temperature at your location. You have an old-fashioned glass thermometer in which a column of colored fluid rises and falls with the temperature—an analog device. First, you decide how often to read the thermometer—the *sampling rate*—and choose an interval of one hour because that is often enough to detect changes but not so often that it wastes your time. Choosing the sampling rate is always a compromise; frequent sampling produces a more accurate representation, but it produces more data to process. Next, you record the readings using numbers—digits—in sequential order. You have performed the function of converting information from an analog device into digital form; but there is an error, as shown in Figure 6.4.

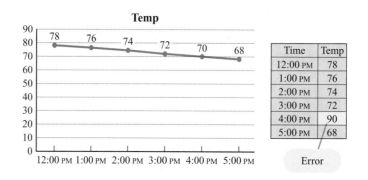

FIGURE 6.4

Falling temperature sampled hourly with an error at 4 pm.

Correcting Errors

Let's assume that you send this sequence of numbers representing outdoor temperatures sampled each hour to someone else. The other person who looks at this sequence of numbers notices that one of the numbers—90—is remarkably different from those that came before and after and does not match the gradual downward trend. By applying some basic logic and knowledge of how slowly outdoor temperatures change, the person would conclude that you had made an error in recording this temperature. The person could reject the unusual number and calculate a replacement number that fits the pattern: 70 instead of 90.

Logic like this can be applied to digital representations of audio signals such as voice or music.

Sampling Rates

To convert an analog voltage that represents human speech, the computer measures the voltage thousands of times each second and converts it into a sequence of numbers, as shown in Figure 6.5.

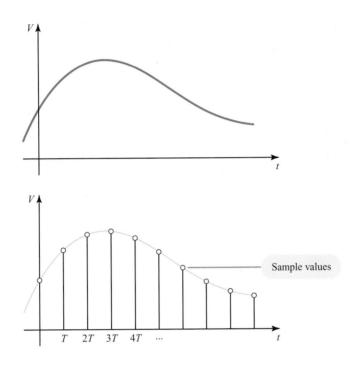

FIGURE 6.5
Sampling of sound waves.

Recall that converting analog systems to a sequence of numbers—A to D conversion—requires compromises between accuracy, speed, and amount of data. A sampling rate of 8,000 samples per second—8,000 Hz—is adequate for understandable human speech, but the higher frequency sounds are missing. Higher sampling rates of 44,100 Hz are used to record music on CDs. The accuracy of the measurement of each sample is determined by how many digits or bits—each 0 or 1 is a bit—are used. Sample values recorded with 8 bits are less accurate than samples recorded with 16 bits.

to listen to examples of sampling rates

You can play sample files that were recorded at different sampling rates and accuracies. You need to have speakers or headphones to hear the examples.

1 **Start a browser. In the Address box, type** `cs.cf.ac.uk/Dave/Multimedia/` `node150.html` **and then press** `↵Enter`. If this Web page has changed and this option is not available, go to `communication.howstuffworks.com/` `analog-digital3.htm` read the page, and then capture the last chart on the page.

2 **Scroll down to** *AUDIO DEMO: Comparison of Sample Rate and Bit Size.* **In the table, click** *44 KHz 16-bit* **to download a sound file.** Notice that the file size is 3.5 Mb or 3,500,000 bits. Once the file is downloaded, the media player associated with that type of file on your computer displays. Look for a Play button that usually has an arrow on it.

3 **Click the Play button and listen to the audio file.**

4 **Repeat this process with the 11 KHz 8-bit file.** Notice the difference in quality.

5 **Move the pointer to the title bar of the player's dialog box. Drag the dialog box to a position next to the table of links, as shown in Figure 6.6.** Notice that the links you have played have changed color.

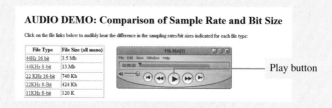

FIGURE 6.6
Samples recorded at different rates and accuracies.

6 **Use the Snipping Tool to capture this screen and save it as** `U3Ch06SampleStudentName` Alternatively, users of Windows XP can press the Print Screen (PrtScn) button on the keyboard and paste the captured screen into a word processing document. Users of Macintosh computers can press Command + Control + Shift + 3 to capture a screen image to the clipboard and paste it into a word processing document.

7 **In the upper right corner of each open dialog box or window, click the Close button** 🗙. **Submit your snip as directed by your instructor.**

Attenuation

When a signal travels through glass or air, it loses some of its energy and becomes weaker. This weakening is called ***attenuation***. If the difference between the two voltages in a digital transmission diminishes for some reason—becomes attenuated—by transmitting the signal over long distances, a ***repeater*** can generate new signals that have the appropriate voltages that match the original digital signal.

Comparison of Analog and Digital Signals

Unlike an analog representation of audio signals that was typical of early audio systems, digital sequences can be examined to detect errors and replacement values can be calculated.

Some advantages of using digital signals to communicate:

- Errors can be detected and corrected.

- It is easier to correct for attenuation.

- Digital signals can be compressed and decompressed by a computer to reduce transmission speed requirements. (Recall from Chapter 4 that this is what a codec does.)

Disadvantages:

- The accuracy depends on the sampling rate.

- Higher sampling rates produce more data that must be transmitted.

- Compromises must be made between the sampling rate and the amount of data recorded.

- Noticeable time lags can occur in synchronous communications if there is too much data to transmit or encode using current technology.

Long-Distance Communication

Digital signals are preferred for sending data over long distances where it is likely that a signal will become weaker or mixed with signals from other sources. Another factor that favors the use of digital signals for long-distance communication is the availability of an alternative to copper wires: fiber-optic cable. Recall that fiber-optic cable consists of strands of very pure glass. To send a digital signal through a fiber-optic cable, the voltages that represent binary numbers are applied to a ***laser diode***—a solid crystalline device that converts electricity to a narrow beam of light of one color—where one of the two voltages causes the diode to emit light, as shown in Figure 6.7, and the other does not. A laser diode is a binary device—the presence of light and its absence are its two states—so it can be used to represent digital information.

The digital signal is converted from two voltages to flashes of light that travel down the glass fiber. At the receiving end, a ***photodetector*** converts the flashes of light back into two voltages that can be used by a computer. Because the wavelengths of light are extremely short and diodes can be turned on and off very quickly, the amount of data that can be transmitted over fiber-optic cables is much higher than other transmission methods. This makes it possible for telephone companies to replace thick cables that used many pairs of copper wire with thin fiber-optic cables that had far more capacity.

FIGURE 6.7

Laser diode converts one of the two voltages into light.

Hybrid Systems

A high-speed digital system requires a microprocessor at each end of the connection to convert signals from analog to digital and back again, and also to correct and compress the data. It requires transmission media as well—like fiber-optic cable—that can transmit data at high rates. The telephone system is a good example of how a mature technology is transitioning to a computerized, all-digital system. Its parts are being replaced with digital systems wherever it is practical and cost effective. The transition began with computerized switching using large, centralized computers. In the next phase, main transmission lines connecting these computers were replaced by digital transmission methods that included microwave radio and fiber-optic cable.

Today's telephone system consists of a mixture of old analog equipment transmitting analog signals, analog devices transmitting digital signals, and all-digital devices. The telephone companies are replacing copper wire with fiber-optic cable in smaller branches of the network, but it is less cost effective to do so because the cables have more capacity than most homes need. The final, relatively low-traffic branch of the system that makes the final connection to the customer's home or place of business is called the *last mile*.

Digital Radio

Radio waves are *electromagnetic (EM)* waves. EM waves are a combination of electric and magnetic fields that are capable of propagating themselves through space without the need for wires or cables. Traditional radio broadcasts use two analog methods of modulating EM waves to transmit audio signals. One of the methods varies the strength—*amplitude*—of the signal to represent the air pressure waves of voice or music, as shown in Figure 6.8. This method is called *amplitude modulation (AM)*.

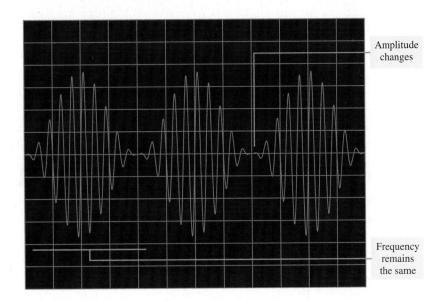

Amplitude changes

Frequency remains the same

FIGURE 6.8
Amplitude modulation.

Other sources of EM waves, such as lightning, produce EM waves in the same frequency range used by AM radio stations but are much greater in strength than the EM waves from a radio station. AM receivers do not have the ability to distinguish between radio signals and those produced by other sources, so AM radio is subject to interference. FM radio stations vary the frequency of the EM wave to simulate audio signals. These FM signals are less affected by large amplitude EM waves from lightning, but they are still analog and do not take advantage of the capabilities of signal processing to correct errors and remove other forms of noise or interference.

The frequencies of EM waves used by analog radio can be used to transmit analog and digital signals at the same time. Computers are utilized to combine the signals at the source. A traditional analog receiver does not recognize the digital component, but a digital radio receiver can separate the digital component and play it instead of the analog component. This method is called *in-band on-channel (IBOC)* and has the advantage of being backwardly compatible with existing analog radios. Radio stations that transmit digital signals are referred to as *digital radio* or *high-definition (HD) radio* because of the reduced static and noise in digital signals. Digital radio would not be practical without the ability to put low-cost digital-signal processors in the radio receivers.

Digital Television

Traditional television uses analog devices to convert images into signals and then back again into images. The same digital technologies that provide better-quality audio for music and radio are being applied to television to improve the quality.

Digital Images

Recall from Chapter 4 that video is a series of still images. An image is converted into a sequence of numbers by using an array of small photo detectors on which the image is focused by a lens. Each photo detector converts the brightness of the light at its location into a voltage. The voltage is measured and the measurement is converted into a binary number.

Color

A voltage is produced for each of three colors: red, green, and blue. The human eye detects these three colors, and the human brain interprets combinations of their brightness as other colors and shades. Humans can distinguish approximately ten million different colors and shades. If each color is recorded using an 8-bit binary number, 256 levels of brightness—shades—can be recorded. The possible combinations of 256 shades of each of 3 colors is more than 16 million, which is enough to represent all of the colors humans can perceive. This level of recording is called *true color* on computer monitor settings.

Resolution

The size of the photo detectors in the array and their spacing determines the amount of detail that can be captured—the resolution. Each small element of the picture that is recorded by a photo detector is called a *picture element* or *pixel*. Digital cameras are often rated by how many pixels their images are divided into. For example, a 6-megapixel camera would use smaller and more numerous photo detectors than a 3-megapixel camera.

Display of Digital Images

If you take out a magnifying glass and take a close look at a flat-panel monitor, you can see that it is divided into triplets of colored bars, as shown in Figure 6.9. At its maximum resolution setting, the monitor uses one triplet of color bars for each pixel of the image.

To display the digital image, the numbers that represent the brightness of each color are transmitted to the appropriate color bar in each pixel. The result is a full-color reproduction of the image, as shown in the close-up in Figure 6.10.

When you choose a *resolution setting* for a computer monitor, you are choosing how many of these triplets are assigned to each picture element. The highest resolution possible for a particular monitor uses one triplet of color bars for each pixel. The monitor setting does not increase the resolution—detail—of the image. Choosing a higher resolution setting on the monitor results in the pixels of an image occupying less of the total screen and makes them appear smaller. Computer monitors are designed to be viewed from about two feet away, so the individual color bars must be small enough so that they are not visible as separate bars. A typical resolution setting for a 17-inch computer monitor is 1280×1024. These numbers represent the number of pixels across and down.

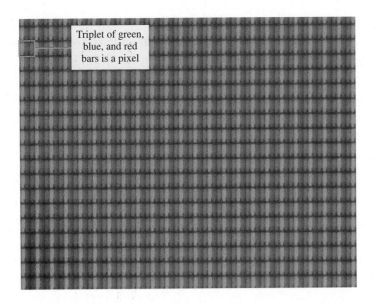

FIGURE 6.9
Computer screen close-up.

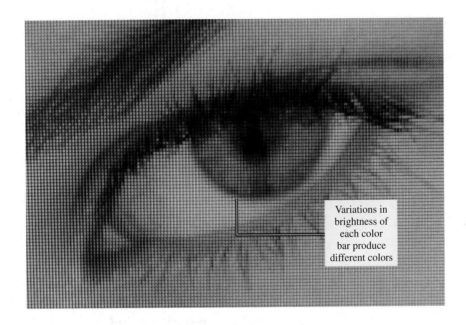

FIGURE 6.10
Image comprised of pixels.

Screen Refresh

If an image is flashed into the human eye, the image will persist in the eye and brain for a short time. If the next image is flashed before the previous one fades away, the image will appear to be continuous. The image on a computer screen is really a series of images. The rate at which they are replaced is called the **refresh rate**. If the refresh rate is too low, it might appear to flicker for some people. Older monitors refresh the screen 60 times per second, and recent model monitors refresh the screen 75 times per second.

A computer converts a sequence of numbers into a two-dimensional image by dividing the pixels up into rows and sending the three color numbers to each triplet in the row from left to right. When it reaches the end of the first row, the computer can skip a row and proceed to do every other row and then start over near the top of the screen to do the remaining rows. This method is used to reduce flicker and is called **interlaced**. If the process does each row in order from top to bottom, it is called **progressive**.

Computer Monitors

Television sets that came before the flat-screen models are analog devices. They use three beams of electrons called **cathode rays** to scan across colored phosphorescent dots on the front of a large vacuum tube—a **cathode ray tube (CRT)**—to reproduce an image, as shown in Figure 6.11. The strength of the beams varies with the brightness of the color. These television sets display images in 525 rows of pixels that are refreshed in alternate rows—interlaced—30 times a second.

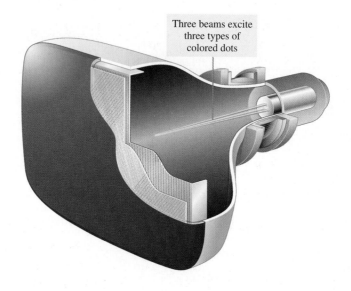

Three beams excite three types of colored dots

FIGURE 6.11
Cathode ray tube.

The resolution available on traditional television was not good enough for use from a foot or two away. Computer makers adapted the analog television CRT for use with computers by redesigning them to display more pixels and with faster refresh rates. Instead of 525 rows of pixels, a typical 17-inch CRT computer monitor displays 768 lines when the monitor is set to 1024×768, and the monitor refreshes the screen 60 to 75 times per second. Note that television resolutions are usually given as references to the number of rows without mention of the number of pixels across. To use an analog CRT monitor, the computer had to convert the digital data that represented the image into an analog signal that was sent to the monitor using a *video graphics adapter (VGA)* connection, as shown in Figure 6.12.

FIGURE 6.12
Analog video monitor connection.

International Television Broadcast Standards

Analog television transmissions are standardized. The use of 525 lines and 30 interlaced frames per second is part of the standard set by the *National Television System Committee (NTSC)*, and it is used in North America, Central America, parts of South America, Japan, the Philippines, South Korea, and Taiwan. The *phase alternating line (PAL)* standard uses 625 lines and 25 frames per second; it is used in most of Western Europe, Western and Southern Africa, Asia, and Australia. The *Séquentiel couleur à mémoire (SECAM)* standard also uses 625 lines but differs in the way it handles color and audio. It was developed by the French and the Soviets and is used in countries formerly controlled by those two powers. See Figure 6.13.

Digital Monitors

CRT monitors have been replaced in most new computer systems with flat-panel displays, most of which use *liquid crystal display (LCD)* technology. Each liquid crystal changes transparency based on the strength of the voltage applied to it, which allows either red, green, or blue light to pass through that appears as colored bars, as shown previously in Figure 6.9.

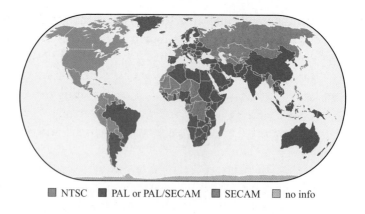

■ NTSC ■ PAL or PAL/SECAM ■ SECAM ■ no info

FIGURE 6.13

Three major analog TV systems.

FIGURE 6.14

Digital video monitor connection.

Newer model computers have monitor outputs—called ***digital visual interface (DVI)***—for digital signals that are sent directly to the LCD monitors, as shown in Figure 6.14.

HD Televisions

The size of an analog television was limited by the size and weight of the glass tube in the CRT. New flat-panel televisions using LCD or similar technologies do not have that limitation and can be much larger. However, if a traditional television signal that only has 525 lines is displayed on a large screen, the pixel size is too large and the image looks grainy or fuzzy. Large television screens require images that have smaller pixels and more of them. To meet this need, newer television broadcasts containing digital images—***high-definition television***

(HDTV)—have more lines of pixels. The resolution of the images displayed on HDTV are assigned codes that indicate the number of lines of pixels and if all the lines are displayed sequentially—progressive—or half at a time—interlaced. For example, a computer that creates a video image that is 1280×720 pixels using a progressive display is 720p.

Because these images are digital, they can be compressed using digital signal processors at the transmission location, and because microprocessors are relatively cheap and small, they can be placed in each new television to decompress the digital signal and distribute it to the elements of the screen.

New HDTV units are very similar to flat-panel computer monitors. Many of them have VGA or DVI ports into which you can plug a laptop or desktop computer; then you can use the HDTV as a very large monitor to display videos from YouTube or other video content that is available on a computer.

The HDTV can be connected to digital devices with a high-speed connection that does not require compression, called a ***high-definition multimedia interface (HDMI)***, as shown in Figure 6.15.

FIGURE 6.15
Digital component connection.

Another advantage of digital television systems is that they can adapt to many different combinations of lines and refresh rates. New standards for digital television are provided by the ***Advanced Television Systems Committee (ATSC)***.

to view the range of available digital TV signals

1 Start a browser. In the Address box, type `www.atsc.org/communications/resources.php` and then press `↵Enter`.

2 On the Web page, click DTV Answers.

3 Near the bottom of the screen, click *Frequently Asked Questions*.

4 Choose one of the questions and click it to display the answer. Use the Snipping Tool to capture this screen and save it as `U3Ch06HDTVStudentName`

5 In the upper right corner of each open dialog box or window, click the Close button [X]. Submit your snip as directed by your instructor.

Digital Video Recorders

A digital television signal is a series of binary numbers that is similar to the data that your computer stores on its hard drive. A device called a digital video recorder (DVR) has a hard drive like a computer on which television programs are recorded for viewing at a later time. A DVR is a computer in a different form. It can be programmed to record shows when you are not home, and it can often record more than one program at a time. Most DVRs are combined with a tuner that allows selection of stations from the cable or satellite service provider, as shown in Figure 6.16.

FIGURE 6.16

DVR and cable tuner.

Some DVR models can be connected to the Internet via an Ethernet cable or wireless home network. They can be programmed to download and store videos on the DVR during the night or while a person is at work, using the *video on demand* feature.

Digital Video Discs

Audio and video signals can be converted to digital signals and recorded on optical discs. Because video recordings have much more data than audio-only recordings, special techniques are used to get as much digital data as possible onto a disc. The ***digital video disc (DVD)*** technology records digital signals as areas on a plastic disc that either reflect or disperse a laser beam to represent the two states of a binary number. High-definition video requires even more data storage capacity. A format called **_Blu-ray disc_** has emerged as the dominant new standard for recording HD video, as shown in Figure 6.17.

FIGURE 6.17

Blu-ray disc.

Interactive Video Games

Interactive video games allow a player to send digital signals to the computer from handheld input devices or from wireless devices, as shown in Figure 6.18.

FIGURE 6.18

Digital remote control.

Integrated Home Entertainment Centers

The devices that comprise a home entertainment center—HDTV, DVR, digital audio system, and interactive game player—use computers and Internet connections to integrate multiple modes of communication, as shown in Figure 6.19.

FIGURE 6.19

Computers integrated into home entertainment equipment.

►►► lesson
two | Becoming More Mobile

As computers and special-purpose microprocessors became smaller and cheaper, they reached the point where they would fit in devices that are easily portable. In this lesson, you find out how very small computers make it possible to navigate and to communicate without wires, using devices that are small enough to carry in your pocket.

Global Positioning System

If you are moving about, it is usually necessary to know where you are. This can be a challenge if you are driving in a new area or are boating where there are few landmarks. The U.S. military developed a navigation system in the 1960s and 70s that used radio signals from satellites to accurately locate ships and airplanes. In 1983, a version of the military system was made available for civilian use, and companies responded by making small units that combined radio receivers and maps to show you exactly where you are.

To make a system that would work in three dimensions from anywhere in the world—a *global positioning system (GPS)*—four satellites needed to be viewable from anywhere on earth, which poses a problem because the earth itself gets in the way. To overcome this complication, 24 satellites—not counting spares—orbit the earth in six different orbits. Each of the satellites orbits the earth twice a day, and they are far enough above the earth so that at least four of them are above the horizon at any time from any place on earth, as shown in Figure 6.20.

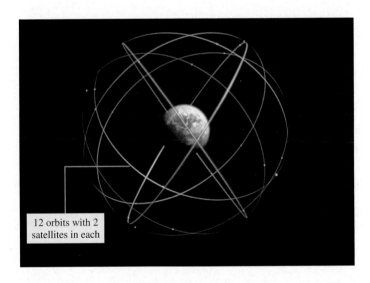

12 orbits with 2 satellites in each

FIGURE 6.20
GPS satellites.

A GPS receiver has an antenna and amplifier that can detect signals from the GPS satellites. GPS receivers can be combined with mapping software to display your exact location and provide driving and boating information in a device that is small enough to fit on the dashboard, as shown in Figure 6.21.

FIGURE 6.21
GPS navigation device.

First-Generation Mobile Phones

One of the limitations of using wires or cables with a phone system is the lack of mobility. Low-cost, compact computers have made it possible to carry a telephone in your pocket and do so without wires. Mobile phones are competing with wired phones to provide connection over the *last mile*. Mobile phones are really two-way radios. To understand the issues related to mobile telephones, some background information is needed about how radio waves are used for communication.

Wireless Devices

Recall that radio waves are electromagnetic (EM) waves that propagate themselves through space without the need for wires or cables; devices that use them for communications are called wireless. EM waves can be created by moving electric charges back and forth on a wire—an **antenna**—but once the EM waves are created, they move outward without wires, as shown in Figure 6.22.

The rate at which the charges move back and forth in the antenna is the frequency, which is measured in **hertz (Hz)**. One hertz is one EM wave per second. EM waves used for communication have frequencies from about 10,000 hertz up to 300 billion hertz. Frequencies of EM waves are often measured in **megahertz (MHz)**, one million cycles per second, or **kilohertz (kHz)**, one thousand cycles per second.

FIGURE 6.22

EM waves travel outward from the antenna.

The same antenna can be used to send and receive. Because the waves spread out in all directions from most antennas that are creating the waves, the receiving antennas intercept only a tiny fraction of the original energy put into the waves, and the waves must be made stronger—*amplified*.

Analog EM Waves

EM waves can be used with analog devices to represent audio if a property of the EM waves varies continuously in a similar manner to the air pressure of sound waves. A common way to use EM waves as analog signals is to vary the frequency to match the variation in sound waves. The devices used for this purpose start by generating an EM wave at a particular frequency. The frequency can be increased or decreased slightly to correspond to changes in air pressure, which is called *frequency modulation (FM)*, shown in Figure 6.23.

Role of the Government

The *Federal Communications Commission (FCC)* allocates ranges of EM frequencies for different public uses. The FCC specifies what frequency a broadcast station can use so that it does not overlap with the signal from an adjacent station. The FCC can allocate the same frequency to different stations if they limit the power of the stations so that their signals are too weak to detect within each other's locations.

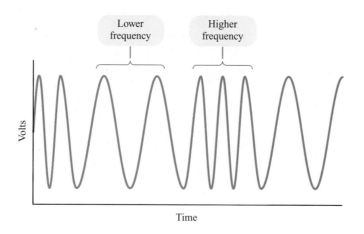

FIGURE 6.23

Frequency changes with sound or voice.

The FCC used a similar strategy for mobile phones. In 1983, the FCC assigned the range of EM frequencies from 824 MHz to 894 MHz—called the **800 band**—for use by analog mobile phones. This range is divided into bands that are .03 MHz wide to allow for frequency modulation above and below the central frequency. The channels are separated by .045 MHz to avoid interference between calls. This system is called the **advanced mobile phone system (AMPS)**. It was advanced in 1983, but there are now other, more advanced, systems in use.

Cells

A mobile phone is a portable two-way radio. It has an antenna that is used to receive and transmit EM waves. The FCC allocates 832 separate frequencies for mobile phone use in a city. Each phone needs two frequencies so that both parties in a conversation can talk and listen at the same time; this is called **full duplex**. The pair of frequencies is called a **channel**. If mobile phones used one, large antenna for an area, the antenna could only provide service to about 400 users at a time.

One way to get around this limitation is to severely limit the power of the transmissions so that they only travel a few miles, which allows for use of the same frequencies in several different locations in the same city. This technique is used to make mobile telephone service practical. Instead of using a centralized antenna to transmit a one-way signal like the commercial broadcast stations do, the mobile telephone system uses many antennas. The antennas are usually mounted high above nearby buildings on towers, and the antennas are often called **cell phone towers** or just **towers**. The area around each tower can be thought of as a six-sided area called a **cell**. The coverage areas are really circles, but the six-sided image makes it easier to visualize because each cell is adjacent to six other cells, as shown in Figure 6.24. The cells typically cover ten square miles of area, and the towers for the same service provider are roughly seven miles apart.

Each cell is allocated 56 pairs of frequencies that are different from those allocated to the six adjacent cells. A mobile phone that is designed to work in this system is called a **cell phone**.

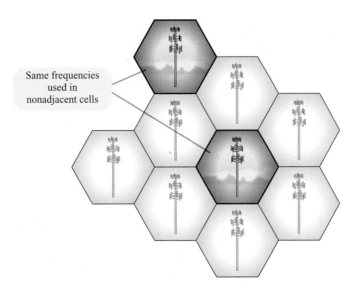

Same frequencies used in nonadjacent cells

FIGURE 6.24

Adjacent cell towers use different frequencies.

Control and Identification

Some of the pairs of frequencies—control channels—are reserved for managing the connections between the tower and the mobile phones. Recall from Chapter 5 that this control channel is also used for texting. Each cell phone service provider is assigned a *system identification (SID)* code by the FCC. Each antenna in a company's system broadcasts its SID using the control channel. When a cell phone is turned on, it checks the control channel frequencies to see if an antenna that belongs to its service provider is close enough to use.

To correctly identify each cell phone, an *electronic serial number (ESN)* is programmed into the phone when it is manufactured. When the cell phone is purchased, it must be *activated*; this includes recording a *mobile identification number (MIN)*—based on the telephone number assigned to that phone—and the phone's ESN into the phone's memory. The SID of the service provider is also added to the phone's memory.

Each cell phone tower in a particular area is connected to and controlled by the *mobile telephone switching office (MTSO)*. The MTSO has a computer that manages connections between the towers and individual phones in the area, and it connects the cell phones to the rest of the telephone network—the public switched telephone network (PSTN)—as shown in Figure 6.25.

When a cell phone is turned on near one of the company's towers and the phone receives the appropriate company SID, the phone transmits its identification number (MIN) and its serial number (ESN) which are received by the tower and forwarded to the computer in the central office (MTSO). The computer compares the MIN to a database of current customers to confirm that this phone is one of theirs. It makes note of the tower that it is nearest to in a database, in case a call for that phone comes in. It also compares the MIN and ESN to confirm that this phone was legitimately activated. The phone transmits its MIN periodically, and the MTSO updates its location in the database as needed.

If a call comes in for a phone in the area served by a particular MTSO, the computer looks up the phone in its database and determines which tower is nearest. The computer uses a control channel frequency to send a ring signal to the phone. If someone answers, the MTSO assigns a pair of unused frequencies to the call for the duration of the call. This system relies on

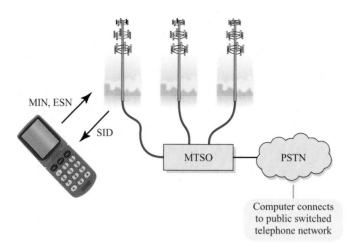

FIGURE 6.25

First-generation mobile phone identification.

the computing power of a central computer at the MTSO, with limited capability from the mobile phone, and is called *first-generation (1G)* technology.

Managing Movement Between Cells

The signal from a mobile phone can be picked up by more than one tower, but the signal will be stronger at the closest tower. The computer at the MTSO compares signal strength if it receives the same MIN from more than one tower, and it assigns it to the tower with the best signal. If the phone is moving, the relative signal strength changes as it gets farther away from one tower and closer to another. The programming in the computer projects the trend in changing signal strength and chooses a new pair of frequencies available at the next tower. When the moving phone gets closer to the next tower, the computer at the MTSO transfers the call to the next tower and sends a signal to the phone over a control channel to switch to the new pair of frequencies. The computer can do this so quickly that the participants in the call usually do not notice.

Dead Zones

EM waves can be blocked by buildings, metal enclosures, or hills. An area in which the mobile phone cannot connect to a cell tower is a *dead zone*. Because service providers often have their own cell towers, the dead zone for one provider might not be a dead zone for a different provider.

to locate dead zones

Service providers register their towers with the FCC. This information is public knowledge and can be accessed on websites like Mobiledia.

1 **Start a browser. In the Address box, type** `cellreception.com` **and then press** ⏎Enter.

2 **Scroll down to *Dead Spot Search* and read the paragraph.** The title is also a link.

3 **Click *Dead Spot Search.*** The *Cell Phone Dead Spots* page displays. This is a collection of complaints from cell phone users about specific locations where reception is poor for particular providers.

4 **On the map, click the state in which you reside. Scroll down to the table. In the table heading, click Location.** The postings are sorted by zip code, as shown in Figure 6.26. Notice that there are many pages of complaints in most states. Because they are sorted by zip code, you can click the pages listed to locate your own zip code.

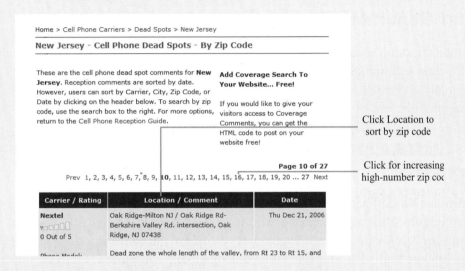

FIGURE 6.26
Dead zone complaints by zip code.

5 **Try different pages of complaints to find a complaint from your zip code or one in your state.**

6 **Use the Snipping Tool to capture this screen and save it as**
U3Ch06ZoneStudentName

7 **In the upper right corner of each open dialog box or window, click the Close button ⊠. Submit your snip as directed by your instructor.**

If the mobile phone moves into an area where its signal does not reach the tower, the call is interrupted; it is a ***dropped call***. A call might be dropped if the phone moves into a cell when all of that cell's frequencies are in use.

Limitation of First-Generation Cell Phones

First-generation cell phones were limited by the number of frequencies available to only 56 active calls per cell in most systems. As cell phone use became more popular, dropped calls became more common due to lack of available frequencies.

Another problem was lack of security. Special receivers called *scanners* are available that check several different frequencies to find which ones are in use and then allow the user to listen. The scanner can also intercept the MIN and ESN that are broadcast by the mobile phone, which can be used to make unauthorized calls.

Second-Generation Digital Mobile Phones

As computers became smaller and more powerful, they could be placed in the mobile phone itself. The same technologies that allow computers to send binary data over phone lines that were originally designed for analog signals can be used with mobile phone systems designed to use analog modulations of EM waves.

Emergency Calls

The traditional wired telephone system assumed that the telephone was in a fixed position. The telephone number was associated with a physical address so that if you knew the telephone number from which a call originated, you knew the location of the caller. In North America, you can call 911 on a telephone and your call will automatically be routed to an emergency call center. Even if you cannot speak, the computer at the telephone switching center can provide the number from which the call originated and the billing address for that number.

The FCC mandated an update to the 911 emergency call system known as the *wireless Enhanced 9-1-1 (E9-1-1)*. They required cell phone operators to provide a method of pinpointing the location of a cell phone to within 50 to 100 meters for 911 calls made from a cell phone. Companies responded by placing a GPS receiver in many cell phones so that emergency responders could locate a caller using a mobile phone, as shown in Figure 6.27.

There are other methods that can meet this requirement, such as comparing the strength of the phone's signals at several towers, but the GPS solution has another benefit. Each cell phone that has GPS also has an inexpensive clock that is extremely accurate because it is constantly updated by the *atomic clocks*—clocks that use the vibration of atoms to regulate time—in satellites. This accurate timekeeping method can be used to synchronize the computer in the phone with the computer at the tower.

Sharing the Same Channel

When you use a *second-generation (2G)* mobile phone, a built-in computer samples your voice and digitizes it. The digital signal is compressed using a codec. The binary signal is transmitted to the local tower by alternating between two frequencies using a method called *frequency-shift keying (FSK)*. For digital telephone conversations, the sampling, digitizing, compression, and decompression can be done by a dedicated processor called a *digital signal processor (DSP)* that is faster than a programmable processor.

FIGURE 6.27
Mobile E9-1-1.

Because the voice signal from each 2G mobile phone is digitized and compressed, its data can be transmitted in about one third as much time as a 1G phone. Second-generation phones contain accurate clocks that are synchronized with the clocks in GPS satellites and the computer at the MTSO, so they share the use of a single channel among several phones. Each phone gets to use the channel, but they have to take turns. Each phone is allowed to use the channel for 6.7 milliseconds (thousandths of a second) to send a burst of compressed data and then waits for each of the other phones to have their turns before sending its next burst. Because this sharing happens so quickly, it goes unnoticed by humans. This method is called **_time-division multiple access (TDMA)_**, and it triples the capacity of each cell in the system.

Adding More Channels

In 1994, the FCC, as well as Industry Canada, assigned the range of frequencies from 1850 MHz to 1990 MHz—the **_1900 band_**—for cell phone use to meet the demand for more channels due to the increased popularity of cell phones. Channels in the 1900 band can be divided into eight time slots using accurate synchronizations between phones and the central computer system.

Sharing Many Channels

The short bursts of digitized and compressed data that represent small portions of a phone call can be exchanged with the tower on any of its channels—not just one. If each short transmission is given a code that identifies it as belonging to a particular call and a time stamp that is very accurate, the computer at the MTSO or the computer in the mobile phone can use any of the channels in that cell that happen to be available at the moment to transmit or receive the call and reassemble it on arrival, as shown in Figure 6.28. This method is called ***code-division multiple access (CDMA)***.

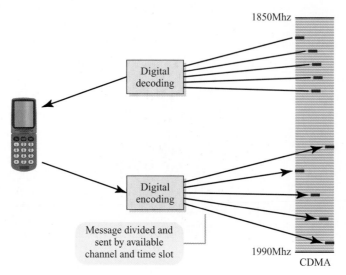

In CDMA, each phone's data has a unique code.

FIGURE 6.28

Code-division Multiple Access.

The TDMA and CDMA methods allow a mobile phone system to transmit approximately ten times as many calls on the same set of frequencies as the first-generation AMPS analog system.

Choosing Modes

When you initiate a call from a mobile phone, the phone uses the control channels to communicate with the MTSO to determine what frequencies and types of service are available from the local tower. It will attempt to use the most efficient and advanced methods first, but if they are not available, it will fall back on the older-generation technologies.

Global System for Mobile Communications

Mobile telephone service in other parts of the world outside North America developed differently. In Europe and parts of Asia, mobile phone services use different ranges of EM frequencies, methods of time-sharing signals, and encrypted data. Approximately 80 percent of the mobile phones in more than 200 countries use the **global system for mobile communications (GSM)** standard. The GSM standard uses time-sharing (TDMA) methods, and it uses encryption to make the calls more secure. A phone that is designed for use with GSM contains the subscriber's indentification and subscription information on a small flash-memory card called a **subscriber identification module (SIM)** card, as shown in Figure 6.29, instead of using the ESM that is built into the phone.

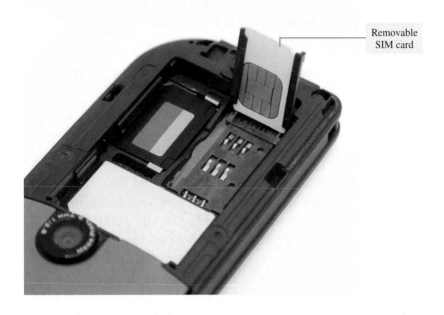

Removable
SIM card

FIGURE 6.29
Cell phone with SIM card.

GMS was designed to provide a common standard for use by different manufacturers of cell phones and by different service providers. To change service providers using a GSM phone, you simply have the SIM card reprogrammed with the new service provider's codes. If you buy a new phone, you can transfer the SIM card to it and sell your old phone.

GSM phones are available in the U.S. from a few companies, but those companies often prevent customers from using the same phone on a different service by **locking** the phone—programming it to prevent exchange of SIM codes for use with a competitor's service.

to learn more about unlocking GSM phones in the U.S.

Some service providers lock GSM phones to prevent their use on other services even if the user buys the phone from another source.

1 **Start a browser. In the Address box, type** `thetravelinsider.info/roadwarriorcontent/unlockingfaq.htm` and then press ⏎Enter.

2 Scroll down to Contents. Under Contents, to the right of the first link, *What is a SIM and what is unlocking,* click the small arrow. The display jumps down the page to display the section on this topic.

3 On the browser's toolbar, click the Back button to return to the Contents area of the page.

4 Use this method to read the first five topics.

5 With the topic *Is it legal to unlock my phone* displayed, use the Snipping Tool to capture this screen and save it as U3Ch06UnlockStudentName

6 In the upper right corner of each open dialog box or window, click the Close button ▄X▄. Submit your snip as directed by your instructor.

Mobile phone systems in Europe use different frequency ranges. Instead of using the 800 and 1900 bands, they use the 900 band (880-960 MHz) and the 1800 band (1710 to 1880 MHz). Phones designed to send and receive in the 800 and 1900 bands will not work in Europe, and phones that only send and receive in the 900 and 1800 bands do not work in the U.S. Phones are available that can use all four bands and three modes—AMPS, TDMA, and GSM. These phones will work almost anywhere in the world.

Second-generation phones are capable of connecting to the Internet at speeds similar to those of the old dial-up systems used with analog telephones by using *general packet radio service (GPRS)*, with data transfer rates of 56 kbps (kilobits per second) to 114 kpbs.

Third-Generation Digital Mobile Phones

Third-generation (3G) mobile phones require processors that are almost ten times more powerful than 2G phones so that they can use more advanced time- and frequency-sharing techniques to increase the amount of data that can be exchanged between the phone and the MTSO. Three of the these techniques are:

- *CDMA2000*—an advanced version of code-division access that achieves data transfer rates of up to 4.8 Mbps (megabits per second)

- *WCDMA*—*wide band code-division multiple access* to attain data transfer rates of about 2 Mbps

- *TD-SCDMA*—*time-division synchronous code-division multiple access* to transfer data at rates up to 2 Mbps

These data transmission rates make it possible to use a 3G phone for low-quality video calls, live updates of maps that coordinate with the built-in GPS receiver, and playing downloaded music. They can download a 3-minute-long song in MP3 format in as little as 15 seconds.

to find out what type of mobile phone service is available in your area

In the U.S., there are several different service options that range from early analog service to third-generation service using international standards.

1 **Start a browser. In the Address box, type** `wirelessadvisor.com` **and then press** ⏎Enter.

2 **Under Find Service, to the left of the Submit button, type a zip code for an urban area, and then click the Submit button.** Alternatively, click the link below the box and select a major city from the list.

3 **Scroll down the list and observe the acronyms used to describe the services and which frequency bands each service uses.**

4 **Return to the previous Web page , enter your local zip code, and then click Submit.**

5 **Scroll to display some of the options in your area. Use the Snipping Tool to capture this screen and save it as** `U3Ch06ServiceStudentName`

6 **In the upper right corner of each open dialog box or window, click the Close button** **X** **. Submit your snip as directed by your instructor.**

Fourth-Generation Mobile Phones

It is reasonable to anticipate that computers will continue to get smaller, cheaper, and faster; the result will be faster communications between mobile phones and the rest of the network. The next generations of mobile phones will have data connection speeds that rival or exceed wired connections. Internet connectivity using the same TCP/IP protocols that are used on the Internet will allow mobile phones to function as mobile computers, with all the features that a desktop computer has now.

A 4G phone by Hitachi, as shown in Figure 6.30, became available in Russia in the fall of 2008.

This generation of mobile phone is really a mobile computer, and the distinction between a computer and a phone is disappearing. As mobile phones continue to increase in computing power and the connection speeds match wired computers, they are in a position to replace traditional computers. The main limitation that prevents this is the small size of the phone's input and output devices, but that is likely to change soon.

FIGURE 6.30

Next-generation mobile phone.

▶▶▶ *lesson*
three | Input and Output Devices Becoming Virtual

Recall that the four basic functions that identify a computer are input, memory, processing, and output. An advanced cell phone has a processor and memory that are limited by the size of the phone and the life of its battery. These limitations can be offset if it has high-speed communication with a network server where files can be stored and processor-intensive tasks can be perfomed. The remaining limitation is the size of its screen and keyboard. New input and output devices are on the way that can remove those limitations.

Virtual Keyboards and Monitors

One method of removing the limitations of bulky physical monitors and keyboards is to replace them with projected images.

Virtual Keyboards

A traditional keyboard is a device that converts the action of depressing a key into a binary number that the computer can use to represent the letter or number on that key. A keyboard is usually large enough to accommodate all of a person's fingers at the same time to facilitate rapid input. The physical keyboard can be replaced by an image of a keyboard that is projected on any flat surface: a *virtual* keyboard. A video camera can record the position and motion of a person's hands on that surface, and special programs can interpret those motions as keystrokes to produce the same input as if the person were typing on a physical keyboard, as shown in Figure 6.31.

FIGURE 6.31

Projected keyboard.

Virtual Monitors

A desktop computer monitor is normally much larger than the screen on a mobile phone. To overcome this limitation, a high-resolution screen mounted close to the eye—shown in Figure 6.32—can appear to be a large-screen monitor floating in space in front of the viewer.

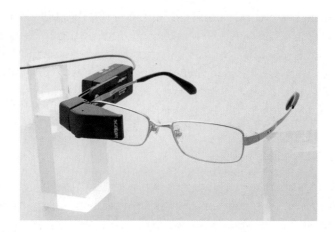

FIGURE 6.32
Virtual monitor.

Inputs to the Brain

The next stage in making computers more mobile is to eleminate the keyboards and monitors entirely and replace them with direct interactions with the human nervous system. Development of these technologies is in the early stages. The resulting devices will be particularly helpful to people who cannot use their hands, eyes, or ears with traditional input and output devices.

The human brain does not function like a digital computer. Instead of simple switches made of crystals that have three connections, a nerve cell—a ***neuron***—can have thousands of branches that connect with other nerve cells, as shown in Figure 6.33.

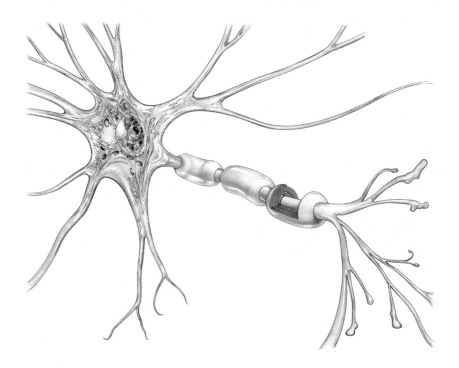

FIGURE 6.33
Illustration of a neuron.

The human brain has about one hundred billion—100,000,000,000—neurons, each of which is connected to approximately seven thousand other neurons. This extremely complex set of connections is more complicated than scientists can understand in detail at this time. They are still in the early phases of mapping and discovering ways to connect directly to this extraordinarily complex information-processing and storage system.

Hearing with Computers

One way to provide input to the human nervous system is to send electrical pulses to the organs that convert external analog inputs like sound and sight into nerve pulses. The human ear is a type of analog signal converter. The eardrum vibrates in response to variations in air pressure waves. It is connected by small bones to nerve cells in the *cochlea* that convert the motion into nerve impulses, as shown in Figure 6.34.

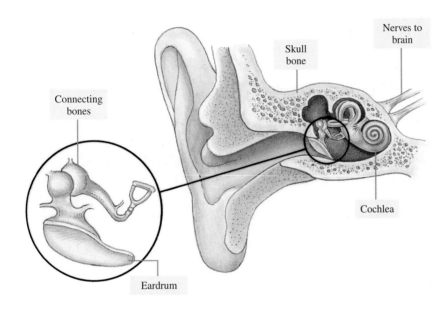

FIGURE 6.34

Ear converts sound pressure waves into nerve impulses.

If the eardrum or connecting bones are not functioning, scientists have developed a technique for using a small computer—a *cochlear implant*, shown in Figure 6.35—to convert sound waves into electrical pulses that the cochlea can convert into nerve impulses.

If an alternate method of hearing can help the hearing impaired, the same technology might enable someone with normal hearing to hear higher or lower frequencies than normal or to listen directly to digital radio broadcasts.

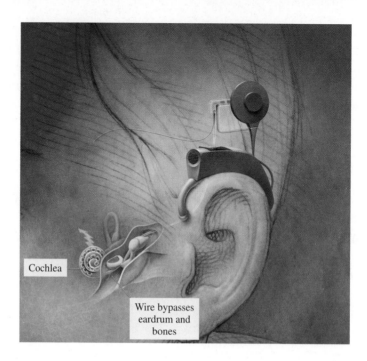

FIGURE 6.35

Cochlear implant.

to learn more about cochlear implants

1 **Start a browser. In the Address box, type** `www.nidcd.nih.gov/health/ hearing/coch.asp` **and then press** `↵Enter`.

2 **Scroll to the section titled *How does a cochlear implant work?* and read the section. Use the Snipping Tool to capture this screen and save it as** `U3Ch06CochlearStudentName`

3 **In the upper right corner of each open dialog box or window, click the Close button** `X`. **Submit your snip as directed by your instructor.**

Vision with Computers

A similar project is under way to provide artificial vision for people who have lost their sight due to damage to parts of the *retina*—the part of the eye that converts an image into nerve impulses. A video camera is mounted on the frame of a pair of sunglasses. The camera is connected to a microprocessor behind the ear that transmits a radio-frequency EM wave to a receiver inside the eye, as shown in Figure 6.36. The microprocessor translates this video image into impulses that are sent to an array attached to the back of the eyeball where part of the retina is still functional.

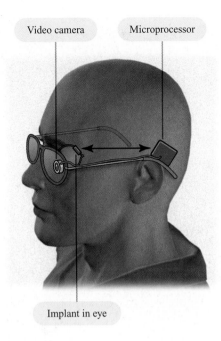

Video camera

Microprocessor

Implant in eye

FIGURE 6.36
Artificial retina.

If an alternate method of vision can help the visually impaired, the same technology might enable someone with normal vision to see in other ranges of the EM spectrum such as infrared and ultraviolet. The visual output of a computer could be perceived directly without a monitor.

Output by Interpreting Electrical Activity of the Brain

Neurons communicate with each other using a combination of chemical and electrical signals. The movement of charged particles in the brain's neurons creates electromagnetic (EM) waves that can be detected outside a person's body. By placing an array of small antennas around the brain, as shown in Figure 6.37, scientists have associated different parts of the brain with different types of activities such as mathematics.

Microprocessors that are smaller, faster, and more powerful than their predecessors can be placed in headsets that can sense brain activity, interpret facial expressions, and manipulate virtual objects in video games, as shown in Figure 6.38.

If the electrical activity of the brain can be interpreted as actions that move virtual objects in a video game, those actions can be converted by a computer into electrical voltages that control motors. These motors can move wheelchairs or mechanical devices that replace hands or limbs, as shown in Figure 6.39. If this process becomes more sophisticated, it could be used as an output method to control cars, airplanes, or any other mechanical device by using thoughts to execute commands or actions.

The traditional idea of a computer consisting of a system unit with a processor and memory, a keyboard, and a monitor is becoming obsolete. The next generation of computers might consist of a unit even smaller than a cell phone that uses a small microphone to pick up your voice and connection devices that provide virtual images and sounds while interpreting your brain activity as commands.

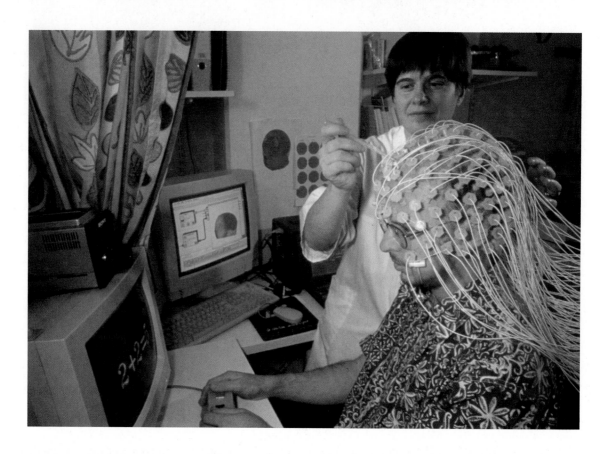

FIGURE 6.37

Sensing mathematical activity in the brain.

FIGURE 6.38

Brain-wave input device.

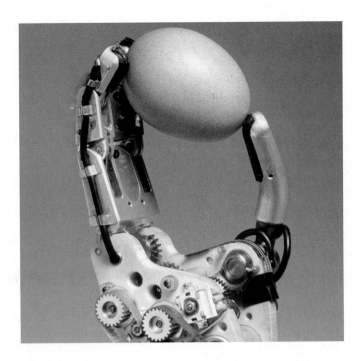

FIGURE 6.39

Mechanical hand controlled by nerve impulses.

Changes of this type will affect the way we use desktop space in the office, how we control the mechanical devices in our lives, and where we work and play. If you keep informed about the progress of these trends, you can anticipate how they might affect you personally.

▶▶▶ *lesson*
four | Prudent and Responsible Practices

In spite of the rapid changes that are affecting the physical shape and mobility of the computer, the way computers are used must be guided by the same principles of prudent and responsible behavior that have worked in the past. This final lesson is a summary of the practices that help make living online at work or at home safe and effective—even if the form and mobility of the computer changes.

Protecting Data and System Integrity

Users of a computer system must be able to trust the output. To trust the system, the programs must be functioning correctly and the data they use must be correct. To maintain this trust, users must be vigilant against efforts by people with malicious intent to place unauthorized programs on the computer or to alter the data.

Protecting System Integrity

The Federal Trade Commission provides a framework for companies to use to protect the integrity of their computer systems in order to protect the information they contain about consumers. These guidelines can be used for individual systems or for businesses:

- Identify the internal and external risks to security, confidentiality, and integrity.
- Design and implement safeguards to control the risks.
- Adjust the security plan according to the results of testing.
- Oversee the information-handling practices of service providers or other people who have access to your computer or its records.

To stay informed of external risks, you can make use of expert advice from the government. The FBI keeps track of the top 20 most commonly exploited vulnerabilities of computer systems and provides information on how to protect your system from them.

Standard practices for protecting computer systems include:

- Use antivirus and antimalware software and their automatic update features to protect against known threats from viruses, worms, spyware, and other malware.
- Update application software such as Microsoft Office products regularly to repair security flaws as they are discovered.
- Use firewall software to intercept threats from known sources.
- Do not use wireless LAN connections unless they are encrypted.
- Stay informed about breakouts of new viruses from a reliable source—not from rumors that could be hoaxes.

Protecting Data

If an attack gets past the system defenses, there are policies and procedures to follow that can limit the damage. Begin by recognizing the types of threats to data:

- It can be stolen and removed from your possession.
- It can be copied without your knowledge.
- Some of it can be destroyed.
- It can be altered subtly so that it contains errors that are hard to find, making a whole database unreliable.
- Incorrect information can be substituted without your knowledge, which you might incorrectly affirm to be accurate, thus harming your reputation.
- It can be used to commit a crime such as impersonating someone.
- It can be used to blackmail someone if it is sensitive information.

Whether the data is yours or is the property of the company you work for, you should recognize its value and take appropriate steps to protect it, such as:

- Restrict use to authorized persons for approved purposes
- Protect passwords or other codes. If you use a password on a public computer, restart it when you are finished.
- Make backup copies on media that will last for the intended period
- Encrypt sensitive data to prevent tampering

- Report breaches of security, even if the data seems to be intact
- Follow procedures for identifying, isolating, and removing infected files
- Restore uncompromised data from backup systems

Protecting and Supervising People

If you are in a position of responsibility, you must use your knowledge of living online to protect others from external threats. The rights to individual freedom of expression must be balanced against the need to protect children and prevent harmful activities like harassment and bullying.

Protecting Children

If you are a parent, you have an obligation to protect and to supervise the activities of underage children. You can choose to selectively block—*filter*—a child's access to sites on the Internet. These are some methods and tools available for meeting your obligations:

- Set up a user account for each child with its own password so that filter settings will be child-specific.
- Use filtering options.
    - Client-side filters: Install programs that monitor and filter activity.
    - Service-provider content filters: Choose an ISP that offers content filtering.
    - Server-side filters: Determine if organizations where the child searches the Internet—such as schools—use filters on network servers to limit access.
    - Use search engine settings such as those in Internet Explorer to filter websites.
- Monitor behavior by visual observation to determine if the type of activity and time spent is appropriate.
- Be alert for addictive behavior that is characterized by the inability to stop, or limit participation to reasonable times. The addiction can be to game-playing or use of social networking, alternative-reality sites, or excessive texting.
- Monitor online activity with tracking software that records all sites visited and time spent.
- Be aware of practices used by predators to gain access for illegal purposes.

to visit the Department of Justice Website on Child Exploitation & Obscenity

The Department of Justice maintains a Web page with information about how to protect children and report illegal activity.

1 **Start a browser. In the Address box, type** `www.fbi.gov/publications/pguide/pguidee.htm` **and then press** `⏎Enter`**.** Notice the extra *e* in the name of the Web page—pguidee.htm.

2 Scroll down and read several of the paragraphs that describe signs of at-risk children. Choose one to capture.

3 Use the Snipping Tool to capture this screen and save it as
`U3Ch06FBIStudentName`

4 In the upper right corner of each open dialog box or window, click the Close button
X . Submit your snip as directed by your instructor.

Protecting Employees

If you are a supervisor at an organization, you have an obligation to the company to protect it from lawsuits arising from inappropriate or illegal behavior by employees and to protect employees from inappropriate or illegal behavior by other employees or by outsiders. You can work with the network administrator or your Internet service provider (ISP) and human affairs department to establish guidelines for employee behavior and your role in supervising them. Be alert for addictive behavior that carries over into the workplace, such as game-playing, use of social-networking sites, gambling, or viewing pornography. Work with your network administrator to respond quickly to external attacks on the system. If computers are compromised, use backup files and computers in other locations to allow your employees to continue to work.

Protecting Privacy

Recognize that if you work at an organization and use the computers, cell phones, or PDAs that the company provides, the organization has a right to monitor your activities and read any files or correspondence if notice is given. In the U.S., this notice might be a paragraph in the employee handbook. Be aware of company policy regarding personal use of computers or communication devices while at work.

When you are using a computer at home, you can limit the amount of personal information that is collected about you by limiting the information you provide voluntarily.

- Use an alias in blogs or social networking sites
- Do not provide personal information such as credit card numbers, account numbers, names of pets, or birthdates in a reply to an e-mail message.
- Do not provide information about relatives—particularly information such as your mother's family name—that could be used as a response to an identification question.
- Use adware software to block cookies used to identify your browsing habits if you do not want the services of targeted advertising.
- Use privacy settings in Web browsers to manage the use of cookies.

Recycle and Use Green Equipment

Responsible use of computers and communications equipment that contain microprocessors includes managing the waste they produce and recycling as many of the parts and materials as possible.

Paper

According to the Environmental Protection Agency (EPA), Americans recycled more than 50 percent of the paper used in 2007. Most paper mills are designed to blend used paper into the process of making new paper. Recycling paper reduces the amount of energy and water needed to make new paper and reduces the need for new landfill space.

Toner and Ink Cartridges

Inkjet printers have cartridges for ink that must be replaced periodically. Some cartridges are simple plastic containers, but others include the device that sprays the ink droplets. The spray heads wear out but can often be used for more than one load of ink. They are not easy to refill by hand, but there are services that will exchange empty ink cartridges for full ones for a fee. Laser printers and copiers use powdered ink called *toner*. Some cartridges can be refilled, or they can be exchanged for refilled cartridges.

Manage eWaste

Used computer equipment that is still functional can be donated to charitable organizations or schools. Discarded computers, cell phones, PDAs, televisions, and radios are called *eWaste*. Because electronic equipment becomes obsolete within a few years, used equipment presents a disposal problem, as shown in Figure 6.40. The devices contain metals and chemicals that are hazardous if the units are burned or buried improperly in a landfill. They often contain precious metals like gold that is used to provide corrosion-free electrical contacts, and they can be recycled profitably. Some firms that recycle eWaste ship the devices to underdeveloped countries where the metals are extracted without proper environmental safeguards. Check with the recycling center you use for eWaste and confirm that it does not export the waste for recycling to countries where environmental protection is not practiced. Erase data storage devices and destroy them physically to prevent theft of sensitive data.

FIGURE 6.40

eWaste is discarded electronic equipment.

Prudent and Responsible Practices

Conserve

The basic concept of conservation is to avoid consuming when there is not a need. You can conserve the fuel used to create electricity by turning off computers at night and on weekends when they will not be in use. If you leave your computer on because it takes a long time for it to start up, you can remove temporary files from your Web browser's cache and remove adware and spyware to speed startup; then turn the computer off when not in use. Many electronic devices have instant-on or standby features, which means that they are not really turned off and are consuming electrical power. Use the computer's operating system power management option to shut down components that are not in use. When you buy paper, choose paper that has recycled content for most purposes, and only use the highest quality paper when the occasion warrants it.

SUMMARY

In this chapter, you learned about the trend toward using digital devices for mobile communications and entertainment. You learned about developments in connecting humans to digital computers to help disabled people and to improve the interface between computers and humans. Finally, you reviewed a summary of practices to enable you to live online safely, securely, and responsibly.

You can extend your learning by reviewing concepts and terms, and by practicing variations of skills presented in the lessons.

KEY TERMS

1900 band	**attenuation**	**digital**
800 band	**binary**	**digital radio**
activated	**bit**	**digital signal processor (DSP)**
advanced mobile phone system (AMPS)	**Blu-ray disc**	**digital video disc (DVD)**
Advanced Television Systems Committee (ATSC)	**cathode ray**	**digital visual interface (DVI)**
	cathode ray tube (CRT)	
	CDMA2000	**dropped call**
amplify	**cell**	**electromagnetic (EM)**
amplitude	**cell phone**	**electronic serial number (ESN)**
amplitude modulation (AM)	**cell phone tower**	
	channel	**eWaste**
analog	**cochlea**	**Federal Communications Commission (FCC)**
analog to digital (AD) converter	**cochlear implant**	
	code-division multiple access (CDMA)	**filter**
antenna		**first generation (1G)**
atomic clock	**dead zone**	

frequency

frequency modulation
(FM)

frequency-shift keying
(FSK)

full duplex

general packet radio service
(GPRS)

global positioning system
(GPS)

global system for mobile
communications (GSM)

hertz

high definition (HD) radio

high definition television
(HDTV)

high-definition multimedia
interface (HDMI)

in-band on-channel
(IBOC)

interlaced

kilohertz (KHz)

laser diode

last mile

liquid crystal display
(LCD)

locking

megahertz (MHz)

microprocessor

mobile identification
number (MIN)

mobile telephone switching
office (MTSO)

National Television System
Committee(NTSC)

neuron

phase alternating line
(PAL)

photo detector

pixel

progressive

refresh rate

repeater

resolution

resolution setting

retina

sampling rate

scanner

second generation (2G)

Séquentiel couleur à
mémoire (SECAM)

subscriber identification
module (SIM)

system identification (SID)

time-division multiple
access (TDMA)

time-division synchronous
code-division multiple
access (TD-SCDMA)

toner

transistor

true color

video graphics adapter
(VGA)

virtual

wide band code-division
multiple access (WCDMA)

wireless

wireless Enhanced 9-1-1
(E9-1-1)

CHECKING CONCEPTS AND TERMS

MULTIPLE CHOICE

Circle the letter of the correct answer for each of the following.

1. Which of the following would produce
   the most accurate digital representation
   of an analog event? [L1]
   a. lower sampling rate
   b. frequency modulation
   c. higher sampling rate
   d. amplitude modulation

2. Why does digitizing a signal make it possible to make corrections? [L1]
   a. A computer can compare each value to
   its neighbors in the sequence and
   detect values that are probably incorrect and then replace them.
   b. Computers can work with analog
   values directly to make comparisons.

c. Binary numbers are more accurate than the numbering systems that use ten digits.

d. Digital signals have more possible values than analog signals.

3. What is the role of a repeater in a long-distance transmission? [L1]

a. retransmitting the signal as exactly as possible

b. providing multiple paths on adjacent strands of the same cable to provide redundancy

c. restoring the original strength of the signal and sending it on its way

d. copying the original signal and then sending it a second time so the two can be compared at the destination to see if either of them was changed

4. How does time-division multiple access (TDMA) make it possible to transmit more calls over the same phone lines? [L2]

a. The call is compressed, parts of it are transmitted over different frequencies, and then it is reassembled.

b. A compressed version of the call takes less time, so different calls can take turns using the same frequency.

c. The time allotted to each call is limited based on the amount of traffic in the cell.

d. The minutes available to each caller at the lowest rate are allocated to different times of the day.

5. How does code-division multiple access (CDMA) make it possible to transmit more calls over the same phone lines? [L2]

a. The call is compressed, parts of it are transmitted over different frequencies, and then it is reassembled.

b. A compressed version of the call takes less time, so different calls can take turns using the same frequency.

c. The time allotted to each call is limited based on the amount of traffic in the cell.

d. The minutes available to each caller at the lowest rate are allocated to different times of the day.

6. How is the identity of the user determined with a GSM phone? [L2]

a. The person's universal telecommunications identification (UTI) number is programmed into the phone's memory when it is activated.

b. The electronic signature of the phone is combined with the phone's electronic serial number (ESN) to create a mobile identification number (MIN) that identifies the user.

c. The user must enter the mobile identification number (MIN) when the phone is first turned on, and this number is transmitted when the phone is in use.

d. The identification of the caller and service provider is recorded on the SIM card and broadcast by the phone when it makes contact with the tower.

7. How is the identity of the user identified with a first-generation phone using AMPS? [L2]

a. The person's universal telecommunications identification (UTI) number is programmed into the phone's memory when it is activated.

b. The electronic signature of the phone is combined with the phone's electronic serial number (ESN) to create a mobile identification number (MIN) that identifies the user.

c. The user must enter the mobile identification number (MIN) when the phone is first turned on, and this number is transmitted when the phone is in use.

d. The identification of the caller and service provider is recorded on the SIM card and broadcast by the phone when it makes contact with the tower.

8. When you choose a higher-resolution setting for a computer monitor, what happens? [L1]

   a. You can see more detail in the image.

   b. The image appears smaller on the screen. *Tighter/sharper*

   c. The image has less detail.

   d. The image gets bigger on the screen.

9. Which analog television standard is used the most in Western Europe and how does it differ from the NTSC standard? [L1]

   a. SECAM; it has fewer lines per screen than NTSC

   b. PAL; it has fewer lines per screen but more images per second

   c. ATSM; it has more lines per screen and it uses a progressive scan

   d. PAL; it has more lines but fewer images per second

10. What is a possible problem with recycling old computers or televisions that could actually harm the environment more than disposing of them in a landfill? [L4]

   a. Nothing—disposing eWaste in a landfill is the worst choice.

   b. Older electronic devices use more toxic materials than new ones, and reusing them exposes people to those toxins more than buying new equipment.

   c. Some eWaste is sent to other countries where it is processed without environmental controls. *mercury phosphrus*

   d. If an old CRT monitor is crushed, it releases gasses that attack the ozone layer.

MATCHING

Match each term in the second column with its correct definition in the first column by writing the letter of the term on the blank line in front of the definition.

_C_ 1. Cochlear implant

_F_ 2. Amplitude modulation

_A_ 3. Cathode ray tube

_J_ 4. Channel

_B_ 5. Dead zone

_D_ 6. Electronic serial number

_I_ 7. Global system for mobile communications (GSM)

_E_ 8. Time-division multiple access (TDMA)

_G_ 9. Code-division multiple access (CDMA)

_H_ 10. eWaste

A. Analog display device

B. Area without cell phone service

C. Device that converts sound into electrical pulses the ear can convert into nerve pulses

D. Identification number of a particular cell phone

E. Method of sharing a frequency between phones by taking turns using the frequency

F. Vary the strength of a signal to represent an analog event

G. Method of distributing a call across several frequencies

H. Discarded computers, cell phones, and televisions

I. Standard for mobile communications in most countries

J. Pair of frequencies.

Skill Drill exercises reinforce chapter skills. Each skill reinforced is the same, or nearly the same, as a skill presented in the chapter. Detailed instructions are provided in a step-by-step format.

Each exercise is independent of the others, so you can do the exercises in any order.

1. Compare Sampling Rates

The sampling rate must be high enough to capture the pattern of change.

To learn more about the importance of choosing the right sampling rate, follow these steps:

1. Start a Web browser. In the **Address** box, type `help.adobe.com/en_US/Soundbooth/2.0/` and then press ⏎Enter.

2. Under *Using Soundbooth CS4*, to the left of *Digital audio fundamentals*, click the plus sign to display the submenu.

3. On the submenu, click **Understanding sound**. Read this page.

4. On the submenu, click **Digitizing audio**. Read this page.

5. Scroll to the section titled **Understanding sample rate** and display the chart that shows the waves and the effect of high and low sampling rates.

6. Use the Snipping Tool or alternative screen capture method to capture this screen and save it as U3Ch06RateStudentName

7. In the upper right corner of each open dialog box or window, click the **Close** button. Submit your snip as directed by your instructor.

2. Learn More About Automobiles, GPS, and Cell Phone Integration

Automobile companies offer services that provide information to drivers using a combination of GPS, cell phone technologies, and live operators.

To learn more about this integrated information service, follow these steps:

1. Start a Web browser program. In the **Address** box, type `auto.howstuffworks.com/onstar.htm` and then press ⏎Enter.

2. On the first page, click the Play button on the video to watch this one-minute explanation of how the OnStar system works.

3. After watching the video, under **Inside this Article**, click **5. OnStar Controversy**. Read this page. Scroll the screen to display an inset box titled **The Competition**.

4. Use the Snipping Tool or alternative screen capture method to capture this screen and save it as U3Ch06StarStudentName

5. In the upper right corner of each open dialog box or window, click the **Close** button. Submit your snip as directed by your instructor.

3. Emergency GSM Cell Phone Number

The GSM standard uses the same emergency number anywhere in the world where there is GSM standard service.

To learn about calling emergency services on a GSM cell phone, follow these steps:

1. Start a Web browser. In the Address box, type `allheartattack.com/ utils/emergency-numbers.php` and then press `↵Enter`. This site provides emergency contact information for heart attack victims.

2. Under **Emergency phone numbers**, there is a list of links to regions of the world. Below that list are two paragraphs that describe how mobile phone users with GSM phones can get emergency service anywhere by dialing just one number—112.

3. Scroll down to display those two paragraphs and read about the requirement for a valid SIM card.

4. Use the Snipping Tool or alternative screen capture method to capture this screen and save it as `U3Ch6EmergencyStudentName`

5. In the upper right corner of each open dialog box or window, click the **Close** button. Submit your snip as directed by your instructor.

EXPLORE AND SHARE

Explore and Share questions are intended for discussion in class or online. Look for information that is related to the learning outcomes for this chapter as directed. Submit your answers as directed by your instructor.

1. The control channel can be used to turn on the microphone in a cell phone without the user's knowledge. This technique was used in 2006 by the FBI as a variation on the traditional wiretap. Use a Web browser and go to a search engine site like Google.com. Search for the keywords `FBI cell phone tap` Choose an article on this topic from a reputable news source and read it. Copy the Web address of the article and save it in a blank word processing document. Prepare to share what you learned about this subject and to provide the address of your source. Submit your answer and the file as directed by your instructor. [L4]

2. Some efforts to recycle eWaste actually result in more ecological damage than throwing the computers and television sets in the dumpster. Find out more about international trade in recyclable eWaste. Use a Web browser to go to `ngm.nationalgeographic.com/2008/01/high-tech-trash/ carroll-text` Read this article and make notes on what you learn. Use a search engine to discover more about this topic. Prepare to share what you learn and to provide the address of your source. Submit your answer and the file as directed by your instructor. [L4]

3. There is more than one approach to using computers to process images and send them to the brains of visually impaired people. One system uses a computer to convert images into sounds. Learn more about these options and share what you discover. Start a browser and go to `www.artificialvision.com` Near the top of the page, there are links labeled **brain implant** and **retinal implant**. Use these links and other links on the site to explore

the topic. Find out the differences between an auditory system, a brain implant, and a retinal implant. Make notes on what you learned. Prepare to share what you learned about this site. Submit your answer and the file as directed by your instructor. [L3]

IN YOUR LIFE

In Your Life questions are intended for discussion in class or online where you can share your personal experience. Restrict your answers to the topics described in each exercise. Submit your answers as directed by your instructor.

1. The GPS unit in a cell phone can be used to track and report its location. This service is available to individuals as well as the government. You can track the location of a child's cell phone. Learn more about this option by starting a Web browser and going to accutracking.com At the top right of the screen, click the **DEMO** button. On the next screen, under Demo Login, click the **Login** button. A sample screen displays showing two phones that are being tracked. Click on one of them to display the dialog box. In the dialog box, click **View History**. A map with locations and paths displays. Scroll down to display the part of the table that has a log of each location. Use the Snipping Tool or alternative screen capture method to capture this screen and place it in a word processing document. Record your thoughts about this product in that document below the screen capture. Save the file as U3Ch06TrackStudentName Submit the file as directed by your instructor. [L2]

2. Learn more about unlocking a GSM phone. Start a browser and go to thetravelinsider.info/roadwarriorcontent/unlockingfaq.htm Scroll down to **Contents**. Under **Contents**, to the right of the first link, *What is a SIM and what is unlocking*, click the small arrow. Read this section. Use the browser's Back button to return to the Contents menu. Use this procedure to read the first five topics, finishing with *Is it legal to unlock my phone?* Form an opinion about unlocking a GSM phone purchased in the U.S. from a company that locks the phone's SIM card. Open a word processing document and write down your thoughts. Quote a few portions of this website and provide the link to your source. Save the file as U3Ch06UnlockStudentName and then submit it as directed by your instructor. [L2]

3. You may know someone who has hearing or vision loss or who has lost the use of parts of their body because of nerve damage. Learn more about how computers are helping people to regain the functions of hearing, sight, or use of limbs. Pick one of these areas. Use a Web browser and search engine to find information about the topic of your choice. Open a word processing document and use it to record what you find. Copy or capture images from websites and record the Web address of each source. Describe what you learn about how computers are helping disabled people, in the same document as the pictures. Obtain information from at least three different websites. Save the file as U3Ch06DisabledStudentName and then submit it as directed by your instructor. [L3]

RELATED SKILLS |

Related Skills exercises expand on or are related to skills presented in the lessons. The exercise provides a brief narrative introduction, followed by instructions in a numbered-step format that are not as detailed as those in the Skill Drill section.

1. Learn More About Control by Brain Waves

To learn more about controlling your environment using your thoughts, follow these steps:

1. Start a Web browser and go to `emotiv.com`
2. Near the top of the screen, click the **News** tab. Read or watch at least one of the news items about this product.
3. Click the **Products** tab, and then click **product demos**. Watch the video on using facial expressions to control a wheelchair. This video takes less than two minutes.
4. Under **Product Demos**, watch **Emotiv Detections**. When you get to the screen titled **Emortal: Online Portal**, pause the playback.
5. Use the Snipping Tool to save an image of the screen that shows the **Emortal** title. Save it as `U3Ch06BrainStudentName`
6. **Close** all open windows without saving any changes. Submit the file as directed by your instructor.

2. Find Out About Using Satellite Phones

Unlike a cell phone, a satellite phone links directly to satellites in low earth orbit and provide connections to remote areas not served by cell phones.

To learn about satellite phones, follow these steps:

1. Start a Web browser and go to `telestial.com`
2. At the left of the page, click **Satellite Phones**. Read the two paragraphs on this page.
3. Near the bottom of the Web page, in the **Satellite Phones Rental** section, click **Find out how it works**.
4. Scroll down to show the table of rental rates.
5. Use the Snipping Tool to save an image of the screen that shows the Iridium phone rental rates. Show it as `U3Ch06IridiumStudentName`
6. **Close** all open windows without saving any changes. Submit the file as directed by your instructor.

3. View GPS Satellite Orbits

To view the orbits of GPS satellites and other communication and navigation satellites, follow these steps:

1. Start a Web browser and go to `science.nasa.gov/Realtime/jtrack/3d/JTrack3D.html`

2. Under **Satellite Tracking**, click **J-Track 3D**. A window opens that shows the earth and the numerous satellites that are in orbit around it.

3. On the menu bar, click **Satellite**, and then on the menu, click **Select**. Another small window opens.

4. Drag the windows so that they are side by side.

5. In the **Satellites** window, click the name of a satellite.

6. In the **JTrack 3D** window, observe that the orbit of the satellite you selected is shown in red.

7. In the **Satellites** window, scroll down to the satellites whose names begin with GPS. Click one of those satellites.

8. Use the Snipping Tool to save an image of the screen that shows the JTrack3D window and the Satellites window side by side. Save it as U3Ch06OrbitStudentName

9. **Close** all open windows without saving any changes. Submit the file as directed by your instructor.

DISCOVER

Discover exercises give students general directions for exploring and discovering more advanced skills and information. Each exercise is independent of the others, so you may complete the exercises in any order.

1. **Learn More About Protection Against the FBI's Top 20 Security Risks** Open a blank word processing document and save it as U3Ch06Top20StudentName Start a browser and go to www.sans.org/top20/ Under **Client-side vulnerabilities in:** click **C2. Office Software** to jump to that section of this long Web page. Alternatively, scroll down to section C2. Scroll down to display the column chart of the number of vulnerabilities in Microsoft Office. Use the Snipping Tool or alternative screen capture method and paste the image of this page into the word processing document saved as U3Ch06Top20StudentName. Return to the previous page. Repeat this process for two more of the links listed. Finally, from the original page, click the **Best Practices for Preventing Top 20 Risks**. A list of seven steps displays. Capture this screen and paste it into the word processing document. The document should have four screen captures. Save the file and close it. Submit the file as directed by your instructor.

2. **Learn About the Next Generation of Cell Phones** The first 4G phone became available in November 2008 from HTC for release in Russia. Start a browser and go to a search engine such as Google.com. Search for articles on 4G cell phones Use an advanced search to limit your search to articles that have been published in the last month or in the last six months. Compare the data speeds available with the 4G technology and compare them to GPRS and 3G. Use the Snipping Tool to capture a screen that shows a 4G phone. Paste the image into a word processing document. Below the image, describe new features that are available on this generation of phone, and include the Web addresses of the sites from which you obtained the screen and any other information that you cite. Save the file as U3Ch06FourGStudentName Submit the file as directed by your instructor.

ASSESS YOUR PROGRESS

At this point, you should have a set of skills and concepts that are valuable to an employer and to you. You may not realize how much you've learned unless you take a few minutes to assess your progress.

1. From the student files, open **U3Ch06Assess**. Save it as U3Ch06AssessStudentName

2. Read each question in column A.

3. In column B, answer Yes or No.

4. If you identify a skill or design concept that you don't know, refer to the learning objective code next to the question and the table at the beginning of the chapter to find the skill and review it.

5. Print the worksheet if your instructor requires it. The file name is already in the header, so it will display your name as part of the file name.

6. All of these skills and concepts have been identified as important by surveying hundreds of individuals working at over 200 companies worldwide. If you cannot answer all of the questions affirmatively even after reviewing the relevant lesson, seek additional help from your instructor.

Glossary

800 band Range of frequencies from 824–894 MHz

8.3 convention An early DOS file-naming convention that used up to eight letters or numbers to the left of a period and up to three characters to the right of a period

1900 band Range of frequencies from 1850–1990 MHz

3-D pie chart A 3-dimensional disk that is divided into wedges that resemble pieces of a pie

A

AAC (.aac) Popular audio compression method

absolute cell reference In a formula, a reference to a cell location that is stored as a given row and column and does not change when the formula is filled

activated Process of recording the service provider's SID and the user's MIN into a phone

active cell The cell where data will display when you type

active-matrix display An LCD monitor type that charges each pixel as necessary

ActiveX Programming language suitable for automating functions on Web pages

ActiveX controls Small programs developed by Microsoft that add functionality to existing programs

adaptive computer device Input devices designed for special needs of people with different types of disabilities

address bar Displays your current location in the folder structure as a series of links separated by arrows

address book Feature that stores a list of names and e-mail addresses with other information

address box Area of a browser in which the Web address is entered

administrator Top level of computer access that enables a person to add or delete programs, add users, and make other significant changes

add-on Program that extends the capability of an application

advanced mobile phone system (AMPS) Early standard for 1G mobile phones

Advanced Research Projects Agency (ARPA) Government agency that created a network of computers named ARPANET that was the forerunner of the Internet

Advanced Television Systems Committee (ATSC) Standard for high definition TV

adware Programs that display advertising without the user's permission

Aero The advanced graphical user interface introduced in Vista

algorithm A set of instructions that a computer can follow to accomplish a task

alignment The horizontal placement of text, whether it is between the left and right margins in a Word document, in a cell on an Excel worksheet, on a PowerPoint slide, or in a graphic object

All Programs Option on the Start menu that displays all installed programs

alpha version The first version of a software program; it comes before beta testing

Alternate (Alt) key Key on the keyboard intended for use with other keys to provide new functions

American Psychological Association (APA) One of two commonly used styles for formatting research papers and reports

American Standard Code for Information Interchange (ASCII) A group that chose which eight bit numbers would represent letters, decimal numbers, and special function characters

amplify Make stronger

amplitude Strength of a wave

amplitude modulation (AM) Varying the strength of a signal

analog An electronic signal or system that varies in time in a way that is similar to the event it is portraying

analog to digital (A to D) converter A device that takes an analog input, such as a voice recorded by a microphone, and converts it to a digital signal

anchor A symbol that indicates the paragraph with which a graphic object is associated

and Logical operator that requires that all criteria be met

animation The process of making objects on the screen move; in PowerPoint, controls how text and other objects come onto the screen during a slide show

antenna Device that conducts charged particles to generate or receive EM wave energy

appliance A computer that is dedicated to a particular task or function

application program Programs with which you can accomplish tasks such as word processing, photo editing, or sending e-mail

application service provider (ASP) Software provided online for special purposes on a license or per-use basis

application software See *application program*

archive Inactive storage

archiving Removing from active use to a storage location

argument A value or expression used by the function, which instructs Excel how to execute the function

ARPANET Network of computers managed by the Advanced Research Projects Agency

asynchronous Communications that do not require the participants to take part at the same time

asynchronous digital subscriber line (ADSL) Type of fast connection to the Internet provided by telephone companies

atomic clock Time-keeping device that uses vibrations of atoms for high accuracy

attenuation Weakening

auction Offer for sale to the highest bidder

AutoArchive Feature for automatically moving files from active use to inactive storage

AutoComplete A feature that begins to complete a cell entry based on other entries in the same column

AutoFit Automatic process to adjust the width of a column or height of a row to fit the largest content

automatic teller machine (ATM) Computer terminal that can dispense cash and accept deposits

AutoRecover A feature that saves a copy of open files at regular intervals to create a version of the file that can be recovered in the event of a computer malfunction

B

backbone Connections between networks

backdoor Program that bypasses normal security measures to allow outside access

backlight Fluorescent light used with LCD panels

backwardly compatible The ability of a newer version of a program to open and display files that were created using an earlier version of the program

bandwidth Range of frequencies used for transmission

bar chart Uses horizontal rectangles whose length represents the value of the data

bar code reader Device that reads a series of vertical bars and spaces that represent a code that can include price and inventory information

BD-R A Blu-ray disc that can be recorded one time

BD-RE A Blu-ray disc that can be erased and recorded many times

BD-ROM A Blu-ray disc that is read-only

beta tester Person who evaluates a prerelease version of software

beta version Early version of the software released to a limited audience for testing

bibliography A list of sources used in a report, which are listed at the end of the document

binary System that has two states that can be represented using zeros and ones

biometric device A security device that can match a user's biological information—comparing fingerprints, retinal scans, or voice prints—with patterns stored in a database to confirm the identity of authorized users

bit (b) A single digit—either a zero or a one—in a binary number

bitmap (.bmp) Rectangular array of picture elements where each has a number to indicate color

blind carbon copy (Bcc) The address to which a copy of an e-mail message is sent that is not revealed to the other recipients

blog Online personal journal, short form for *weblog*

blogosphere Collection of all blogs

Blu-ray Optical disc technology that enables you to save 25 GB on a single-layer disc and 50 GB on a dual-layer disc that is the standard for recording HDTV

Bluetooth A wireless standard used for short distances. Used to connect cell phones and headsets, MP3 players and headphones, and wireless keyboards and mice

body The main part of an e-mail message containing the principle information to be conveyed

body language Communication by gestures and body position

Bookmarks List of website addresses for future reference

Boolean logic Formal rules for making decisions

boot To start the computer

borders Lines on the edges of the cells

bots Automated programs

bridge Connection between two similar networks that use the same protocols

broadband Using multiple signals of different frequency on the same medium to provide fast Internet connections that are always active

broadband coax Type of coaxial cable that can carry signals farther than normal coaxial cable

browser Program that displays Web pages

buffer Memory used to store data temporarily while downloading

bug Errors found in programs that cause the program to fail to complete its operation successfully

build Subdivision of a version used for large software projects

bullet A symbol—often a small round dot—that precedes items in a list

bulleted list A list of information that is in no particular order; each item in the list is preceded by a small symbol or bullet point

bullet point A line of text that is preceded by a small dot or other symbol

burn To write data to an optical disc

business-to-business (B2B) Exchanges between two businesses

business-to-consumer (B2C) Exchanges between businesses and consumers

byte (B) A group of eight bits used to represent characters, decimal numbers, and other special characters

C

cable modem Device that separates data from television signals

cache Temporary storage area

call center Group of people at one location who use audio communications to provide service

callouts Shapes that have a pointer and that contain text

CAPTCHA Distorted word that is recognizable by humans but not computers

carbon copy (Cc) Duplicate of the message

cash flow analysis The process of tracking money coming in and going out

cathode ray Beam of electrons

cathode ray tube (CRT) Analog imaging device that uses a beam of charged particles in a glass vacuum tube that uses an electron beam to create pictures on the end of the tube that is covered with light-emitting phosphors

CDMA2000 Advanced code-division access standard used in 3G phones

CD-R Optical disc to which data may be written

CD-ROM Optical disc from which data may be read

CD-RW Optical disc from which data may be read and to which data may be recorded and rewritten

cell The intersection of a row and column in a worksheet or a table or the area around a mobile phone tower

cell address The column letter and row number that are used to identify a cell in an Excel worksheet

cell phone Mobile phone that uses the cell system

cell phone tower Antenna used in mobile phone systems

cell reference In Excel, the identification of a specific cell by its intersecting column letter and row number

center Text that is aligned horizontally in the middle of an area

central processing unit (CPU) The "brains" of the computer; performs calculations and controls communication in the computer

certificate authority (CA) Entity that warrants the identity of a member

chain e-mail Messages intended to be duplicated and forwarded

channel Pair of frequencies used for full-duplex communications

chat Text-based exchange that takes place when both parties are present

checksum The total of the numbers in a packet

Children's Online Privacy Protection Act (COPPA) Law that protects the rights of children on the Internet

chip Another term for microchip

cipher text Encoded document

circuit breaker Safety device to disconnect electric power

circular reference An error in a formula that is caused when the cell that contains the formula results is included in the formula argument either directly or indirectly

circuit switching Wires that make up a circuit are connected at a central location

citation A reference in a text to the source of the information

classified ad Advertisement that is categorized

click through Using a hyperlink to get to another Web page

client Computer or program that requests services from a server

clip art Images used to illustrate a variety of topics that come with Microsoft Office or are obtained from other sources

clock A device that sends out pulses used to coordinate computer component activity

clock speed The rate at which the clock circuit emits pulses

Close button Closes a file or the application if only one file is open

clustered column chart Groups columns together for convenient comparison between values of the same type

coaxial cable Wire within a tube of metal, both of which are insulated

cochlea Portion of the ear that converts pressure into nerve impulses

cochlear implant Device that converts sound waves into electrical signals that are transmitted to the cochlea where they are converted to nerve impulses

codec Program or hardware that codes and decodes files to make them smaller

code-division multiple access (CDMA) Method of distributing a call over available frequencies

code group Subset of a coded message

column chart Uses vertical rectangles whose height represents the value of the data

column heading In the Computer window Content pane, identifies the columns; click on the headings to sort the file list

Command key Macintosh key similar in function to the Alternate key on other keyboards

command-line interface A way of interacting with the operating system using the keyboard

comment A note that an author or reviewer adds to a document that displays in either a balloon-shaped graphic or in the Reviewing pane

compact disc (CD) Portable, round optical storage medium

compact flash card Removable electronic memory that does not need power to retain data; typically used in digital SLR cameras

comparison operators Symbols that are used to compare two values

compatibility mode Office 2007 files that a saved with a previous version file format

compression Method of reducing file size

Computer In the Computer window, a toolbar that provides buttons to perform common tasks

computer-based training (CBT) Training that is delivered and assessed using a computer

Computer Security Resource Center (CRSC) Government site for security information

conditional formatting A selected format that is applied if a criterion is met

consumer-to-consumer (C2C) Exchanges between individuals

Content pane In the Computer window, displays the contents of the folder selected in the Navigation pane—the active folder

context sensitive Choices that display on a shortcut menu that are related to the specific area in the window or document where you clicked

contextual tabs A tab that contains tools that are related to the selected object and only displays when a related object is selected

Contrast ratio The range between the darkest black on the screen and the brightest white

Control (Ctrl) key Key on the keyboard intended for use with other keys to provide new functions

control channel Frequency used to manage mobile phones

Control Panel A set of options that sets default values for the operating system

cookie Text file that contains identification numbers

Copy A command used to duplicate selected data and place it in temporary storage for use in another location in a file or in another file

copyright The legal right of the artist, author, composer, or playwright to exclusive publication and sale of artistic, literary, musical, or dramatic work

country code top-level domain (ccTLD) Two letter code that designates a country at the end of a URL

course management system Software that provides components of a class, either online or in combination with face-to-face instruction; usually provides a syllabus, calendar, lectures, chatrooms, a gradebook, and other features

crimeware Program designed to steal information for the purpose of impersonation in order to gain financially

crop To hide a portion of an image by removing unnecessary parts of the image

cumulative total Also known as a *running total*; the sum of the current value plus the previous total

currency Standard unit of value

currency format Similar to accounting format but it places the currency symbol next to the number on the left

Cut A command that removes text or images from its original location and makes it available for use in another location

cybercafé Place that serves food and drink and provides Internet access

D

data Raw, unprocessed facts and figures

database Lists of data organized in tables where each column is a type of information and each row is one person, event, or interaction

database management system (DBMS) A relational database that controls large amounts of data, and provides data security, multi-user access, and can be customized to fit the user's needs

database server Manages requests for data from a database

data source A mail merge file that contains organized data that includes names, addresses, and other information necessary to merge with a document for mailing purposes

dead zone Area without cell phone service

debugging The process of removing bugs or errors from a software program

decryption Reversing the encoding process to make a message readable

default printer The printer that a document is sent to when the Print button is clicked

defragment Rearrange data on a hard disk so that files are written on adjacent sectors

denial of service (DOS) Overloading a server with requests for service so that it denies service to legitimate users

desktop The basic screen from which Windows and applications are run. The desktop consists of program icons, a taskbar, a Start button, an optional Windows Sidebar, and a mouse pointer

desktop computer A personal computer that fits well in an individual workspace but is not mobile

desktop publishing Creating professional-quality newsletters, flyers, brochures, and booklets on a PC; also a type of software

device driver A small program that is written to provide communication instructions between a peripheral device and the computer's operating system; also called a *driver*

Device Manager Windows dialog box that provides information about devices connected to the computer

dialog box A box where you select settings and choose what actions you want the computer to take

dial-up Connection to the Internet that uses telephone voice circuits

diff Feature that highlights changes made to a document

digital Uses digits; typically refers to a binary system

digital radio Broadcast radio that includes a digital signal

digital signal processor (DSP) Microprocessor that is dedicated to converting and compressing signals

digital signature Identifying characteristics that are encrypted with a private key

Digital Subscriber Line (DSL) Digital subscriber line; uses high-pitch tones people cannot hear to transmit data

digital to analog (D to A) converter A device that takes a digital file, such as an image from a digital camera, and converts it to an analog signal

digital light processing (DLP) Projection technology that uses thousands of mirrors that are controlled by the computer

digital single lens reflex (DSLR) Semi-professional and professional still cameras that use interchangeable lenses and give the photographer complete control over the photography process

digital versatile disc (DVD) See *digital video disc*

digital video disc (DVD) Optical storage that can be recorded in layers on both sides; also called *digital versatile disc*

digital video recorder (DVR) Video recording and replay device that uses a hard drive

digital video interface (DVI) port A standard digital video interface that used to connect video sources to digital monitors or display devices

digitizing tablet Flat surface with an array of crossed wires built into the surface that can sense the vertical and horizontal position of a pointing device

direct deposit Electronic transfer between the employer's bank and the employee's bank

direct mail Advertisements sent by postal service

direct marketing Advertisement that uses direct mail

directory harvest attack (DHA) Attempt to create a list of valid e-mail addresses

disc Optical media such as CDs and DVDs

disintermediation Removing intermediate steps, people, or processes

disk Magnetic media such as hard disks and floppy disks

Disk Operating System (DOS) An early operating system with a character-based interface

distance education Teaching students who are not physically present using communication technology

distributed database Related records stored on more than one computer

distributed processing Dividing a task into component parts that can be distributed to other computers

docking station Device into which a camera or other device is attached to transfer data to a computer

document Word processing file; the main work area in the Microsoft Word window

documenting Providing information about the source, author, and creation date of a workbook

document scanner Scanner that can scan a number of individual pages of text but that cannot be used to scan books or magazines

domain name A unique combination of a domain name and top-level domain

domain name server Computer that provides a directory that relates domain names to host computers

Domain Name System (DNS) The combination of an easy-to-remember domain name and the numerical address of its host computer

dongle A device resembling a USB drive needed to connect a computer to a Bluetooth wireless device on computers without built-in Bluetooth capabilities

Do Not Call registry List of phone numbers maintained by the U.S. government of people who do not want to be solicited by phone

dot matrix printer Type of impact printer

dots per inch (dpi) Measure of printed image quality; usually the higher the number of dots per inch, the better the image quality

double-data-rate 2 (DDR2) A type of SDRAM typically used in personal computers

drag See *drag-and-drop*

drag-and-drop A technique for moving text, an image, or other object from one location to another by selecting an item and dragging it with the mouse to a new location

driver See *device driver*

dropped call Interrupted connection resulting in a lost connection between callers

dual boot The option of selecting an operating system when you turn the computer on

dual-core processor A multi-core processor with two processors

dumb terminal A communication device with a keyboard and monitor that depends on another computer for processing and storage

DVD-ROM Optical disc that is read-only; uses the digital versatile disc method of encoding data

DVD-RW A rewritable DVD

DVD-R/RW (+R/RW) One of two competing DVD formats

E

E1 Transmission capacity equivalent of 30 twisted pairs of telephone lines (European)

e-book An electronic book that can be read on a computer or a special e-book reader

edit Revise and change information

e-learning Education that uses a computer to deliver instruction

electronic learning (eLearning) Computer supported education

electromagnetic (EM) Waves of energy comprised of electric and magnetic fields

electronic commerce Doing business online

electronic data interchange (EDI) Standard for exchanging billing and invoices

electronic mailing list (e-list) List of e-mail addresses

electronic serial number (ESN) Code programmed into a cell phone for identification purposes

electrostatic plotter A plotter that can print large graphics, similar to a laser printer

e-mail Electronic mail

embedded chart A chart that is on the same worksheet as the data

embedded operating system Compact, efficient, and often single-purpose operating systems that are used in computer appliances and special-purpose applications, such as an automobile, an ATM machine, or a portable media player

em dash Name for a long dash in a sentence that marks a break in thought, similar to a comma but stronger

emoticons Symbols that indicate emotions

Encrypt Document A command that enables you to set a password for a file

endnote A reference that is placed at the end of a document or section of a document

end-user license agreement (EULA) Software license that you agree to when you purchase and install commercial software

enterprise resource planning (ERP) Set of applications that automate coordination of separate processes and functions in an organization

ergonomics Applied science of equipment design to reduce operator fatigue and discomfort

Ethernet Standard for connecting a network; usually refers to a twisted pair cable

eTrust Privacy certification service

euro European Union's currency

eWaste Discarded electronic equipment

exchange rate Adjustment factor for the difference between currency values

Extensible Markup Language (XML) Framework for writing a language as simple text along with information on how the application software should interpret that text

external social network (ESN) Social network that is available to everyone

external hard drive A hard drive that plugs into a computer, usually using a USB connection

extranet Local area network connected to another over the Internet by a secure connection

extrapolation To extend a trend beyond the known data

F

fair use Rule that allows use of copyrighted material for certain purposes without paying royalties

Favorites In the Computer window, a list of commonly used folders; in a browser, it is a list of website addresses for future reference

Federal Communications Commission (FCC) Government agency that allocates EM frequencies for public use

feed aggregator RSS reader that displays RSS files

fiber optic cable Glass strands used to carry data as flashes of light

field In a template, e-mail message, or database, a predefined area where a specific type of data is entered, such as file name, page number, or date. In Access, the smallest useable fact collected for each record; a category of data

field area An area on a document that is coded to insert a specific value

field placeholders Field names that are inserted to reserve spaces for the final data that will be inserted during the mail merge process

file compression program Program that reduces the size of files

file extension The letters following a period after a file name that identifies the type of file and often the software that was used to create it

file server A networked computer that stores and finds files or data, delivers the information to the user, and manages updates to the files

File Transfer Protocol (FTP) Rules for transferring files between computers over the Internet

fill handle In Excel, the small box at the lower right corner of a selected cell that is used to fill content across a row or down a column

filter To display only data, Web pages, or incoming messages that meet certain criteria

Find A command that is used to locate a word, phrase, or specific formatting

finite element analysis Dividing a model into small elements and calculating how they interact to simulate behavior of a real system

firewall Software that can block unwanted or unsafe data transmission

FireWire High speed connection developed by Apple and used for data transfer

first line indent A paragraph style that extends the first line of a paragraph to the right of the rest of the paragraph

first generation (1G) First cell phones

flame Insulting or provocative posting

flame war Exchange of insults or flames online

flash drive See *USB drive*

flash hard drive Hard drive that uses flash memory and has no moving parts. They use less energy, break down less frequently, and generate less heat than magnetic hard drives

flash memory Memory with no moving parts; retains its information after the power is removed. Flash memory is used for such things as USB drives and camera digital picture storage

flat panel Thin display that often uses LCD technology

flat screen CRT display with a less curved screen

flatbed scanner Device to transfer documents or pictures one sheet at a time

Folders list At the bottom of the Computer window Navigation pane, displays a list of folders that are contained within the selected folder

font A set of numbers and letters that have the same design and shape

footer An area at the bottom of a page reserved for information that should appear on every page

footnote A reference that is placed at the bottom of the page

form Access object that is used to input, edit, or view data, typically one record at a time

format The appearance of a document

formatting marks Characters displayed to represent keystrokes when you press ⏎Enter, Tab⇄, or Spacebar but which do not print

formula Symbolic representation of mathematical process

formula bar The area on a worksheet that displays the contents of the active cell

forward Sending a received message to a subsequent address

fragmentation Files stored on the hard disk as separate parts in nonadjacent tracks

frames per second Rate at which video images are displayed

fraud Hoax that is intended to make personal gain from another person

freeware Software that is copyrighted by the programmer but for which there is no charge

frequency The number of variations of the medium per second

frequency modulation (FM) Changing the frequency of an EM wave

frequency-shift keying (FSK) Method of sending binary data using two frequencies

friend-to-friend (F2F) File sharing between acquaintances

full duplex Ability to send and receive simultaneously

function A prewritten formula that is used to solve mathematical problems or manipulate text fields

Function (Fn) key Key on notebook keyboards intended for use with function keys to provide additional functions

G

gadget Small program—such as a currency converter, a calendar, or a clock—that displays in the Windows Sidebar

gallery A list of potential results

gamepad A game controller held in both hands with buttons and control sticks, which is used to play computer games

gateway Connection between different networks

general packet radio service (GPRS) Data connection used with 1G and 2G mobile phones

generic top-level domain (gTLD) General category

gigabyte Approximately a billion bytes

global positioning system (GPS) 3D location system using satellites as reference points

global system for mobile communications (GSM) Standard for mobile phone connections used in most countries outside North America

gold version The final copy of software at the end of the beta process

google Act of searching for information, typically using the Google search engine

Graphic Interchange Format (GIF) Image storage format that uses only eight bits of data for each picture element

Graphical User Interface (GUI) A program interface that includes screen elements such as dialog boxes, windows, toolbars, icons, and menus—that is manipulated with a mouse and keyboard to interact with the software

graphics tablet See *digitizing tablet*

grayscale Shades of gray that represent color, which are applied to slide images when they are printed

gridlines Lines that separate cells

group A collection of related commands on a tab that enable you to interact with the software

H

H.261 Early video compression standard

H.264/MPEG-4 Part 10 Recent video compression standard

H.320 Standard for video conferencing over public switched telephone networks, digital , T1, and satellite networks

H.323 Standard for video conferencing over LANs

H.324 Standard for video conferencing over standard telephone lines and 3G mobile telephones

hacker Clever programmer

handheld computer A small computer that fits in a pocket or purse

handout A printable output in PowerPoint that displays one to nine slides to a page for the purpose of providing an audience with a copy of a presentation

hanging indent A paragraph style that leaves the first line at the left margin, and the rest of the lines of the paragraph to the right of the first line

hard disk Magnetic media made of metal; part of a hard drive

hard drive Device to read and write hard disks; usually the main storage device in a computer

head Devices in a hard drive that read and write data in magnetic form on a stack of thin metal disks

header An area reserved at the top of a document for information that should appear on every page in a document; also the label at the top of a column or at the left of a row of data

header area The top part of the e-mail form used for identifying the recipients and subject

heading In Excel, the number at the far left of a row or letter at the top of a column used to identify a location on a worksheet

heat sink The radiator fins attached to a processor that help cool the processor when a fan is running

hertz Measure of frequency equal to one repetition per second

high-definition multimedia interface (HDMI) Connector used to transfer digital signals

high definition (HD) radio Digital radio

high definition television (HDTV) Television system that uses digital signals

hoax Lie intended to convince someone of the reality of something that is not real

home page Primary Web page with links to other pages in a group, or the page displayed first when a browser opens

hop-off gateway Device that connects the data networks to the public switched telephone network

horizontal (category) axis Bottom border of the chart with category labels

host Computer that contains a program or file

hot thread Most active Web discussion

hot-swappable Can change connected devices without shutting down the computer

hyperlink Text or an object that that you click to connect to another file, location or Web page where information is located

Hypertext Markup Language (HTML) A language that is used to create Web pages that can be viewed in a Web browser

Hypertext Transfer Protocol (HTTP) Rules used to move Web pages on the Internet

I

IBM compatible Platform that used Intel processors and DOS or Windows operating systems

identity theft Impersonating someone online for fraudulent purposes

impact printer Transfers ink to the paper by striking an ink-impregnated cloth ribbon

in-band on-channel (IBOC) Method of adding digital signal to analog signals using the basic frequency

indent To move text in from the left and/or right margin

infected State of computer security has been compromised by malware

information Data that has been processed so it is organized, meaningful, and useful

information bar Displays at the top of a window to warn you of security issues related to files that you want to open

infrared (IR) light Form of invisible light used to send signals or data

ink-jet printer Creates an image on paper by spraying ink on a page

input The action of adding instructions and data to a computer

insertion point Position where input will go; a blinking vertical line on your work area that indications where text or graphics will be inserted

insourcing Having work done in the same country

instant messaging (IM) Exchange that takes place over the Internet when both parties are present

integrated circuit (IC) Arrays of transistors and other electronic devices that perform a function

interest rate The amount charged to borrow money

interlaced Refreshing an image by refreshing half of the lines at a time

internal hard drive The main storage device in a computer

internal rate of return (IRR) A financial measurement that is used to evaluate an investment and is comparable to the percent interest you earn on a savings account

internal social network (ISN) Social network that may be joined by invitation only

International Bank Account Number (IBAN) Bank identification number

International Business Machines (IBM) Computer company that popularized personal computers in traditional businesses

International Telecommunications Union (ITU) Standards setting body for international radio and telecommunications

Internet Corporation for Assigned Names and Numbers (ICANN) Organization that coordinates domain names and IP addresses

Internet forum Web-based discussion (see *message board*)

Internet message access protocol (IMAP) The set of rules for either delivering or managing e-mail on the server

Internet Protocol (IP) address Internet protocol number for a computer on the Internet

Internet Service Provider (ISP) Companies that connect individuals or other companies to the Internet

Internet Storm Center (ISC) Emergency-response information for dealing with security breeches

intranet Private network that uses the same communication protocols as the Internet

ISO 6392 code International bank identification number

J

Java Programming language suitable for automating functions on Web pages

Joint Photographic Experts Group (JPEG) Very popular image format that allows variable compression

joystick Pointing device which is a rod connected to a track ball

jumpers Connectors that fit over pairs of pins

junk e-mail Unsolicited and unwanted e-mail (see *SPAM*)

justified Text that is aligned evenly between the left and right margins; the spaces between words are adjusted to ensure that the text aligns evenly

K

key Information used to encrypt or decrypt messages

keyboard shortcut Pressing two keys at a time to perform an action

keylogger Program that records keystrokes

keyword search Strategy for selecting Web pages that contains certain words

kilohertz (KHz) One thousand hertz

L

land An unmarked spot on a CD that represents the number 1

landscape A horizontal page orientation that is wider than it is tall

laptop computer A mobile computer that can be used anywhere and can run on batteries when a power outlet is not available; also called a notebook or portable computer

laser diode (LED) A solid crystalline device that converts electricity to a narrow beam of light that is one color

laser printer Uses a light beam to transfer images or text to paper where powdered ink is attracted and melted onto the paper

last mile Reference to the smallest branches of a branching structure

layout The arrangement of placeholders on a slide

leader Dots or other marks that provide a visual connection between widely separated text

leader character The dot, dash, or other character used in a tab leader

leader line A graphic that connects a label to a chart element

left-aligned Alignment on the left margin, with the right edge of the paragraph uneven

legacy Older model or version

legend Identifies the data series on a chart

libel A false and malicious publication printed for the purpose of defaming a living person

line chart A chart that uses lines whose height on the vertical axis represents the value of the data

line spacing The distance between lines of text in a paragraph—1.15 is the default line spacing in Microsoft Office Word 2007

linklog Blog devoted to links to other blogs or sites

Linux An operating system for personal computers based on the UNIX operating system

liquid crystal display (LCD) Type of digital display that uses electric fields to change the transparency of liquid cells to pass red, green, or blue light to create an image; typically much thinner than older-style monitors

live preview A technology that shows the a preview of formatting changes on selected text or graphics before it is applied

Local Area Network (LAN) Group of connected devices that are usually close to each other

Lock mode Command from the Shut Down menu that enables a person who wants to leave the computer for a little while without logging off to come back to his or her own personal settings without having to log on again

locking Preventing the user from using a GSM phone with another provider

log Off Command from the Shut Down menu that closes personal settings and requires you to supply your username and password to log on again before using the computer

lossless Compression method that recovers all the details in a file after coding and decoding

lossy Compression method that permanently loses details of a file during coding and decoding

lumen Measure of brightness of light sources

M

Macintosh (Mac) Model of personal computer by Apple Corporation

mail merge A Word feature that joins a main document and a data source to create customized letters, labels, or envelopes

mail server Manages delivery and submissions of electronic mail

main document In a mail merge, the document that contains the text and formatting that remains constant

mainframe computer Large computer systems, usually very reliable and secure, used to process large amounts of information

malware Software that is designed with malicious intent

manual column break An artificial break between columns to control the flow of text

manual line break An artificial end to a line without creating a new paragraph

manual page break An artificial break between pages to control the flow of text, also referred to as a hard page break

margin The space between the edge of the paper and the text

Mark as Final A command that changes a document to Read-only status

markers Small rectangles on a line chart that identify each data point

maximize The process or button that increases the size of a window to fill the screen

Maximize/Restore Down button Expands a window to fill the screen or restores it to its previous size

media player Plays audio or video files of many different formats

megabyte Approximately a million bytes

megahertz (MHz) One million hertz

megapixel Measurement of the number of pixels (in millions) in a digital camera image

memory Integrated circuits designed to store data before and after it is processed by the CPU

message board Web-based discussion

MHTML format (MIME HTML) HTML code used in single-file Web pages

microchip Integrated circuit for computers

microcomputer Another term for a personal computer

minicomputer At one time, the category of computer between a workstation and a mainframe; used primarily as file and Web servers

microprocessor In personal computers and workstations, the central processing unit (CPU) that consists of millions of transistors

microSD card Removable flash memory that does not need power to retain data; typically used in point-and-shoot cameras, smartphones, and PDAs

Microsoft Office A suite of applications that perform tasks commonly used in an office environment, such as writing documents, managing finances, and presenting information

minimize The process or button that hides a window and represents the window with a button on the taskbar

mixed cell reference Cell location where either the row or the column remains constant, but not both

mobile identification number (MIN) Code derived from the ESN and assigned telephone number

mobile telephone switching office (MTSO) Coordination center of the cell phone system in an area

moblog Blog designed for use on mobile devices

modeling Using formulas to simulate the behavior of real systems

modem Device that translates small voltage switches from a computer into two tones on a telephone line

moderator Person who has administrative rights to an e-list and can delete members or postings

Modern Language Association (MLA) One of two commonly used styles for formatting research papers and reports

monitor Display device used with computers

Mosaic Early Web browser

mouse Pointing device that moves on the desktop and controls a screen pointer

mouse pad Pad to give traction to the rubber ball in a mouse

movie clips Animated clip art or video clips

Mozilla Firefox Early Web browser

MP3 (.mp3) Popular audio compression method

multi-core processor Multiple processors on a single chip

multimedia messaging service (MMS) Extension of the short message service that manages transfer of text plus audio and video files

N

Name box The area on the Excel window that displays the cell address or name of the currently active cell

namespace File that contains the definitions and relationships of an XML file

nanoseconds Billionths of a second

National Television System Committee (NTSC) Analog TV standard used in North America and several other countries

Navigation pane The area on the left side of a folder window that enables you to view the folder structure in a vertical list. In the Computer window, displays the Favorites list and the Folders list

netiquette Rules of appropriate behavior on the Internet

Netscape Popular Web browser

network Group of connected devices

network license A software license that allows anyone on the network to use a piece of software

network server Manages flow of data between computers on the network

neuron Nerve cell

node Any device on the network

nondisclosure agreement An agreement not to share the product's new features with anyone else during beta testing

nonprinting characters See *formatting marks*

non-volatile memory Memory that does not need constant power to function

Normal view The main view in PowerPoint that is used to create a presentation

not Logical operator that reverses a true or false value

Notes pane In PowerPoint, in Normal view, the portion of the window at the bottom that is used to create notes for the speaker

notification area An area on the right side of the taskbar that keeps you informed about processes that are running in the background, such as antivirus software, network connections, and other utility programs; it also typically displays the time

null Empty or nonexistent

numbered list A list of items preceded by numbers that are arranged in a particular order—chronological, importance, or sequence

Num Lock key Key on the keyboard that toggles the function of the numeric keyboard keys from navigation to numeric functions

O

Occupational Safety & Health Administration (OSHA) An agency in the Department of Labor

Office button A button that displays commands related to files

Office Clipboard A temporary storage area in Microsoft Office applications where copied or cut text or images are stored

on demand Available on request

OpenOffice Suite of productivity applications available for free download that works with Linux, Windows, and Mac platforms

open source The source code for software that is free to distribute and use that meets the criteria of the open-source initiative

opening post (OP) First posting in a thread to start the discussion on a topic

operating system A type of software program that determines how the processor interacts with the user and with other system components

optical character recognition (OCR) Software that converts images of text on paper into editable electronic text

optical mouse Mouse that detects motion using the reflection of a beam of light

option button Element of a page that can be toggled on or off to record a choice

Option key Macintosh computer key that is similar to the Control key on other computers

opt out Choose not to participate

or Logical operator that requires that either or both criteria are met

OS X An Apple Macintosh operating system

output The process of displaying, sharing, or otherwise communicating information that has been processed by the computer

outsourcing Having work done in another country

P

packet Group of about 1,000 bytes of data that includes addressing and error-checking labels

parenthetical citation A citation in the MLA style that uses the author's last name and the page number, surrounded by parentheses

passive-matrix display An LCD monitor type that scans and refreshes the screen a row or column at a time

password A code used to identify a user to grant access to the network

Paste A command that inserts copied or cut text or images in a new location

Paste Options A button that displays formatting options for recently pasted text

patch A software program that modifies and existing program to repair minor problems

patent Protection for an invention

payload Program that is carried by malware that performs a function

peer-to-peer Relationship between computers that are connected directly to each other without the use of a network server

pen plotter A plotter that uses individual pens and different colored inks to create large line drawings

peripheral Device attached to the system unit or case

personal computer A computer typically operated by one person who can customize the functions to match personal preferences; sometimes called a microcomputer

personal digital assistant (PDA) Appliance that tracks calendars, tasks, and contact information; often supports e-mail functions

Personal Information Manager (PIM) Software that tracks calendars, tasks, and contact information that may be expanded to include other functions such as e-mail

petabyte Approximately a quadrillion bytes

phase alternating line (PAL) Analog TV standard used in Europe and many other countries

phishing Fraudulent attempt at tricking someone into divulging sensitive or private information

photo detector Device that converts light into electrical voltage

photoblog Blog devoted to photos

pie chart Uses a circle to represent the whole of a group of data and slices to represent how each piece of data contributes to the whole

pin To attach a program to the Start menu

pit An indentation burned into a CD that represents the number 0

pixel A single picture element or subdivision of a picture

placeholders Preformatted areas that define the type of information to place in each area on the slide

plain text Decoded or original document

plain text format Document format that saves the text and paragraph marks, but none of the text or paragraph formatting

platform The combination of a particular operating system and the processor that it controls

plug-and-play Windows feature that recognizes new hardware and automatically searches for the correct software driver to install the new hardware

plug-in Program that adds functionality

plug strip Device with several power outlets

podcast Distribute multimedia files over the Internet

point (pt) Measurement for font size; one point is one seventy-second of an inch

point-and-shoot camera Small, inexpensive digital still camera with mostly automatic functions

pointing stick A pointing device that senses directional pressure

point-of-sale (POS) terminal A type of dumb terminal used for managing and recording transactions

pop-up A window that appears when activated from a Web page

port Connection device on the computer

Portable Document Format (PDF) A document format developed by Adobe that can be read on most platforms, but cannot be edited without special software; maintains document formatting, graphics, and layout

Portable Network Graphics (PNG) Graphics format designed for the Web

portal Web site that is an entry point to a variety of services and information

portrait A vertical page orientation that is taller than it is wide

post office protocol (POP) The rules for delivering e-mail

power strip An extension cord with a box of additional electrical receptacles

present value Amount of the loan before it has been repaid

primary key field Unique identifier field in a database table

primary storage The type of storage that is used while the computer is processing data and instruction; also known as memory

print driver Software that communicates between the computer and the printer

print on demand (POD) Ability to print books as required

print queue A waiting area for documents that have been sent to the printer

print server Manages printing requests from network computers

private branch exchange (PBX) Device for routing telephone calls within an organization and connecting to the telephone company

private key Non-published information used to encrypt or decrypt a message that cannot be used to reverse the process

probe Sensor used to explore places that are unsafe or not easily accessible

processing Manipulating data according to a set of instructions to create information that can be stored

programmable Computers that can change programs

programmer A person who writes computer programs

programming The process of writing software

programs See *application program*

progressive Refreshing an image by refreshing each line sequentially from the top

projector Projects monitor image for group viewing

Properties A command that displays the document properties, which includes the author, document title, subject, keywords for searching, or other information

protocol Group of rules

proxy server Security software or device that requests Internet services using its own identity to hide the address of the computer that is actually requesting the service

public key Published information used to encrypt or decrypt a message that cannot be used to reverse the process

public switched telephone network (PSTN) Older circuit switching telephone system

Q

quad-core processor A multi-core processor with four processors

query In a database, a set of criteria intended to extract the records and fields that would answer a particular question and display the table with only those records

Quick Access Toolbar A customizable toolbar to the right of the Office button that contains the Save, Undo, and Repeat/Redo buttons

Quick Launch toolbar An area to the right of the Start button that contains shortcut icons for commonly used programs

Quick Style gallery A list of available styles in a document; found on the Home tab

QuickTime (.mov) Video compression method from Apple Computer

qlog Blog devoted to answering questions

R

radio Electromagnetic waves

radio frequency ID (RFID) A device that enables remote retrieving of information using radio waves

random access memory (RAM) Integrated circuits that work with the CPU

range A contiguous group of cells that are identified by the cell at the upper left, a colon, and the cell at the lower right

readme File with notes from programmers on changes made since the manual went to press

read-only A file that can be opened and read but not edited

really simple syndication (RSS) Method of delivering content to subscribers using XML

record Database information about one person, item, place, object, or event divided into fields and displayed in a single row of a data source

Redo A command that reverses the action of the Undo command

reflector E-mail address to which a message is sent that will be distributed to the e-list

refresh rate Frequency of replacement of images

registry Company that manages a top-level domain

relational database A type of database that divides data into several tables that can be related to each other by a common field; Access is a relational database

relative cell reference Cell location that is stored as a certain number of rows and columns from the currently selected cell

relay A device that uses an electromagnet to connects circuits

release to manufacturing (RTM) A software version following beta testing that is sent to the companies that process the product for distribution

remote control Wireless control unit typically used with an appliance such as a music player, a television, or a media center on a computer

Repeat A command that repeats the previous action

repeater Device that amplifies and retransmits a signal

Replace A command that replaces found text or formatting with new text or formatting

reply New message automatically addressed to the original sender

reply to all New message automatically addressed to the original sender and those to whom it was copied

report The Access object that is used to summarize information for printing and presentation of the data

resolution The level of detail on a computer monitor, measured in dots per inch for images and pixels for monitors

resolution setting Choice of pixel size to display on a computer monitor

response time The amount of time it takes to change the color of a pixel on an LCD monitor

restore down Process or button that reduces the size of a maximized window

restore point A representation of the state of your computer's system files at a particular point in time

Restrict Permission A command that enables you to specify the users who have permission to read, change, or have full control over a document

retina Part of the eye that converts light into nerve impulses

reverse auction Request for lowest bid to provide a service or quantity of goods

Reviewing pane A pane at the bottom or side of the screen that displays comments and tracked changes

revision history Log of changes

revolutions per minute (rpm) Rate of spin of a disc

Ribbon The area at the top of a Microsoft Office 2007 window that contains groups of buttons for the most common commands used in applications

rich text format (RTF) A universal document format that can be read by nearly all word processing programs and that retains most text and paragraph formatting

right-aligned Text that is aligned on the right margin, with the left edge of the paragraph uneven

robot A mechanical device programmed to perform special functions

rootkit Program that gives outsiders access to a computer and administrator rights

rotation handle A small green circle that displays at the top of some graphic objects that is used to rotate the object in a circle

router Computer that selects the route that data should take

R-squared (R^2) value A measure of how well the calculated trendline fits the data; the closer the number is to 1, the better the fit

S

Safari Web browser by Apple

Safe Mode A method of rebooting a computer that runs only the essential parts of the operating system, and does not load many of the utilities that typically run in the background

salutation Courteous recognition or greeting

sampling rate Frequency of measurement

sans serif fonts Fonts that do not have lines or extensions on the ends of letters and are often used as headings and titles and for shorter documents

scanner Device to transfer documents and pictures into a digital format; also, a device that checks several different frequencies to detect and receive those that are in use

scanning Act of transferring a document or picture to a digital format one line at a time

screen saver A moving image that displays on a monitor after a set period of inactivity

ScreenTip A description that displays the name of a screen element, button, or area on a window

scroll bar Horizontal or vertical bars that enable you to navigate in a window, menu, or gallery by manipulating the display of content within the window

scroll box A box in scroll bars that can be used to drag a work area up and down or left and right; it also provides a visual indication of your location in the work area

search engine Program that displays links to Web pages that meet search criteria

second generation (2G) Cells phones using digital transmission

secondary storage Type of storage that is used to record information for later retrieval, and does not require constant power to retain the information that is stored

Secure Digital (SD) card Removable flash memory that does not need power to retain data; typically used in point-and-shoot cameras, smartphones, and PDAs

Secure Sockets Layer (SSL) Rules for using cryptographic methods to provide secure communications over the Internet

self publishing Using affordable software to create and distribute books

sensor Device that reacts to changes in the environment and produces an electrical signal that corresponds to the change

Séquentiel couleur á mémoire (SECAM) French and Soviet analog television standard

serif fonts Fonts that have lines or extensions on the ends of the letters and are typically used for large amounts of text

server A powerful computer that provides a service, such as running a network or hosting an Internet site

service pack Major software updates that are just short of an upgrade

shareware Software that can be used for a trial period but must be paid for if used regularly

Shift key Key on the keyboard used to produce capital letters or to be used in combination with other keys to provide new functions

shopping cart Program that aggregates orders on a commercial Web site

short message service (SMS) Wireless service for sending short messages

shortcut menu When you click the right mouse button, a list of actions that displays related to the area on which you clicked

Sigma (∑) Greek letter associated with the Sum function

signature block Name, title and contact information at the end of a formal message

simple mail transfer protocol (SMTP) The rules for structuring and sending e-mail

simple payback period The number of years that it takes to recover the cost of an investment, which is a measure that is commonly used to compare investment alternatives

single-spaced Line spacing set to 1.0 that has no additional space between lines of text in a paragraph

site license A software license that allows anyone in an organization or group to use a piece of software

sizing handle Small squares and circles that display around the perimeter of an object that are used to resize the object and which indicate that the object is selected and can be moved, resized, or formatted

sketchlog Blog of portfolio drawings

Sleep mode Command from the Shut Down menu that shuts down nearly all of the power to the computer but keeps power to the CPU and to RAM, while greatly reducing energy consumption

slide Screen intended for projection (see *slide show*); the main work area in PowerPoint

slide master Slide layout images that contain all of the placeholder formats for each slide layout within a theme, which are used to change theme formats for all slides

Slide Master view In PowerPoint, a view that contains each slide layout, where you can change placeholder formatting characteristics for the selected theme

Slide pane In PowerPoint, in Normal view, the center pane that is used to enter slide content

slide show Series of screens used to present ideas to an audience

Slide Show view The view that is used to display slides electronically using a computer and overhead projector

Slide Sorter view In PowerPoint, thumbnail slides images displayed on a single page that is used to rearrange slides and add transitions

Slides/Outline pane In PowerPoint, in Normal view, the left pane that is used to display thumbnail images of the slides or an outline

slope The angle of a straight line compared to horizontal

small caps A text effect that displays the capital letters in a normal manner but the lowercase letters as capital letters that are approximately 3/4 height

Small Computer System Interface (SCSI) A peripheral connection method used for high-speed data transfer

smartphone A cellular telephone that has a small keypad and can run software applications, store and play music, display pictures, and send and receive email; often includes features of PDAs

SmartArt A diagram that creates a visual representation of concepts and information; use it to illustrate hierarchies, steps in a process, relationships, cycles, or lists

social network Social groups that are interconnected on the Internet

software Written instructions that direct a computer's processor on how to complete tasks; also called *programs*

source code Computer program in text form before it is translated into machine code

spacing after Space added between paragraphs when the enter key is pressed

spam Unsolicited bulk messages

speaker notes A printable output in PowerPoint that provides a copy of the slide image and related notes for the speaker during a presentation

spider Automated program that searches for Web pages

spim Form of spam directed at instant messaging services

sponsored links References to Web pages that are placed with highly ranked websites for a fee

spoofing Replacing the name of the originator of a message with a name from a contact list to disguise the origin

spreadsheet Generic term for financial data arranged in rows and columns with formulas that can recalculate automatically if values in cells change

spyware Program that records and reports user activity to an unauthorized party

star Configuration of connections that radiate from a central location

Start menu List of programs or menus of programs displayed by clicking the Start button on the taskbar

status bar Displays information about the document or other file on which you are working

storefront software Programs that enable a Web site to sell goods and services

style Combinations of formatting characteristics that are grouped together and named, and then are applied with a single click

stylus A pen-like input device that is used to tap a touch screen

subscriber Member of an e-list

subscriber identification module (SIM) Flash memory card in a mobile phone that records the subscriber's identification information and the provider's SID

subscript Characters that are placed below the regular text in a line

subwoofer Audio speaker designed for low range sounds and music

Sum A function that chooses adjacent cells that contain numbers, adds the values, and displays the total in the cell that contains the SUM function

supercomputer Extremely fast computers used for research, modeling, and large-scale data analysis

superscript Characters that are placed above the regular text in a line

supply chain Sequence of steps that produce products and deliver them to the consumer

surge suppressor Protects the computer from pulses of higher-than-normal electric voltage

S-video port Port on the video card that enables you to connect your computer to cable and view television programs

switch user mode Command from the Shut Down menu that closes personal settings and allows another user to log on

switchboard operator Person who made the connections between circuits in early telephone systems

symmetric key Information used to encrypt and decrypt the same message

synchronous Interactions between parties that are present at the same time

synchronous dynamic random access memory (SDRAM) Type of memory typically used in personal computers (see *double-data-rate 2 [DDR2]*)

synonym A word that is similar in meaning

syntax The order of arguments in a function

system administrator Person who controls the computers

system clock Circuits that keep time in the computer

system identification (SID) Code assigned to each cell phone service provider

system restore Process of reinstating a previous set of values used by the operating system

system unit The part of the personal computer that contains the central processing unit

T

T1 Transmission capacity equivalent of 24 twisted pairs of telephone lines

table The Access object that stores the data that makes up the database; each table stores a set of related data; inn Word a list of information set up in a column-and-row format; in Excel data that is organized into adjacent columns and rows and define as a table

tablet computer A laptop computer designed to enable the user to write on the screen as a mode of input

tab stop A location on the horizontal ruler to which you can move the insertion point by pressing the Tab key; used to align and indent text

tabs On the Ribbon, used to access commands related to a category of actions for each application

taskbar Displays the Start button and the names of any open files and applications. The taskbar may also display shortcut buttons for other programs

telecommute Go to work electronically rather than physically

telework Work from home

Telnet Program to allow remote login over the Internet

templates Preformatted and designed documents that can be used repeatedly

terabyte Approximately a trillion bytes

terminator Required device at the end of some types of buses such as SCSI connections

texting Sending text messages between mobile digital devices

theme A collection of design elements, fonts, colors, and graphics that create a uniform look for a presentation, Word document, or Excel worksheet

thesaurus A research tool that provides a list of synonyms

third generation (3G) Mobile telephone system that provides high-speed data and Internet access on cell phones

thread Postings on a topic

thumb drive See *USB drive*

thumb mouse A portable mouse that uses a trackball operated by the thumb

thumbnail Icons that display a small representation of a file, or a slide

time-division multiple access (TDMA) Method of sharing the same frequency by dividing its use into time slots

time-division synchronous code-division multiple access (TD-SCDMA) Advanced version of CDMA used in 3G phones

title bar The bar at the top of a window; often displays the program icon, the name of the file, and the name of the program. The Minimize, Maximize/Restore Down, and Close buttons are grouped on the right side of the title bar

toggle A button that activates or deactivates a feature or command

toner Dry ink used with copiers or laser printers

top-level domain (TLD) Group of domain names

touch pad A small, rectangular, flat area below the space bar on many notebook computers that performs the functions of a mouse

touch screen Input device that senses touch on a monitor

track ball A pointing device with a moving ball in a cradle

Track Changes A feature that records changes and comments made to a document by others

trademark A word or symbol that indicates ownership of a product or service that is reserved for exclusive use by the owner

transformer Converts electrical voltage from high to low or low to high

transistor An electronic device that can switch on or off in response to an external signal

transitions Added to slides to control the direction, timing, speed, and manner in which slides enter and exit the screen during a slide show

Transmission Control Protocol/Internet Protocol (TCP/IP) Rules used to control the transmission of packets on the Internet

Transport Layer Security (TLS) Rules for using cryptographic methods to provide secure communications over the Internet that followed SSL

trendline A calculated line that can be extended to predict values beyond the end of the data

trial version Software that is intended for temporary use to evaluate a product

Trojan Program that disguises itself within another program that the user agrees to install

true color System that can display all of the colors that the human eye can perceive

tumbleblog Blog that contains a mixture of media types

twisted pair Two insulated wires that are wrapped around each other

type A USB Connector on the upstream or computer side of the cable

type B USB Connector on the downstream or device end of the cable

U

Undo A command that reverses one or more previous actions

Unicode A code that uses up to 32-bit numbers to represent characters from numerous languages, including the older ASCII codes

Uniform Resource Locator (URL) Unique name used as an address on the Internet

uninterruptible power supply A device that uses batteries to keep a computer running when the power fails

Universal Serial Bus (USB) Connection method that replaces many other types of peripheral connectors

Unix Popular operating system on mainframe computers; the basis for the Linux operating system on personal computers

update Changes to a version of software to fix problems or add minor feature improvements

upgrade Replaces current version with a newer one that has significant changes

USB 1.1 First version (see *Universal serial bus*) of USB

USB 2.0 Second version (see *Universal serial bus*) of USB

USB drive Flash memory that plugs into a USB port on a computer

USB hub Provides multiple USB ports and may provide additional power

user name a name that is unique on a particular computer system

utility program Small program that does one task

V

venture capitalist Someone who loans money to startup companies in exchange for part ownership

vertical (value) axis The left side of the chart used to indicate the magnitude of the value of the data

video graphics adapter (VGA) Digital to analog adapter to use analog monitors with digital computers

video graphics array (VGA) port A personal computer display standard

video on demand (VOD) Download video at a time chosen by the viewer

video RAM (VRAM) Dedicated video memory

Views Different ways to display data on the screen

virtual Having the appearance of reality

virtual memory Space on a hard disk used to supplement physical memory

virtual team Group whose members are separated by time or distance

virus Program that makes copies of itself and distributes them as attachments to files or e-mail

vlog Blog devoted to discussions of videos

voice gateway router Device that connects the LAN and PBX to the phone company

Voice-over-the-Internet Protocol (VoIP) Audio conversation using Internet packets

voice recognition Ability to convert speech into digital files or commands

voice synthesizer Software that translates electronic words into spoken words

volatile memory Memory that needs constant power to function

W

WAV (.wav) Popular uncompressed audio file format

Web archive, single file Combined elements of a Web page saved as one file

Web cams Video camera intended for use over the Internet

webcasting Broadcasting video online

Web crawler Program that examines Web pages and gathers data about them

Web log (blog) A personal online journal

Web page A document that is written in HTML and displayed by a browser

Web server Computer that runs software that provides Web pages and runs scripts

website Collection of Web pages

what-if analysis Process of substituting values to see the effect on dependent calculations

Wide Area Network (WAN) Network of devices some of which are much farther away

wide band code-division multiple access (WCDMA) Advanced version of CDMA used in 3G phones

wiki Server program that allows users to collaborate to create the content of a website

Wikipedia Online encyclopedia that uses wiki

window Rectangular area of the screen with a title bar, Close and Minimize buttons, and a Maximize/Restore Down button

Windows Name of Microsoft's operating system that uses a GUI

Windows-based applications Programs that are written to work on computers that use a Microsoft Windows operating system

Windows Explorer The program within Windows that displays the files and folders on your computer

Windows Sidebar An area on the side of the screen that displays information you want to access quickly. Gadgets are added to the Windows Sidebar that display information such as weather or stock market data

wire transfer Electronic transfer of money

wireless Radio waves used instead of wires

wireless application protocol (WAP) Rules for connecting mobile devices to the Internet

wireless Enhanced 9-1-1 (E9-1-1) Enhanced emergency calling service that locates mobile phones

wireless fidelity (WiFi) Wireless standard used to connect computers and peripherals

WMA (.wma) Popular audio compression method

WMV (.wmv) Video compression method from Microsoft

word The unit of data with which a processor can work

WordArt A feature that turns words into a graphic that can be moved, resized, and modified to create decorative text

word processing The process of using a computer to write, store, retrieve, and edit documents

word size The amount of data that is processed in one operation

wordwrap As you type, the text on the line moves to the right, and words move down to the next line as necessary to adjust the spacing on the line to remain within the established margins

work area The area on the screen where you enter text, numbers, or graphics to create a document, a worksheet, or presentation slides

workbook A collection of worksheets in a spreadsheet program

worksheet The main work area in Excel, which is a grid of rows and columns, generically referred to as a spreadsheet

workstation A high-powered personal computer designed for specific tasks, such as graphics, medicine, and engineering; the term is also sometimes used to describe a networked personal computer

World Wide Web The resources and users on the Internet that are using the Hypertext Transfer Protocol

WorldWideWeb Name of Berners-Lee's first Web browser (see *World Wide Web*)

worm Malware program that duplicates itself on a network

X

X-Y scatter chart Similar to a line chart but it forces equal intervals on the horizontal axis

Z

Zoom bar A bar that is used to change the magnification of the document or worksheet

Photo Credits

COVER

Courtesy of www.istockphoto.com

CHAPTER 1

CO-01	Mike Agliolo\Photo Researchers, Inc.
Fig. 1.1A	istockphoto.com
Fig. 1.1B	Phil Degginger\Getty Images Inc.-Stone Allstock
Fig. 1.1C	Jim Pickerell\Stock Connection
Fig. 1.4	Underwood & Underwood/Corbis
Fig. 1.5	istockphoto.com
Fig. 1.7	George Washington School of Engineering and Applied Science
Fig. 1.8	Shutterstock
Fig. 1.9	istockphoto.com
Fig. 1.10	Phil Degginger\Getty Images Inc.-Stone Allstock
Fig. 1.11	Jim Pickerell\Stock Connection
Fig. 1.14	NSW
Fig. 1.15	Stephan Savoia\AP Wide World Photos
Fig. 1.17	© US Robotics
Fig. 1.18	Skyways Internet Services and Computers
Fig. 1.19	Gyula Matics\istockphoto.com

CHAPTER 2

CO-02	istockphoto.com

CHAPTER 3

CO-03	Amanda Rhode\istockphoto.com
Fig. 3.2	istockphoto.com
Fig. 3.5	istockphoto.com

CHAPTER 4

CO-04	Images.com
Fig. 4.24	istockphoto.com

CHAPTER 5

CO-05	Vasko Miokovic\istockphoto.com
Fig. 5.1A	Jon Feingersh
Fig. 5.1B	Sherwin Crasto\Corbis/Reuters America LLC
Fig. 5.24	Ryan McVay\Getty Images, Inc.-Photodisc.
Fig. 5.25	Jon Feingersh
Fig. 5.30	Sherwin Crasto\Corbis/Reuters America LLC
Fig. 5.33	Tammy Bryngelson\istockphoto.com

CHAPTER 6

CO-06	Mike Agliolo\Photo Researchers, Inc.
Fig. 6.1A	Tim Ridley © Dorling Kindersley
Fig. 6.1B	Pascal Goetgheluck\Photo Researchers, Inc.
Fig. 6.7	Photograph courtesy of NASA
Fig. 6.8	istockphoto.com
Fig. 6.9	© Daniel Rutter/Dan's Data
Fig. 6.10	Tim Ridley © Dorling Kindersley
Fig. 6.11	© Dorling Kindersley
Fig. 6.12	Twilight Images\Alamy Images Royalty Free
Fig. 6.13	Wikipedia, The Free Encyclopedia
Fig. 6.14	istockphoto.com
Fig. 6.15	istockphoto.com
Fig. 6.16	istockphoto.com
Fig. 6.17	Sony Electronics, Inc.\Newscom
Fig. 6.18	© Aaron Harris/AP Wide World
Fig. 6.19	Christian J. Stewart\istockphoto.com
Fig. 6.20	European Space Agency/CE/Eurocontol/ Science Photo Library/Photo Researchers, Inc.
Fig. 6.21	© Douglas Keister/CORBIS All Rights Reserved
Fig. 6.22	istockphoto.com
Fig. 6.27	Peter Steiner\Alamy Images
Fig. 6.29	istockphoto.com
Fig. 6.31	Martin Meissner\AP Wide World Photos
Fig. 6.32	Scalar Corporation
Fig. 6.33	© Dorling Kindersley
Fig. 6.34	Peter Bull © Dorling Kindersley
Fig. 6.35	Scott Bodell\Phototake NYC
Fig. 6.39	James King-Holmes\Photo Researchers, Inc.
Fig. 6.40	istockphoto.com

Index

Secure sockets layer (SSL), 98
Security
  behaviors, monitoring of, 213–214, 272
  children, protecting, 271–272
  contact information, 107, 108
  crimeware, 162–163
  data risk reduction, 212–213, 269–271
  defenses, 164–168
  digital signatures, 98, 115
  malware, 161–162
Self publishing, 106
Servers, 12–13
  domain names, 20
  e-mail, 183–184
  host, 13, 20
  networks, 12
Shopping cart, 100
Short message service (SMS), 147–148
Signals, analog *vs.* digital, 237–238
Signature blocks, 194
Simple mail transfer protocol (SMTP), 124
Sketchlogs, 138
Skype, 146
Smartphones, 124–125
Snipping Tool, 20, 51
Social networking, 152–153, 201
Software
  desktop publishing, 106
  open source, **156–157**, 178
  storefront, 106
Source code, 25, 42, 156
Sources, citing, 74–75, 85–86
Spam, 133
Spiders, 61
SPIM, 163
Sponsored links, 62, 76, 77
Spoofing, 161
Spybot, 108
Spyware, 108, 118, 162
Star configuration, 7
Storefront software, 106
Streaming, 141–142
Subscriber identification module (SIM), 259
Subscribers, 135
Supply chains, 212
Surge suppressors, 213
Switchboard operator, 8
Symmetric keys, 96–97
System administrators, 36, 164–165
System identification (SID) code, 253
System integrity, protecting, 270

T

T1 (DS1) connections, 28
TCP/IP, 9–11
TD-SCDMA, 260
Telephone calls
  e-mail as documentation of, 195
  emergency, 256, 279
  unwanted, 107
  VoIP, **144–147**, 201–202
Telephony, 7–8
  analog, 232–233
  digital systems, 254–256
  hybrid systems, 238

Internet connection types, 26–28
Internet financing by, 34
mobile phones (*See* Cell phones; Mobile phones)
PSTNs, 201–202, 263
satellite, 281
Television, 239–246
Telework/telecommuting, 207–209
Telnet, 11
Text messaging, 147–148, 193, 200
Third-generation (3G) mobile phones, 260–261
Thread, 136
Time-division multiple access (TDMA), 257–259
Toner, recycling, 273
Towers, 252
Trademarks, 75
Transistors, 233–234
Transmission control protocol/Internet protocol (TCP/IP), 9–11
Transport layer security (TLS), 98
Trojan horse, 162
Troubleshooting
  e-mail, 131–132
  FTP, 74
  Web page elements, copying, 69
  Web pages, 53, 60
True color, 240
Tumbleblogs, 139
Twisted pairs, 13–15

U

Uniform resource locator (URL), 17, 53
Uninterruptible power supply (UPS), 145
User name, 35–36

V

Venture capitalist, 104
Video
  conferencing, 204–206, 225–226
  on demand (VOD), 199–200, 246
  games, interactive, 247–248
  Internet viewing of, 34, **139–142**
  recorders, digital, 199, 246
  VGA connections, 243
  voting, 221–222
Virtual teams, 207
Viruses, 161
Vision, artificial, 266–267
Vista. *See* Windows Vista
Vlogs, 138
Voice gateway router, 202
VoIP (Voice over Internet Protocol), 144–147, 201–202
Voting, 221–222

W

Watts, Duncan, 152
WCDMA, 260
Web browsers, 51
  encryption, 98
  navigating, 52–55
  plugins, 57
  settings, modifying, **57–59**, 82

Webcams, 146
Webcasting, 199–200
Web crawlers, 61
Weblogs, 138–139, 150, 173, 198
WebMD, 149
Web pages
  AutoComplete feature, 55–56
  content evaluation, 76
  content retrieval marking, 66–71
  creating, 71–73, 83
  displaying, 22, 24
  downloading, 70–71
  elements, copying, 67–69
  ethics, 76–77
  filtering, 271–272
  history, 56–57
  hosting, 73–74
  printing, 69
  refreshing, 54
  searching within, 65
  source code, viewing, 25, 42
  sources, citing, 74–75, 85–86
  sponsored links, 62
  storage (cache), 54, 55
  as storefront, 100
  troubleshooting, 53, 60
Web server (host), 13, 20
Websites
  blocking, 77–78, 110–111
  described, 52
  digital signatures, 98, 115
  trusting, 110–111
Wide area network (WAN), 15–16
Wiki, 157
Wikipedia, 157–160, 168, 178
Windows Defender, 108–109
Windows Meeting Place, 225–226
Windows Vista
  firewall settings in, 45
  screen captures, 20
  Windows Defender, 108–109
Windows XP, 20, 45
Wireless (radio), 13–15
  connections, 29
  devices, 250–251
  digital systems, 238–239
  GRPS, 260
  HD, 239
Wireless application protocol (WAP), 148
Wireless Enhanced 9-1-1 (E9-1-1), 256, 279
Wire transfers, 93–95, 114–115
Word
  citations, 75, 85–86
  e-mail connection to, 129
  Web pages, creating, 71–73
Workplace safety, 216
World Wide Web (WWW), 23–25
Worms, 161

X

XML, 142

Y

Yahoo!, 61, 130, 146
YouTube, 139